Psychoanalytic Perspectives on Identity and Difference

Every day, clinicians encounter challenges to empathy and communication while struggling to assist patients with diverse life histories, character, sexuality, gender, psychopathology, cultural, religious, political, racial and ethnic backgrounds. Most writing pertaining to ideas of similarity, discrepancy and 'the Other' has highlighted differences. *Psychoanalytic Perspectives on Identity and Difference: Navigating the Divide* offers a different focus, emphasizing points of contact, connection, and how divisions between people can be transcended.

In-depth case material, astutely elucidated by diverse theoretical approaches, furnishes stimulating ideas and valuable suggestions for facilitating a meeting of minds and psychological growth in patients who might otherwise be difficult or impossible to engage. Exploring how psychoanalysts can navigate obstacles to understanding and communicating with suffering individuals, topics covered include internal experience of likeness and difference in the patient and in the analyst, and how analysts can find echoes of themselves in patients.

Psychoanalysts and psychotherapists will appreciate the importance and value of this wide-ranging, groundbreaking exploration of these insufficiently addressed dimensions of human experience.

Brent Willock is President of the Toronto Institute for Contemporary Psychoanalysis, Board Member of the Canadian Institute for Child and Adolescent Psychoanalytic Psychotherapy and on the faculty of the Institute for the Advancement of Self Psychology.

Lori C. Bohm is Supervising Analyst, Faculty and former Director at the Center for Applied Psychoanalysis and Intensive Psychoanalytic Psychotherapy Programs at the William Alanson White Institute. She is Psychotherapy Supervisor in the Clinical Psychology Doctoral Program at the City University of New York.

Rebecca Coleman Curtis is Professor of Psychology at Adelphi University, Faculty and Supervisor at the William Alanson White Institute and Supervisor at the National Institute for the Psychotherapies.

Psychoanalytic Perspectives on Identity and Difference

Navigating the Divide

Edited by
Brent Willock, Lori C. Bohm
and Rebecca Coleman Curtis

Routledge
Taylor & Francis Group
LONDON AND NEW YORK

First published 2017
by Routledge
2 Park Square, Milton Park, Abingdon, Oxon OX14 4RN

and by Routledge
711 Third Avenue, New York, NY 10017

Routledge is an imprint of the Taylor & Francis Group, an informa business

© 2017 selection and editorial matter, Brent Willock, Lori C. Bohm, & Rebecca Coleman Curtis; individual chapters, the contributors

The right of the editor to be identified as the author of the editorial material, and of the authors for their individual chapters, has been asserted in accordance with sections 77 and 78 of the Copyright, Designs and Patents Act 1988.

All rights reserved. No part of this book may be reprinted or reproduced or utilized in any form or by any electronic, mechanical, or other means, now known or hereafter invented, including photocopying and recording, or in any information storage or retrieval system, without permission in writing from the publishers.

Trademark notice: Product or corporate names may be trademarks or registered trademarks, and are used only for identification and explanation without intent to infringe.

British Library Cataloguing in Publication Data
A catalogue record for this book is available from the British Library

Library of Congress Cataloging in Publication Data
Names: Willock, Brent, editor. | Bohm, Lori C., editor. | Curtis, Rebecca C., editor.
Title: Psychoanalytic perspectives on identity and difference : navigating the divide / edited by Brent Willock, Lori C. Bohm and Rebecca Coleman Curtis.
Description: Abingdon, Oxon ; New York, NY : Routledge, 2017. | Includes bibliographical references and index.
Identifiers: LCCN 2016022515 | ISBN 9781138192546 (hardback : alk. paper) | ISBN 9781138192539 (pbk. : alk. paper) | ISBN 9781315543857 (e-book)
Subjects: LCSH: Identity (Psychology) | Difference (Psychology) | Psychotherapy. | Psychoanalysis.
Classification: LCC BF697 .P754 2017 | DDC 155.2--dc23
LC record available at https://lccn.loc.gov/2016022515

ISBN: 978-1-138-19254-6 (hbk)
ISBN: 978-1-138-19253-9 (pbk)
ISBN: 978-1-315-54385-7 (ebk)

Typeset in Times New Roman
by Saxon Graphics Ltd, Derby

Contents

Acknowledgements ix
Contributors xi

Introduction 1
LORI C. BOHM

PART I
The internal experience of likeness and difference in the patient 9

1 **Identifying/disidentifying** 11
  BRENT WILLOCK

2 **Negotiating the different/alike divide in the treatment of shame** 22
  GLADYS GUARTON

3 **The transition from adolescence to adulthood in psychotic patients and their families: a framework for assessing recovery** 28
  BARRI BELNAP

4 **Neuroticism is the way home** 48
  MARK EGIT

5 **An unpublishable paper** 59
  HARRIETTE KALEY

PART II
The work of the therapist to find him or herself in the patient 67

6 Reluctance to finding myself in the other:
 treating an alleged paedophile 69
 SUSAN KOLOD

7 On intersubjective firsts in the analytic third:
 becoming a subject in the presence of the other 76
 IONAS SAPOUNTZIS

PART III
Cultural, racial and cognitive/emotional divides 85

8 Our not-so-hidden shame: lack of ethnic diversity in the
 field of psychoanalysis 87
 JOHN V. O'LEARY

9 Finding their way home: the struggle of the Australian
 Aboriginal people to become one people within one nation 95
 JANICE A. WALTERS

10 The autistic core in Aboriginal trauma:
 breaking down or breaking out of the autistic defence 105
 NORMA TRACEY

11 A bicultural approach to working together:
 conversing about cultural supervision 118
 TRUDY AKE AND SARAH CALVERT

12 Identity amongst differences: a personal account of a
 pakeha psychologist working in a New Zealand
 Māori Mental Health Service 128
 INGO LAMBRECHT

13 The good son: psychotherapy with a 65-year-old man
 with the diagnosis of Asperger syndrome 136
 SUSAN ROSE

14 Creativity, identity and social exclusion:
  working with traumatized individuals 144
  MARILYN CHARLES

PART IV
Internal experience of likeness and difference in the therapist 163

15 An autobiographical account of the analysis of an analyst
  who endured complex childhood trauma 165
  JOHANNA TIEMANN

16 Same old story? Consistency and change in the analyst's work
  over time 171
  MICHAEL STERN

17 The analyst as patient: working from both sides of the divide 179
  EMILY FUCHECK

18 The contrapuntal play of paradox: likeness and difference
  in the theories of Otto Rank 192
  CLAUDE BARBRE

Conclusions:
The universal and the particular in the therapeutic encounter 208
REBECCA COLEMAN CURTIS

Index 212

Acknowledgements

This book's inspiration emerged from creative brainstorming and much hard work by Dr Michael Stern (The Psychoanalytic Society of the New York University Postdoctoral Program), Professor Michael O'Loughlin (Adelphi Society for Psychoanalysis and Psychotherapy), Dr Lori C. Bohm (William Alanson White Psychoanalytic Society), Professor Ionas Sapountzis (Adelphi Society for Psychoanalysis and Psychotherapy), Professor Rebecca Coleman Curtis (William Alanson White Psychoanalytic Society), Dr Rhonda Sternberg (Psychoanalytic Society of the New York University Postdoctoral Program), Margaret Pearl (Aotearoa New Zealand Chapter of the International Association for Relational Psychoanalysis and Psychotherapy) and Dr Brent Willock (Toronto Institute for Contemporary Psychoanalysis). On to the thematic tree – *Identity and difference* – that evolved, our wonderful authors put magnificent leaves. Kate Hawes (Senior Publisher), Kirsten Buchanan (Senior Editorial Assistant), Aiyana Curtis and Charles Bath (Editorial Assistants), Nigel Turner (Cover Designer) and the rest of the outstanding staff at Routledge made this vision a reality.

We thank the following publishers and authors for their kind permission to quote passages from their fine publications: In Chapter 1, W.W. Norton's *Identity and the life cycle* by Erik H. Erikson; in Chapter 4, a selection from The Pisan Cantos, copyright ©1948 by Ezra Pound, is reprinted by permission of New Directions Publishing Corp.; in Chapter 9, thanks to Monica Brown and Emmaus Productions for their kind permission to reprint the lyrics to 'One people, one land', all rights reserved, ©2001; in Chapter 13, a passage from W.W. Norton's *The history of love* by Nicole Krauss (2005).

Contributors

Trudy Ake, BSW, BA. Ngati Tuwharetoa and Ngati Ranginui. Member, Aotearoa New Zealand Association of Social Workers; Private Practice in Social Work and Maori Cultural Supervision, Tauranga, New Zealand.

Claude Barbre, PhD, LP. Professor, The Chicago School of Professional Psychology; Board Member and Clinical Supervisor, The Chicago Center for Psychoanalysis (CCP); Private Practice, Chicago.

Barri Belnap, MD. Psychotherapist/Psychopharmacologist in Private Practice and Staff Member at the Austen Riggs Center, Stockbridge, Massachusetts.

Lori C. Bohm, PhD. Supervising Analyst, Faculty Member and former Director, Center for Applied Psychoanalysis and Intensive Psychoanalytic Psychotherapy, William Alanson White Institute, New York. Psychotherapy Supervisor, Clinical Psychology Doctoral Program, City College of the City University of New York.

Sarah Calvert, PhD. Clinical Psychologist in Private Practice, Auckland, New Zealand.

Marilyn Charles, PhD, ABPP. The Austen Riggs Center, Stockbridge, Massachusetts. President, Division 39 (Psychoanalysis), American Psychological Association; Co-Chair, Association for the Psychoanalysis of Culture and Society; Contributing Editor, *Psychoanalysis, Culture, and Society*.

Rebecca Coleman Curtis, PhD. Professor of Psychology, Adelphi University; Faculty, William Alanson White Institute, New York.

Mark Egit, PhD. Graduate, Toronto Institute for Contemporary Psychoanalysis; Faculty, Toronto Art Therapy Institute; Private Practice, Toronto.

Emily L. Fucheck, PsyD. Supervisor of Psychotherapy, William Alanson White Institute, New York; Associate Editor, *Contemporary Psychoanalysis*; Private practice, New York City and Dutchess County, New York.

Gladys B. Guarton, PhD. Supervisor, Adelphi Postdoctoral Program in Psychotherapy and Psychoanalysis; Private Practice, Great Neck, New York.

Harriette Kaley, PhD. Professor Emerita, Brooklyn College–City University of New York. Former President, Division of Psychoanalysis, American Psychological Association; Board Member, The Psychoanalytic Society (Graduate Society of New York University's Post-Doctoral Program in Psychoanalysis); Independent Practice, New York City.

Susan Kolod, PhD. Supervising and Training Analyst, Faculty Member and Eating Disorder, Compulsions and Substance Abuse Program, William Alanson White Institute, New York; Private Practice, Brooklyn and Manhattan.

Ingo Lambrecht, PhD. Consultant Clinical Psychologist, Manawanui Oranga Hinegaro Ora, Mental Health Service for Māori, Auckland, New Zealand.

John V. O'Leary, PhD. Faculty and Supervisor, William Alanson White Institute; Staff Psychologist, Columbia Presbyterian Hospital.

Susan L. Rose, PhD. Supervisor, Faculty Member and Director, Child and Family Center, and Former Director, Autistic Spectrum Service, William Alanson White Institute, New York; Supervisor of Psychotherapy, Clinical Psychology Doctoral Program, City College of the City University of New York; works clinically with children, adolescents and adult with diagnoses on the Autism spectrum.

Ionas Sapountzis, PhD. Faculty and Supervisor, Derner Institute of Advanced Psychological Studies, Adelphi University, Garden City, New York.

Michael Stern, PhD. Clinical Supervisor, Institute for Contemporary Psychotherapy, New York; Private Practice, New York and New Jersey.

Johanna Tiemann, PhD. Center for Optimal Living, New York; Private Practice, New York.

Norma Tracey, MAASW. Founder, Gunawirra, an organization that works with Aboriginal children and their families in New South Wales preschools.

Janice A. Walters, PhD. Psychoanalyst and Associate Professor of Psychology, Borough of Manhattan Community College of the City University of New York.

Brent Willock, PhD. Founding President, Toronto Institute for Contemporary Psychoanalysis; Board Member, Faculty and Clinical Supervisor, Canadian Institute for Child and Adolescent Psychoanalytic Psychotherapy; Faculty, Institute for the Advancement of Self Psychology.

Introduction

Lori C. Bohm

> We shall assume that *everyone is much more simply human than otherwise* ...
> (Sullivan, 1953, p.32)

My doctoral dissertation was a study of the factors contributing to psychological and physical wellbeing in older adults. Data were collected via a variety of means, including a structured interview. The subjects were residents in independent living settings, some catering to the general public and some designed especially for seniors. As a woman in her late twenties, I was, in some ways, like a cultural anthropologist, spending hours with people many years ahead of me in life who had lived through a range of experiences from mundane to fascinating, some of which I would ultimately know well and others I could only imagine.

As I thought about the themes in the present volume, one man I interviewed for my study came to mind. He was a crusty old fellow, living alone, as he had for many years after the early death of his wife. As a young man, he had fought in World War I, and the atrocities and hardships he had witnessed and participated in were as fresh in his mind as if they had occurred the day before. Before he would agree to be interviewed, he spent an hour or more testing me, trying to determine if I could in any way walk in his shoes, if I could even minimally grasp the horrors that he had experienced, if I could understand what it is like to shoot another person at point-blank range to avoid being killed oneself. He asked, 'How can you think that you can help me or any person if you have never faced what I have faced, if your life is so different from mine?'

I did manage to persuade this man to be a subject in my study, but his interrogation remains with me these many years later. Despite the fact that we were both white Americans, our life experiences made us quite different from one another. He was approaching the end of his adult life; mine had just begun. As an older, and I hope wiser, psychologist–psychoanalyst, I have come to appreciate the myriad factors that make us all quite different from one another, that make each of us unique. Beyond the cultural, racial and ethnic divides, each family is its own mini-culture. Even within the family, each child has his or her own rendition of family life, affected by temperament, fit between the child's personality and that of the parents, by the historical moment and other issues. Some children grow up feeling like outsiders in their own families, while some fit right in. This can be true even in healthy families. People with neglect, abuse or other trauma in their histories are even more likely to grow up feeling different (Van Ijzendoorn, Schuengel and Bakersman-Kranesburg, 1999). It is no wonder that most people seek to affiliate with others they see as like themselves.

As psychoanalysts, we work daily with people whose life experiences and challenges are distinct from our own. Yet, we are able to find ourselves in our patients. We are able to help people very different from ourselves grasp and develop a sense of identity and comprehend and clarify the vicissitudes of their inner lives. How do we do this? How does it work? What do we have to overcome as analysts and as people to accomplish these crucial goals? Are there factors in our patients' histories and backgrounds that may present barriers to successful treatment, and, if so, how can we minimize the potential ill effects of these issues?

Psychoanalytic Perspectives on Identity and Difference: Navigating the Divide is a book about identity and identification and the centrality of these concepts to our work as psychoanalytically oriented clinicians. Although it will address, among other factors, cross-cultural, racial and ethnic diversity, this is not a book about 'othering' or 'the Other'. Rather than focusing on 'who is and what is alien and divergent from the norm, from identity and from the self' (Wikipedia, 2016, online), the book conceptualizes the touch points that help us connect or 'navigate the divide' presented by our differences.

At this historical moment, such a focus is timely and urgent. Globalization affects our daily lives. The Internet and social media expose us to people, experiences and ideas that would have remained foreign less than a generation ago. Thinking about the ways we are 'alike' and 'different' becomes part of the fabric of daily life. Many of the worst human tragedies (wars, genocide) have occurred largely because people see themselves as different (and better) than other people, or feel threatened by people with beliefs and practices that are discrepant from their own. It is therefore essential that we think about the ways in which people who seem very different from ourselves are actually similar, with similar needs and aspirations for themselves and their families. By recognizing our points of connection with people whose culture, ethnicity, socioeconomic status or way of relating to others are different from ours, we may be better able to accept and appreciate the value in our differences.

Four themes

This book on alikeness and difference addresses issues that confront mental health practitioners of all theoretical orientations. The chapters in this book encompass four themes:

1   the internal experience of likeness and difference in the patient, and its ramifications;
2   the work of the therapist to find him or herself in the patient;

3   cultural, racial and behavioural divides;
4   the internal experience of likeness and difference in the therapist.

Within each of these themes, the reader will find rich clinical cases that demonstrate ways of working with issues of likeness and difference and explicate relevant theoretical models. The cases also depict the challenges we face and ways to overcome the barriers to connecting with patients who see themselves as very different or whom we experience that way. As will become clear in the chapters on cultural, racial and behavioural differences, people who are robbed of the opportunity to know fully and positively embrace their unique histories and culture are at greater risk of mental illness and social isolation. Throughout, the therapists work to help their patients find and consolidate a meaningful identity and to feel they have a viable place in their social worlds.

The internal experience of likeness and difference in the patient

All of the chapters in the first section of the book illustrate how patients' internal experiences of likeness and difference impede successful adaptation and/or identity development. The book begins with a chapter by Brent Willock that examines the process of identification and disidentification in two patients, and how this unconscious way of being like rejecting others can interfere in interpersonal relationships. The patients projected unacceptable, dissociated self-experiences into others and then experienced the others as malignant. Through their work with Willock, the patients were able to become aware of the 'not-me' parts of themselves, re-integrate these parts and relate to others more adaptively.

Next, Gladys Guarton points out that navigating alikeness and difference is evident in the two crucial tasks of development: to be able to be differentiated from as well as connected to significant others. When a person experiences intense shame, as do the patients Guarton describes in her chapter, the person feels different, set apart from others. Guarton suggests that this sense of painful difference develops from insufficient attunement on the part of the mothering person during childhood.

Continuing the exploration of development, Barri Belnap proposes a functional model showing how psychotic symptoms in adolescence can function to communicate identity. The symptoms are used by the patient to research and learn age-appropriate goals. Belnap demonstrates how treatment that is focused on the patient's development instead of on psychotic symptom reduction can help the psychotic adolescent move into a more adaptive identity, characterized by curiosity and knowledge-seeking.

In 'Neuroticism is the Way Home', Mark Egit emphasizes the neurotic person's inexorable, unconscious search for an other (the 'object') who gives him or her an experience that repeats (is like) what was painfully felt during childhood. Psychoanalytic psychotherapy can provide a different experience with an other (the therapist as object), which can then free patients to have healthier, different experiences with people in their lives outside of the consulting room.

Harriette Kaley presents her work with a young gay man who wishes to transition to being a woman. That goal was accomplished during the therapy, and the patient was finally able to live in a way consistent with her sense of herself. However, she refused to give permission for her story to be published. Kaley's chapter describes the issues that surfaced as the negotiation around publication took place.

The work of the therapist to find him or herself in the patient

Two chapters focus particularly on this essential element of psychotherapeutic work. In both instances, the therapist at first has difficulty finding her or himself in (identifying with) the patient. Susan Kolod's patient is an older man who was accused of sexually abusing his granddaughter. Despite the fact that the patient was incarcerated and lost his job, the charges were then dropped. His continuing struggle with feeling misunderstood and the need to adjust to the many changes caused by the paedophilia accusation brought him to therapy. Kolod struggled with wanting to know whether the accusations were, in fact, true. In this context, she found it challenging to identify with this patient. A consultation with a self-proclaimed paedophile-turned-author helped her to let this question go; ultimately, Kolod was able to empathize with her patient's suffering. This permitted her to see him as a fellow human being and to provide a healing experience for him.

The beginning of the treatment of a child referred to Ionas Sapountzis for a gender identity disorder felt to the therapist 'as if something was missing', as the little boy tried in odd ways to communicate. Eventually, he began bringing in books of words in a range of foreign languages, languages in which the letter symbols are different from in English. Sapountzis, who is Greek, found himself transported to the time in his own life when he tried to learn German in order to enter the German school in Athens. Only then was he able to connect with the pain of this boy in not feeling good enough and to find himself in the patient. He was subsequently able to stop being preoccupied about finding the 'right way' to reach this boy, whom he had previously seen as difficult to engage, and to simply 'be' with him and to validate what was important to him. The boy ultimately stopped engaging in odd behaviours and made friends at school. As treatment finished, the boy did not appear to have a gender identity disorder. Sapountzis calls upon Winnicott, Ogden, Searles, Stern and others to elucidate the process between himself and his young patient.

Cultural, racial and behavioural divides

The chapters in this part of the book cover arenas of alikeness and difference that are overtly apparent to the observer. However, the intrapsychic meanings of these differences reverberate uniquely for each patient, and for each patient/therapist dyad.

In the first chapter of the third section, John O'Leary bemoans the fact that there is not enough racial diversity in the people who practise psychoanalytic psychotherapy. He urges the field to find ways to appeal more to clinicians of colour, and likewise to the many potential patients who are from diverse racial and ethnic backgrounds. This chapter is respectful of the great value in difference, but posits that people may prefer to be in therapy with clinicians who are similar to themselves racially or ethnically.

Janice Walters describes an extreme rendition of aversion to difference, with the goal of cultural genocide. She tells the history of the Aboriginal people at the hands of the people who colonized Australia. The Aboriginal people were seen as vastly inferior to the white colonizers, who took the children of Aborigines away from their parents and raised them in an effort to rid them of their indigenous ways. These children became known as the Stolen Generation. Walters describes the severe mental illness that often resulted from being torn away from one's parents and culture. Norma Tracey further describes this tragedy and describes a programme for treating these severely mistreated, disrespected and abused people.

In New Zealand, a way of working has developed to aid white (*Pakeha*) mental health practitioners in understanding the Māori culture. Trudy Ake and Sarah Calvert demonstrate this way of working, which is called 'cultural supervision'. In addition to having a clinical supervisor, *Pakeha* practitioners treating Māori patients learn from a cultural supervisor who helps them decipher and comprehend myriad cultural imperatives and differences, truly 'navigating the divide'. Ingo Lambrecht gives a soul-searching, rich description of what it is like to be a *Pakeha* working in the Māori Mental Health Services, and what it has taught him about alikeness and difference.

The remaining two chapters in this section describe work with people whose behaviours mark them as different. Susan Rose discusses her treatment of a man in his sixties with Asperger syndrome, a disorder on the autistic spectrum. People with Aspergers are limited in their ability to comprehend how other people think and what motivates them, a tremendous impediment to functioning in the social world. Through often repetitive interventions, Rose was able to help this man navigate the challenges presented by the illness and death of his mother, to be able to transition to being the helper to his elderly father and to begin to have some insight into how people other than himself think.

Arguing that people who present psychotic symptoms are 'most often driven mad by experiences that push them outside the social order', Marilyn Charles offers a theoretically and clinically rich discussion of psychosis in traumatized individuals. People suffering with psychosis often behave in ways distinctively different from non-psychotic individuals. Like people on the autistic spectrum, people who are psychotic are challenged in their ability to comprehend the social world. Charles believes that how the psychotic person's 'markers of difference are read' by those in their worlds determines whether the person will become alienated from him or herself and others or be able to use his or her differences as creative tools.

Internal experience of likeness and difference in the therapist

Therapists' experiences of feeling alike and different, both while on the job and in life, have important implications for their work. There is precedent in psychoanalysis for clinicians to document their own traumatic journeys and treatments in articles and books (see, for example, Guntrip, 1975; Little, 1990; Stolorow, 2007), often as a way to illustrate theoretical discoveries and suggestions for improving clinical methods. In the first chapter in the final section, Johanna Tiemann describes her own treatment and her recovery from the trauma of having a visible birth defect. By virtue of having been born with a cleft lip and palate, Tiemann always felt different from others, that she was repugnant and that her face represented her inner badness. Her parents' lack of empathy exacerbated her feeling of difference. Tiemann's contribution traces her struggle to find a suitable therapist, one who would not challenge her illogical assumptions, and who could help her experience her similarity with others and rejoin the social world.

In contrast to Tiemann, Michael Stern writes about experiences that are, for the most part, universal. His focus is on the ways in which the therapist is the same and different over time, as a function of length of time in the field and the exigencies of life. Life events, such as parenthood and illness, change us, and years in practice often make us wiser and less rigid about technique.

Emily Fucheck's chapter deals with two ruptures in her relationship with her training analyst, the first of which was repaired; however, the second led to the demise of the treatment. Fucheck discusses the difference between how her analyst dealt with her and how she responded to one of her analytic patients when there was a similar rupture in their work. Fucheck shares her internal process during her own analysis and in her work with her patient in an open, honest way – a contribution in itself.

The final chapter of the book is a complex exploration of the life and work of an outsider psychoanalyst: Claude Barbre explores the theoretical work of Otto Rank, including his similarities and differences with Freud. In particular, Rank understood artists to be people who feel different, like exiles from their own cultures. He believed that creativity was made possible by the 'life-force of the will' and focused on the duality in development, one harkened to by Gladys Guarton earlier in this volume, the tension between the movement towards individuation and the need to be part of the whole. The notion of the will, which originates in the drive for self-actualization, illustrates this tension, as exercising one's will may lead to separation from the group. Barbre discusses the 'contrapuntal play of likeness and difference' in Rank's work and delves into the factors in Rank's early history that contributed to his way of understanding the human condition.

As is clear from this summary, *Psychoanalytic Perspectives on Identity and Difference: Navigating the Divide* is a book that breaks new ground in focusing in wide-ranging ways on this neglected dimension of psychological experience. The rich case material, technical suggestions and ample theoretical explanation make this volume a unique and valuable asset to mental health practitioners as they seek to reach and help all of their patients. The material in the book expands and deepens the understanding of what it means to be 'more simply human than otherwise', making it possible for our patients and ourselves to embrace this essential idea.

References

Guntrip, H. (1975). My experience of analysis with Fairbairn and Winnicott. *International Review of Psychoanalysis*, 2: 145–156.

Little, M.I. (1990). *Psychotic anxieties and containment: a personal record of an analysis with Winnicott*. London: Jason Aronson.

Stolorow, R. (2007). *Trauma and human existence*. New York: The Analytic Press.

Sullivan, H.S. (1953). *The interpersonal theory of psychiatry*. New York: W.W. Norton.

Van Ijzendoorn, M.H., Schuengel, C. and Bakersman-Kranenburg, M.J. (1999). Disorganized attachment in early childhood: meta-analysis of precursors, concomitants and sequelae. *Development and Psychopathology*, 11: 225–249.

Wikipedia, 'Other', online at https://en.wikipedia.org/wiki/Other (accessed 3 July 2016).

Part I

The internal experiences of likeness and difference in the patient

Chapter 1

Identifying/disidentifying

Brent Willock

> The neurotic ego has, by definition, fallen prey to overidentification and to faulty identifications with disturbed parents, a circumstance which isolated the small individual both from his budding identity and from his milieu.
> – Erik Erikson

Childrearing circumstances in which children feel unloved and rejected can trigger a powerful combination of problematic defences: identification with the rejecting object; disidentification with important parts of the self; projective identification of these unacceptable self-states on to others. These pathologically accommodative processes wreak havoc with identity, self-esteem and relationships. In significant ways, afflicted individuals cease being themselves. Becoming the bad object, they projectively perceive others as their disowned, despised selves. Shocked victims of these patients' hostile (second) nature feel they are being regarded very differently from how they view themselves. In analysis, these pathological identificatory processes can be revisited and revised, with significant therapeutic effects.

The visit

Lying on the couch, Lorraine complained about an upcoming houseguest – her teenaged niece.

'What's in it for me?' Lorraine asked bitterly. 'Someone else should shoulder this responsibility. This is the last time I'll sacrifice my weekend for my sister's daughter!'

In the past, she liked this girl, regretting that geographical distance and family dynamics diminished contact. Ordinarily, she would have looked forward to her company, seeing it as an opportunity to strengthen their bond. When I mentioned this discrepancy, Lorraine agreed, but insisted she was in no mood to host her niece.

I wondered if her current antipathy might reflect how she believed her own mother had felt about her when Lorraine was a child, namely that she was an unwanted burden. This idea made instant sense to Lorraine. She realized she was playing the roles of her child self (burdensome niece) and her mother (irritable woman not wanting to be bothered with this youngster).

This interpretation emerged from years of work during which Lorraine's mother was portrayed mostly as an absence. Lorraine knew her mother must have been around because meals appeared. Apart from two cherished memories, this woman did not seem to be a significant, positive presence in Lorraine's memory. In contrast, she recalled a close relationship with her father.

With her niece, Lorraine was repeating rather than remembering (Freud, 1914) an important aspect of her childhood. She was processing, but mostly defending against traumatic experience pertaining to an unavailable, unloving mother via repetition compulsion (Freud, 1920). In this reversed remembering/not-remembering manner, Lorraine could feel like the powerful, unloving victimizer rather than the neglected child. She also felt herself to be the victim of her burdensome child, making this a multifaceted, sadomasochistic scenario.

Individuals who utilize projective identification maintain a tie to disowned parts of themselves. Lorraine's angry connection to her niece sustained an intensely negative mother–child bond. Memorializing her relationship with her mother this way, Lorraine deployed a defence Anna Freud (1948), following Ferenczi (1932), called identification with the aggressor. She became her emotionally unavailable, resentful parent. Identifying with her rejecting mother, Lorraine created a complementary counter-identification with her dependent, unwanted, childhood self, aggressively attributing this self-state to her niece. Using this girl as a toilet-breast (Meltzer, 1967), Lorraine dumped her innocent, needy, devalued, childhood self into her image of her niece. Her niece now represented this feared, unwanted part of Lorraine that Lorraine could attack, underscoring its 'not-me' (Sullivan, 1940) status.

In contemporary Relational psychoanalytic parlance, these introjective/projective processes result in what Jessica Benjamin (1988) calls doer/done-to relationships rather than healthier ones based on mutual recognition. In Lorraine's case, the one done-to (niece) has been transformed into a version of the doer's self that the doer (Lorraine) could not contain. For defensive reasons, misrecognition eclipsed recognition.

Drawing on British Object Relations Theory further enriches our understanding of The Visit. In Fairbairn's (1952) framework, infants internalize bad objects. In subsequent efforts to 'master' this entity, an unholy alliance is forged between the rejecting object (Lorraine's mother) and the antilibidinal ego (the new, nasty Lorraine) against the libidinal ego (projected on to the unsuspecting niece hoping to enjoy a pleasant sojourn with auntie).

In Winnicott's (1969) idiom, Lorraine was enmeshed in subjective object relating (omnipotent projections) as opposed to realistic object usage (Benjamin's recognition). Subjective object relating leaves no room for reflection (Fonagy et al., 2002; Ogden, 1986). The other is not perceived as a separate subject. At most the other is a selfobject (Kohut, 1971), for example, a toilet-breast. Subjective object relating belongs to Klein's paranoid-schizoid realm and Freud's (1915) purified pleasure ego (taking into the self anything attractive, eliminating all that is non-gratifying). In contrast, realistic object usage reflects higher level mentation that corresponds to Klein's depressive position and Freud's reality ego.

Speculating about a death drive, Freud (1920) and his Kleinian followers underscored the need to turn this destructive force outward in order to survive. In the processes I am describing, there is a similar need to redirect the withering power of perceived maternal rejection on to other objects (niece) in order to carry on living. While there is an instinctive basis to this desperate object relating, it is most useful to focus on defensive aspects and aims of these convoluted relational processes. Most psychoanalysts would find these processes more plausible than earlier explanations based on redirecting the death instinct outwards.

Some readers might object to the preceding comingling of Freudian, Kleinian, British Object Relations, Sullivanian and contemporary Relational concepts. They may believe it wrong, or at least inadvisable, to mix terms from different models. In contrast, *Comparative-Integrative Psychoanalysis* (Willock, 2007) favours bringing ideas of diverse schools together. Multiple perspectives mingle well at the comparative–integrative table. Together, they create richer, more useful dialogue and understanding than is possible when feasts are restricted to those belonging to just one school of thought. Even small steps toward creative coexistence can help heal our fractured discipline.

Analysis helps patients move from repeating to remembering, advancing from post-traumatic states and adaptations to healthier modes of being that permit separation, perspective, reflection. In relationship to her niece, I tried to assist Lorraine to progress from doer/done-to, sadomasochistic, paranoid-schizoid object relating to growth facilitating, mutually enjoyable, meaningful, depressive position, recognition and object usage. In accord with Bion's (1970) concept of the container and the contained and the need to use alpha function (reverie) to transform beta elements (unmanageable, raw feelings suitable only for evacuation) into alpha elements that can be retained in the self and used productively, Lorraine transmitted her angry upset about her niece into me, a toilet-breast. Identifying with the harshly attacked girl, I felt uncomfortable imagining the 'reunion' they were about to suffer. Making sense of what was going on in terms of Lorraine's past, I reflected that understanding back to her in a form that proved tolerable, manageable, and useful for reflection and maturation. In keeping with Ogden's (1986) suggestion to rename the depressive position the historical position, we placed Lorraine's intolerable experience in historical perspective, linking then and now, thereby contextualizing and transforming it.

In our next session, Lorraine conveyed her realization that when her niece visited last year the girl had been burdened by worries related to her mother's serious illness. Mother was now doing well and the current visit was 'wonderful'. Having worked through the oppressive phantasy in which she had been entangled, Lorraine became free to participate in a more rational, creative, mutually enjoyable reality.

One evening, Lorraine's niece wanted to watch some age-appropriate television. Believing this would be boring, Lorraine exiled herself to her computer, then thought it might be interesting and enjoyable to spend time with her niece and see what the programme was about. That experience turned out to be very pleasant. Linking this new experience to her past, Lorraine lamented that her mother never would have watched a TV movie with her. She was now remembering rather than repeating. This was a 'holy grail' weekend, Lorraine enthused. It provided a long-sought, historically elusive, mother–daughter experience. Initially unpromising ingredients had been miraculously transmuted into sacred gold. In contrast, Lorraine usually bemoaned angrily that she would (or had been) frighteningly alone all weekend, much as had been the case after her parents' divorce.

As we worked on these problematic processes of identification, disidentification and projective identification, Lorraine frequently began sessions describing some intensely upsetting interaction, saying she looked forward to sorting out 'Who's who?' For example, she went ballistic when her girlfriend asked which route they should take to a restaurant. Lorraine was now aware she could have been performing as someone other than her usual mature self, simultaneously seeing others as other than who they actually were. She considered that with this girlfriend she may have enacted an angry, fed-up, rejecting version of her mother. She also realized she identified with her girlfriend to whom she had assigned the role of dependent, frightened, misunderstood, berated, childhood Lorraine. To make matters even more complicated, and complete, when raging at her girlfriend, Lorraine realized she was also voicing anger at her mother that she had never dared express. Here she believed she was raging at her mother for not taking initiative, planning things carefully and lovingly for her, instead of turning to her daughter to be the responsible, knowledgeable adult.

It was by no means quick and simple for Lorraine to move from pathological, defensive, identificatory object relating through reflection to healthier intersubjectivity. In time, she became increasingly adept at understanding her propensity to create these painful dramas. She was ever more able to figure out what was going on, what the anxieties and unrequited longings were that motivated these defensive processes, and what she could do to transcend these enactments. With these new insights and abilities, she spent less time in furious fantasies and relational entanglements and could more readily repair any damage she caused.

Pathological accommodation (Brandchaft, 2007) relates to Winnicott's (1960) depiction of individuals forging false selves on a compliance basis. Those escaping overwhelming relational conflicts this way often feel inhibited and deadened. In contrast, analysands like Lorraine embrace a more aggressive flight pattern that is disturbingly uninhibited and 'lively'. At times, however, they may exhibit constricted, devitalized features. In love making, Lorraine often felt numb, dead. In adolescence, her family said she was always miserable. Then, she could not verbally express certain emotions and concerns. In analysis, she learned to feel and reflect upon previously unformulated (Stern, 1997), dissociated experience. In so doing, she became increasingly able to communicate with others.

The following vignette from several months later illustrates how significant this progress was in terms of these identificatory processes. A friend distanced herself because Lorraine had challenged her as to whether she really wanted to have a baby. Whenever I speak up, Lorrraine complained to me, I am abandoned by 'mother' (e.g., that friend). Lorraine's lament was very familiar. In this instance, she surprised me by reflecting on the event and concurring with her friend's accusations. 'I am judgemental, insensitive, thoughtless ... sometimes.' She could now accept criticism since the feedback no longer felt so total.

Instead of simply feeling furiously disappointed by her friend, Lorraine now had empathy for her, recalling how that friend's father had brutalized her, while her mother had been such an ineffective protector. She also realized she had challenged her friend because she feared a baby would make 'mother' (i.e., the friend) less available. Even more surprisingly, Lorraine asked who was going to be understanding and loving toward her friend's father and mother whose brutality and absence expressed their own pain. When I acknowledged Lorraine's unexpected empathy for those abusive parents, she surprised me even further by saying they were her, that is, 'insensitive, thoughtless, judgmental, harsh – due to fear and pain'. Even after many decades of practice, changes and growth effected by psychoanalysis can still strike one as almost miraculous.

A day (not) at the spa

Angela enjoyed her friend's daughter since Zoey was a baby. I was, therefore, surprised when Angela, upon receiving a text message, raged that this child, now a young woman, only contacts her when she needs something. Zoey's proposal that they should get their nails done could only mean Zoey wanted Angela to pay. Angela responded that she would not be visiting her aesthetician for some time.

When Angela gained some distance from this event, she shared that mother's mantra was 'If you expect anything from me, you'll get less.' In the shadow of that philosophy, Angela learned to not ask for anything. Reflecting on Zoey's upsetting proposal, Angela remarked, 'I'm my mother to Zoey's/my needs. Mother felt burdened by my slightest needs.' Identifying with her dismissive mother, Angela disowned her needy self, projectively assigning that unacceptable role to Zoey as prelude to rejecting her request. In so doing, she perpetuated her unsatisfying relationship with her own mother.

We had done much work on Angela's relationship with her critical mother. In one model scene (Lichtenberg, 2001), the family doctor told young Angela and her mother that Angela's genital odour meant she needed to wash down there. When they got home, mother tossed a facecloth at her, coldly telling her to use it. On another occasion, she flung a bottle of lotion at her, muttering 'Put it on your legs.' It is surely more than coincidental that Angela's rage toward Zoey pertained to feminine bodily activities that could have given rise to enjoyable bonding, but, as in Angela's childhood, did not. For the moment, reverse repetition ruled but remembering and reflection were beginning to dismantle the power of those pathological identificatory processes.

Realizing what had happened with Zoey, Angela was distressed that she could still be so issued about mother–daughter matters after having worked on them so much in treatment. She felt she must be getting nowhere. Equally noteworthy, I responded, was the fact that she understood what was going on in her feelings about Zoey so quickly. Angela could see this was indeed progress.

Like Lorraine, Angela created many scenes in which she attributed her 'inappropriately requesting' therefore rejected self to others. As she developed the space (in our room and in her mind) in which to ponder these dynamics, she increasingly got a handle on them. As she disidentified with her rejecting mother, shifting from enactment to thinking, she could be more empathic with others, with herself and even with her mother. For example, she looked forward to her son's coming home from college. I reminded her of how she used to dread his return, feeling burdened by his needs, like she believed her mother felt toward her. (When she arrived home from university, mother told her she could not stay with her – unless Angela succeeded in getting child support money from her father.) Angela acknowledged the validity of the contrast I was highlighting, remarking that her new attitude toward her son represented a major turning point. 'Now I know what family means,' she sobbed. Having disidentified with mother, she was free to be a loving parent to her son. Their relationship blossomed.

Dreaming she was kissing a man, Angela felt awkward, not knowing if she was pleasing him. In her associations, she wondered what is expected in relationships, and can she live up to whatever it is. Imagining mother glaring, she continued: 'So many impossible expectations were put upon me. Now in relationships, I become demanding and critical.' She lamented ruining her relationship with Bernard, becoming the mother he could never please. Now she realizes she and Bernard are alike.

> I become mother, judging. You better meet my needs and do it right. No one can meet that. Every time ma entered the house, my stomach knotted. If Bernard had taken me to Rio, I'd have found something else to complain about. I feel exactly like mother. I could never satisfy her, therefore I never got love, therefore I felt empty, therefore I filled that space with anger versus nothingness. Bernard could never fill his mother's needs. I get him now.

Where enactment was, empathy now is, increasingly.

Dylan

Dylan reported a dream of himself 'in two parts' – adult, and child of six or seven years 'seen from the outside'. He characterized this youngster and his own childhood self as unlikable, peevish, defensive. Needing to be other than the loathsome creature he was, Dylan said he became 'profoundly dishonest' in his self-presentation. I asked what the dream child was doing. The grimy kid was just sitting, feeling everyone hated him, Dylan replied. He was a whiney, excuse-making nose-picker rather than being ballsy, out there, taking his lumps, standing up for something.

Seeming to intuit that the self-hatred he was expressing derived from how he felt his mother regarded him, Dylan declared: 'If I was my mother, I'd dislike me after I developed my peanut allergy.' Here he manifested Fairbairn's (1952) moral defence: Better to be a sinner in a world ruled by God than to be an innocent child in a world ruled by the devil. Allying himself with mother hating himself (Fairbairn's rejecting object allying with the antilibidinal ego to attack the libidinal self), Dylan could obtain some 'security'.

While Dylan's description of the boy dripped with disgust and contempt, his dream image evoked in me the Thematic Apperception Test picture of a boy seated on a log cabin's stoop. I told him the boy seemed lonely and unhappy, as if he needed someone to come talk with him, maybe hug him, perhaps engage him in some interesting activity. Dylan agreed, but felt no desire to do that. 'This was a kid I didn't want,' he stated. The boy reminded him of a pathetic Oxfam child with a television voiceover pleading that his parents were dead and the situation was horrific. One doesn't know whether to believe it or change channels to avoid pain, Dylan remarked. 'My dream depicted emotional squalor from which I want to get away. My family was distant, disappointed. They wanted to get rid of me.'

In our next session, Dylan said he felt excited and optimistic after our discussion of his 'divided self' dream. He (mistakenly, or intuitively) thought I had asked if he had any inclination to pick up the young boy, reiterating that he only wanted to distance himself from this despicable creature. He did, however, associate to a female friend who had been dumped by her high school boyfriend. After thirty-five years, they were both divorced, and would soon be 'rejoined' with each other. I wondered if this romantic narrative reflected his longing to be reunited with his childhood self after having dumped him long ago. Dylan accepted this interpretation, alluding to that self being worth holding, then reverted to expressing hatred for needy old people in his doctor's waiting room. A process was beginning wherein he vacillated between disliking and imagining liking hitherto rejected aspects of himself.

For decades, Dylan tormented himself with obsessions that he was homosexual, living a family life lie. His parents would despise his 'true' identity. He imagined they suspected he was gay and hated him for that. Now he shared his insight that homosexual thoughts represent his longing to lovingly reconnect with his self (cf., Freud's [1922] views on homosexuality as narcissistic object-choice).

Nothing of who he really is was acceptable to his mother, Dylan believed. 'I only exist to attend to her needs.' Rewarded for falseness, he always felt separate from that performance, 'empty, not there'. He had identified with her judgmental, undermining manner. He now began thinking he had been wrong to devalue and dismiss old people. He drew inspiration in this regard from his wife's love for her aged mother.

After this shift from contempt to compassion, Dylan reported a dream in which he partied with family and friends in a Detroit home he used to own. Now it was located near my Ann Arbor office. With increasing urgency, he told partiers that since this was no longer his abode, they must not be caught in it. As things began to feel increasingly out of control, the outraged owners arrived. 'How could I be so stupid to occupy their space?' Dylan's body began to shake. I suggested this dream could represent his wish to re-inhabit a former, childhood self he had abandoned. The more he accomplished this re-ownership through our work, the more nervous he became that the 'owners' to whom he had sold out would violently object to his taking back that which he had surrendered. Dylan agreed.

Earlier that session, there was additional evidence that Dylan had been daring to re-inhabit his body. He reported feeling 'flush' upon seeing a handsome man on television. That reaction would usually have spiralled into obsessive thoughts about being gay, therefore loathsome. This time he thought such feelings do not make him gay. 'When I see an attractive man on the street, I have a physical response indicating I am happy to see him and have a reciprocal experience of myself.' Genital warming indicates that 'I exist in my penis and in the rest of me. It's not arousal, but inhabiting. The rest of me thinks of it as betrayal. I shouldn't have that good feeling. As we work together, the enormous ball of homosexuality shrinks.'

The next session, Dylan announced that he used to have to work so hard to feel like one person, battling aspects of himself that did not fit. Reflecting on recent progress, he declared, 'If I die tomorrow, I wouldn't feel I never got a chance to live my life. Before I felt so ripped off. I believed life would end without starting.' As he dis-dis-identified, he became increasingly able to be himself and live his life.

Continuing to address the pressures he felt to conform to alien parental agendas, Dylan dreamt he was at a political convention. A regime was ending. Hitler was there (cf. Laing, 1971). People wanted to know if others, like himself, were friend or enemy. Young Hitler encouraged Dylan to exchange uniforms with him. Dylan felt compromised. To hide who he was, he needed to adopt an anti-Semitic guise. He associated to an admired grandmother, visited by Nazis, trying to flush out, with veiled threats, who was with, versus against, them. Defiantly, she declared, 'I will never help.' Dylan seemed to be searching for a model that would help him stand up for himself in the dangerous times he was revisiting.

Dylan's mother's birth had been preceded by that of an ill brother who had been institutionalized and died after a few years. This tragedy broke Dylan's grandmother's heart. In her nineties, she still obsessed and wept about that son. Dylan began crying. He did not know why he was so moved. He had not known this boy. 'Maybe I liked the child that died.' I suggested he liked the part of himself that had also been sent away and 'died' and was moved that a mother could have such deep, enduring feelings for her son, unlike how he believed his mother felt about him. Dylan concurred: 'There was something wrong with that boy, but he was still loved.'

Dylan could not believe how much he enjoyed presenting a paper at an out-of-town academic conference. In the past, he would have felt overwhelmed, longing to hide. Flying back, a photograph in a newspaper of an athlete initiated an emotional descent concerning gayness, stripping away all his happiness. Recalling that I once said he tends to react to positive experiences negatively, Dylan thought this experience could be another manifestation of self-sabotage. I asked what the athlete looked like. He was handsome, young, perhaps having an expression of longing, sensuality, need. His fit torso stimulated a 'pre-sexual' response that turned into a 'cavern yawning before me, an abyss of danger'.

Dylan's homosexuality seemed to represent a long-standing boyish longing for love that he felt might be safer and more likely to be satisfied with father rather than mother. It was also code for a loathsome, unlovable self. I suggested when he contemplated the photo it may not have represented an other so much as it served as a mirror reflecting a self-image. Dylan agreed that it was as if something had pulled him through that image, something he had lost, like the way people long for their youth and strength. He missed the me he might have been if he had not had that nut allergy and other problems.

Feeling increasingly healthy, Dylan expressed deep gratitude to analysis for having helped him ascend to a state he had never thought possible. After his trip, he could not believe how much he enjoyed work and how efficient he was at it now that he was no longer so agonized. Not only did his zest for work blossom, but so did that other pillar of mental health, love. He talked about loving his wife with greater certainty and depth than had ever been possible. To Freud's criteria, love and work, people often add play. Dylan shared repeatedly how much more he was enjoying sculpting. Some of his art pertained to matters he was working on in analysis.

When he turns against himself, Dylan feels as if he is hurting someone else, someone who deserves the hate. When he feels good about things, this accusatory part arises. Lately, this phenomenon was not so problematic. 'The demon doesn't materialize.' In an earlier analysis, when Dylan was feeling good about the treatment, he would look in a mirror and say, 'You're not going to get away with this. I'm going to make sure you don't get free.' How bizarre this now sounded, he remarked. 'Why did this me hate the me that just wants to enjoy life?'

I said this old mirror story sounded like he had signed a pact with mother and could not get free. 'The Stockholm syndrome for survival,' Dylan responded. When he first heard of that phenomenon, he understood it immediately, whereas others were perplexed by that close relationship between captive and abductor. He said I had rightly referred to an Unholy Alliance between him and mother. It was mother's voice threatening him, although he was the one speaking the lines in the mirror. His relationship with her was good if they both attacked part of him. 'The child part didn't get any air or water.' He said I was also correct that there might be a me on the other side that he might like. 'It all feels spooky.'

'If it weren't for you, I'd be all alone in psychic space,' Dylan shared. His sense that our work relieved psychic isolation seemed like a health-promoting antidote to the pathological alliance he struck long ago with his internalized bad object. Dylan felt it was an enormous development to be breaking away from that unholy alliance. 'Now I see the boulder that has blocked my life. It is so painful to think about having been conscripted into such pervasive self-loathing.' Until now, he reflected, the conscripting force had been immune from prosecution. He resented that most of his life had been wasted, or limited, by self-hatred, despite his having tried so many ways to escape. He was grateful that he was waking up.

As he figured out why he and his mother had become psychically entangled, Dylan no longer felt compelled to demonize her. Instead of blaming anyone else, he felt empowered. Believing he had internalized mother's censure as a way of partnering with her, he saw it as his doing, but not his fault, like Stockholm syndrome. 'If I did it, I can undo it.' The voice speaking to his apartment mirror was 'me fully on board to extinguish the vitality of the other part of me'. He was amazed he bought into that belief so aggressively. He noted that the mean part of him had vitality, courage and determination – qualities he wanted to restore to a more harmonious, whole self. His new freedom to not demonize mother meant he was getting free of her, he believed. She was shrinking to human size. He no longer felt he carried within him an impenetrable recess where the blackness, beyond words and communication, cannot be reached.

Progress is usually accompanied by anxiety and resistance. Not knowing why he was upset, Dylan associated to a movie in which children were torn away from their mothers. I believe he felt analysis caused painful separation between him and his internal mother – a manifestation of the libido's adhesiveness (Freud, 1937, p.241) and attachment to bad objects (Fairbairn, 1952). Dylan felt angry and sad. 'I feel like acting out, picking a fight so I can separate from you and your influence.'

In another dream, Dylan backed out of his underground parking space – a good image for a place in his unconscious where he had deposited a problematic, hitherto static, self-state. He realized he was turning another car with him, like they were glued together. There was a creepy, scraping sound. When he got 'to my or someone's lot', big pieces were missing from the dashboard and the moulding in the steering wheel with its controls. 'Can I still drive?' he wondered. Yes, he could work around these difficulties, though repairs will cost a fortune. 'My interface with the machine is gone.' He associated to mother's thirty-year-old car that she does not want to change. This dream strikingly represented symbiotic enmeshment and the dangers associated with desirable, but difficult separation–individuation (Mahler, 1972).

Summary

Feeling unloved and rejected can prompt children to embark on a defensive sequence in which they: identify with dismissive objects; disidentify with important aspects of themselves; project these unacceptable self states; then devalue, reject, and attack those qualities they now find in others. Drawing on concepts from diverse schools of thought, consistent with the spirit of comparative–integrative psychoanalysis, illuminates this dark, twisted, troubled state of affairs. In treatment informed by the resulting rich rainbow of theoretical constructs, pathological identificatory processes can be revisited, reviewed and revised. During this therapeutic odyssey, revitalized selves are fostered that feel more whole, rational, insightful, authentic, empathic, loving and lovable. 'There were so many years I felt completely dead,' Dylan remarked. 'It feels so different to be alive, to feel alive.'

References

Benjamin, J. (1988). *The bonds of love*. New York: Pantheon.
Bion, W.R. (1970). *Attention and interpretation*. London: Tavistock.

Brandchaft, B. (2007). Systems of pathological accommodation and change in analysis. *Psychoanalytic Psychology*, 24: 667–687.
Erikson, E. (1959). *Identity and the life cycle*. New York: International Universities Press.
Fairbairn, W.R.D. (1952). *Psychoanalytic studies of the personality*. London and Boston: Routledge and Keegan Paul.
Ferenczi, S. (1949). Confusion of the tongues between the adults and the child (the language of tenderness and of passion). *International Journal of Psychoanalysis*, 30: 225–230.
Fonagy, P., Gergely, G., Jurist, E.L. and Target, M. (2002). *Affect regulation, mentalization, and the development of the self*. New York: Other Press.
Freud, A. (1948). *The ego and the mechanisms of defence*. New York: International Universities Press.
Freud, S. (1914). Remembering, repeating and working-through (further recommendations on the technique of psycho-analysis II). In *The standard edition of the complete psychological works of Sigmund Freud*, vol. 12. London: Hogarth Press, pp.145–156.
—— (1915). Instincts and their vicissitudes. In *The standard edition of the complete psychological works of Sigmund Freud*, vol. 14. London: Hogarth Press, 1957, pp.109–140.
—— (1920). Beyond the pleasure principle. In *The standard edition of the complete psychological works of Sigmund Freud*, vol. 18. London: Hogarth Press, pp.1–64.
—— (1922). Some neurotic mechanisms in jealousy, paranoia and homosexuality. In *The standard edition of the complete psychological Works of Sigmund Freud*, vol. 18. London: Hogarth Press, pp.221–232.
—— (1937). Analysis terminable and interminable. In *The standard edition of the complete psychological works of Sigmund Freud*, vol. 23. London: Hogarth Press, pp.209–254.
Kohut, H. (1971). *The analysis of the self*. New York: International Universities Press.
Laing, R.D. (1971). *The politics of the family and other essays*. London: Tavistock.
Lichtenberg, J.D. (2001). Motivational systems and model scenes with special references to bodily experience. *Psychoanalytic Inquiry*, 21: 430–447.
Mahler, M.S. (1972). On the first three subphases of the separation–individuation process. *International Journal of Psychoanalysis*, 53: 333–338.
Meltzer, D. (1967). *The Psycho-Analytical Process*. London: Karnac.
Ogden, T.H. (1986). *The matrix of the mind: object relations and the psychoanalytic dialogue*. Northvale, NJ: Aronson.
Stern, D. (1997). *Unformulated experience: from dissociation to imagination in psychoanalysis*. Hillsdale, NJ: Analytic Press.
Sullivan, H.S. (1940). *Conceptions of modern psychiatry*. New York: W.W. Norton
Willock, B. (2007). *Comparative-integrative psychoanalysis*. New York: The Analytic Press.
Winnicott, D.W. (1960). Ego distortion in terms of true and false self. In D.W. Winnicott, *The maturational process and the facilitating environment*. New York: International Universities Press, 1965, pp.140–152.
—— (1969). The use of an object. *International Journal of Psychoanalysis*, 50: 711–716.

Chapter 2

Negotiating the different/alike divide in the treatment of shame

Gladys Guarton

Being different and alike, understood as being both individuated and connected, makes a person whole. The ability to oscillate comfortably between these two fundamental states is the mark of mental health (see Guarton, 1999). In relationships, both partners must reconcile their needs for agency and communion. Analytic success depends on the ability of both participants to surmount transference–countertransference binds (which Levenson [1994] views as inevitable versions of the master/slave dialectic).

Blatt (2010) described two personality configurations privileging either self-definition or relatedness. The level of development and integration of these two fundamental human dimensions is proportional to the level of self-maturation. Each facilitates the other's development. Exaggerated preoccupation with either results from disruptions in psychological development affecting both dimensions.

Shame is a social emotion that 'sets one apart' (Lynd, 1958). It identifies one as different, lacking, not measuring up to others' or one's own idea of how one should be. Together with dissociation, shame is a common denominator in most patients' difficulties (Bromberg, 2011). Shame, guilt and preoccupation with protecting self-regard and self-worth are typical of Blatt's introjective personality configuration that privileges autonomy and self-definition over relatedness. Paradoxically, one feels different, or set apart, precisely because one has not attained the differentiation, or self-definition, that would provide the sense of worth accompanying the perception that one is measuring up to one's own and/or others' expectations.

Pathological shame often results from relational trauma in the preverbal developmental stage. Children who are taught that their feelings and desires are unacceptable feel humiliated for being the way they are (not just how they behave). Although they try to hide unacceptable feelings and associated shame, shame repeatedly returns in situations reminiscent of the original trauma. This wordless, thoughtless, disorganizing state cannot be escaped. Its exposure engenders further shame.

Schore (1995) sees shame developing when toddlers, in a state of stage-typical excitement and elation, spontaneously express themselves with caregivers, expecting shared positive affect, but encounter facial/affective misattunement.

Adult shame replicates that sudden shift from high arousal to a low arousal, inhibitory, paralyzing state in situations similar to the original. Erikson (1959) also conceptualized shame as rooted in a failure in life's second year. He emphasized identity development characterized by self-doubt, which stalls the emergent sense of autonomy (following the initial developmental stage of trust versus mistrust and preceding the next one, guilt versus initiative).

Similar to Schore, Winnicott (1966, 1968) viewed shame as related to insufficient maternal attunement to the preverbal child. Spontaneous self-expression encounters lack of recognition, indifference or dislike. Feeling cut out of the relationship, the child becomes unable to 'go on being' – unable to express and assert the self. These children grow up relating compulsively by 'being done by the other', dissociating the ability 'to do to the other'. Both abilities must be developed, together with the capacity to oscillate between them, if one is to be creative and relate intimately.

Current research also suggests post-traumatic stress disorders (PTSDs) in soldiers and trauma victims are more severe and chronic in individuals who were prone to shame prior to the traumatic episode. Discussing PTSD, Levine (2010) points out that a third survival strategy of humans and other animals, 'playing dead', is utilized when the better-known flight and fight responses are unavailable. Paralysis, a passive response of last resort for escaping dreaded situations, involves no action, therefore no energy release. Its success depends on the other's behaviour. During treatment, Levine facilitates the patient's ability to take action to escape paralysis and release accompanying pent-up energy.

Converging neuroscientific and attachment research elucidate psychoanalytic theory and practice. They demonstrate that emotional memories, positive and negative, that shape individuals' affective relational patterns are preverbal in origin and remain stored in the unconscious, implicit self, located in the brain's right hemisphere. Psychoanalysis fundamentally involves right-brain to right-brain communication, which is unconscious, affective and experiential rather than verbal and cognitive (Schore, 2009).

Shame and guilt have often been confused. Their distinction is significant in treatment. Shame (Lewis, 1971) is directly self-evaluative. In guilt, the thing done, not the self, is the central object of negative evaluation. This distinction concerning the divergent effects of shame and guilt on the self, on interpersonal relationships – work, intimacy, family – and on the social order has been confirmed empirically (e.g. Tagney and Dearing, 2002). Investigators describe guilt as the more developmentally advanced, adaptive emotion. They highlight its orientation toward others as opposed to shame's self-absorption, which often interferes with relatedness. That shame is strongly linked to depression and suicide (Lewis, 1971) was confirmed by Tagney and Dearing, who point out that shame-prone and depressed individuals share a tendency to make 'internal, stable, and global attributions' (p.117) for negative events, seeing themselves as always to blame for everything. This tendency is more prevalent in women, although it might be argued that shame may be more recognized by women.

This chapter focuses on a group of patients suffering from shame – all women, all achievers, all proud of 'self-sufficiency'. All described their problems as due to difficulty expressing feelings. Some articulated shame as a significant reason for entering treatment. Those who were explicit about suffering from shame could more easily 'tell' the analyst about it, but were terrified of 'showing' it. One changed from lying on the couch to sitting (both her choices), explaining this move was a sign of courage because now she could be 'seen' as opposed to only being heard.

Another exclaimed 'Now that you can see me, I can change!' after we both survived an interaction where she became flustered, paralyzed and disorganized, while I experienced a range of feelings that translated into a prolonged, concomitant paralysis. Being contagious, shame makes the other prone to hide or escape. While looking at her, I partook of her sense of paralysis, helplessness and ineptitude, while unsuccessfully struggling to find a way to do something constructive. We transcended the impasse when I described my experience to her. She responded by describing her experience, including the unprecedented one of 'me staying with her', which she found relaxing and intimate.

As a person and therapist, I have observed how difficult it is to sustain contact with someone experiencing shame. Shame is alienating since it re-enacts situations that felt painfully rejecting and disruptive to ongoing interaction. It compels one to hide and, because historically the other's reaction was also to escape, shame continues to disrupt interactions, fostering further shame.

The fear of showing shame versus telling about it goes to the root of the experience because, in its preverbal origins, it was the significant other's facial expression that was rejecting, and the toddler's nonverbal, unformulated expressions or behaviours caused the rejection. That shame typically occurs in the presence of important others is a reminder of the original trauma when the child was left 'high and dry, all dressed up with no place to go'. In therapy, experiencing the unacceptable, unformulated desire makes the patient feel unworthy, deserving of rejection.

Transference/countertransference enactments involving shame occur rather frequently. They can be understood and resolved retroactively, as long as the mutual experience can be communicated. Mary, a highly religious, responsible, accomplished woman in her fifties, entered treatment because of suicidal despondency when I was in analytic training. She felt deeply ashamed because she had engaged in an extramarital affair and was unable to stop. She could not live with the realization that she had 'two faces, a good and a bad one'. When she looked in the mirror, she actually imagined these images superimposed. Since they haunted her constantly, she contemplated suicide.

It became evident that Mary suppressed her own needs when they conflicted with those of others. She rather compulsively placed herself at their service when she thought they might need her. She avoided expressing anger because she had been taught it could harm others. I understood her suicidal thoughts and her faces as a struggle involving a false self.

As months passed, Mary became increasingly open and involved in our relationship, more free to express a wider range of emotions. On different occasions, she attempted to tell me about a past interaction with me that haunted her. Except for saying I wore a 'green dress' and through her demeanour communicating that the memory was unpleasant, she was unable to verbalize her memory. Weeks later, she said I wore that dress and showed disapproval or displeasure on my face on the day when, in the initial stages of treatment, she stated she had damned herself because she had chosen her lover over God. I remembered her words vividly, together with the consternation I felt related to her self-condemnation, based on her religious beliefs, and my inability to find words to express understanding of her feelings without disputing her beliefs. I described my memory of my experience. She voiced recognition and relief. She stated it was important to make sure I 'saw' her and her feelings, as opposed to judging her in terms of good/bad or right/wrong. She had been afraid of actively 'taking me to task' and finding out the truth of my experience.

The analyst's unwittingly evaluative facial expressions are specifically important to patients with shame because they are received as approval or disapproval of the whole self. I communicated disagreement of Mary's view of herself based on her religious beliefs, together with the uncomfortable feeling of helplessness that accompanied my inability to respond with words. To Mary, this signalled disapproval of her. If I had responded to her pain by simply recognizing it, being with her in the moment, she could have continued to 'go on being'. Instead, my nonverbal demeanour disrupted our connection, separating us into one who was disapproved of and one who disapproved.

Dread of exposure to shame often goes hand in hand with fear of disappointing others' expectations. Audrey entered analysis because she suffered from deep fear of becoming suddenly self-conscious, flustered and paralyzed in action and thought, exposing her inadequacy and, she believed, compelling others to be disappointed in her and for her. She identified this state as panic and/or social anxiety. She narrated painful incidents that occurred between sessions or long ago. The most frightening social situations were casual. Trying to conform to others' relaxation made her tense.

Audrey was appropriately cared for by both parents. She did not view them as close to each other and did not feel understood by them. Consequently, she did not confide emotional concerns to them. They seemed to expect and appreciate her self-sufficiency. Equating this approval with respect, it became the basis of Audrey's self-esteem.

Exploring her fear of disappointing others and herself, Audrey remembered how she felt sorry and embarrassed for her parents when they appeared uncomfortable as a result of being teased or placed 'on the spot' in family and social gatherings. As a toddler, she attempted to defend them when they were teased, but was never 'taken seriously'. She also mentioned early memories when father, with apparent pride, asked her questions in the presence of friends to 'show her off'. She resented these intrusions, but felt she had to 'perform' to make him proud. She grew to fear these questions for fear of disappointing.

Audrey viewed herself as capable in professionally challenging situations, but unable to respond to 'casual and normal' social situations that only called for a simple answer or behaviour without being flustered. Someone in the group asking her to tell a certain story or do something where she would be the centre of attention stimulated pressure to perform. When I asked what happened when she declined these invitations, she suddenly looked uncomfortable, flustered, embarrassed, shifting positions on her chair and looking away. After a long silence and some gentle prodding from me, she said she complied with requests because she was 'supposed to be able to do it'. With palpable amazement, she wondered why she never thought of refusing. Realizing she had always assumed she had to live up to expectations, she left the session smiling, telling me how silly, but powerful, she felt.

These vignettes highlight a common characteristic in patients afflicted with shame. Learning to 'make do' without the other's soothing attunement in early emotional distress, they largely dissociated self-affirmation-seeking desires, and did not develop the trust that accompanies their fulfilment. They prided themselves in self-sufficiency, usually confusing it with independence, or autonomy. Realizing she perpetuated the pursuit of respect and self-esteem instead of the love and intimacy she actually missed, one patient remarked: 'One becomes complicit against one's self.' The fragility of self-sufficiency is exposed when natural desires for connection that became unconscious because they were deemed unacceptable emerge.

Sometimes elation following newly found power of self-assertion may be feared as potentially leading to loss of impulse control. One patient, excited because she finally asserted herself in a group in relation to a family member with a propensity to volunteer my patient's services to the family, bemoaned: 'I am so happy that I did it, and did it well, but I'm afraid I might go manic and maybe hurt people.'

Most relational/interpersonal clinicians agree that treatment of shame calls for integration of dissociated aspects of the patient's self. In psychoanalysis, the process invariably generates mutual enactments that can be detected and resolved through awareness and shared experience. Developing a more solid sense of trusting connection is the basic (slow to be achieved) requirement to combat paralysis and facilitate action which usually alleviates shame but often generates guilt because the new assertiveness is typically felt as aggressive, hurting the relationship. Guilt signals transition to a higher developmental level. The corresponding differentiation between the self and the actions of the self sets the stage for the treatment of conflict, and further negotiation of the mutual needs for assertion and connection.

References

Blatt, S.J. (2010). *Polarities of experience: relatedness and self-definition in personality development, psychopathology, and the therapeutic process*. Washington: American Psychological Association.

Bromberg, P.M. (2011). *The shadow of the tsunami and the growth of the relational mind*. New York: Routledge.

Erikson, E.H. (1959). *Identity and the life cycle*. New York: International Universities Press.

Guarton, G.B. (1999). Beyond the dialectic of love and desire. *Contemporary Psychoanalysis*, 35: 491–505.

Levenson, E. (1994). Beyond countertransference: aspects of the analyst's desire. *Contemporary Psychoanalysis*, 30: 691–707.

Levine, P.A. (2010). *In an unspoken voice: how the body releases trauma and restores goodness*. Berkeley, CA: North Atlantic.

Lewis, H.B. (1971). *Shame and guilt in neuroses*. New York: International Universities Press.

Lynd, H.M. (1958). *On shame and the search of identity*. New York: Science Editions.

Schore, A.N. (1994). *Affect regulation and he origin of the self: the neurobiology of emotional development*. Hillsdale, NJ: Erlbaum.

—— (2009). Relational trauma and the developing right brain: an interface of psychoanalytic self-psychology and neuroscience. In D. Fosha, D. Siegel and M. Solomon (eds), *The healing power of emotion: affective neuroscience, development, and clinical practice*. New York: Norton, pp.112–144.

Tagney, J.P. and Dearing, R.L. (2002). *Shame and guilt*. New York: Guilford Press.

Winnicott, D.W. (1966). Creativity and its origins. In D.W. Winnicott, *Playing and reality*. London: Routledge, 1971.

—— (1968). Playing, creative activity, and the search for the self. In D.W. Winnicott, *Playing and reality*. London: Routledge, 1971.

Chapter 3

The transition from adolescence to adulthood in psychotic patients and their families
A framework for assessing recovery

Barri Belnap

In this chapter I offer a model for how to think about adolescents who have psychosis. This functional model focuses on how things work, based on the assumptions of systems biology and advances in linguistic theory and philosophy of science (Ewens, 1996; Noble, 2008; Polanyi, 2015; Whitehead, 1978). With this model I am interested in showing how *the process of learning* shifts throughout development.

Rather than psychotic symptoms needing to be eradicated, I have become interested in how they function as *prostheses* created from the resources available to support patients in developmental efforts and learning. Premature removal of prostheses before alternatives are available might cause collapse and permanent foreclosure of developmental efforts. This formulation offers the possibility to claim something useful about psychotic resources.

There is much to appreciate and learn from research efforts that assume psychotic symptoms reflect early developmental deficits. However, my observations tracking the effects of first break of psychosis in adolescents and upon their families suggest a different focus. Listening to psychotic individuals facing the transition between adolescence and young adulthood, it appears that current family and developmental dynamics are more relevant than past dynamics or deficits and that what is most at stake for the subject is all that impacts separation, individuation and transition to adulthood. Achievement of these tasks is of primary importance to the adolescent's immediate future.

Defined in functional and neurodevelopmental terms, adolescence is the period spanning age 12 to 25 years, and is distinguished by developmental efforts to achieve capacities needed to address the cognitive, emotional and social needs of adulthood (Somerville, Jones and Casey, 2010). Alarmingly, one role psychosis plays in adolescent patients is to create an impediment to the work of adolescence – in a surprising way. These patients use healthy parts of their minds to *attack their minds* in an attempt to hide and eradicate shameful delusions or eruptions of emotions that put the adolescent at odds with peers and developmental expectations. A loss of functional capacity to address current developmental demands results. The hierarchy of needs shifts from exploring and sharing experience to hiding the growing sense of something terribly wrong with one's mind both from others and from oneself. One patient believed aliens placed a chip in his brain that he needed to 'cut out'. If you watched how he used his mind, it was clear he directed his thoughts and actions toward erasing feelings and ideas that felt alien to him. Being with his friends meant trying to imitate them, to be like them in a way that hid what he really felt inside.

Such attacks on oneself result in an inability to trust personal experience and to use the mind as a tool. Particularly crippling for the adolescent is that such attacks limit the use of social and interpersonal opportunities to reflect on ideas. The question arises whether re-establishing the priority of a developmental focus on the healthy aspects of adolescents in first-break psychosis might minimize these attacks, thereby increasing resilience. Pursuing this question, I began to observe behaviours, psychotic and nonpsychotic, through the lens of how these patients were responding as adolescents undergoing the transition to young adulthood. Through this lens, psychotic symptoms function to bring basic tasks of adolescence into hyperfocus, making visible mechanisms underlying what we refer to as separation, individuation, identity and the role transitions of late adolescence.

The functional model

This model begins by asking what tasks a psychotic state of mind has evolved to address. Psychotic symptoms as prostheses are good enough solutions that hold a place open for growth to occur in the future. They will be replaced over time if learning and development are allowed to happen in a stepwise fashion. To evaluate the effectiveness of treatment focused this way, we would track how well the individual is learning to meet developmental challenges through more effective and mature skills and strategies rather than tracking psychotic symptoms.

One patient described her transition out of psychosis as follows:

> When I was psychotic I said I felt I had the spine of a small child but I was carrying this adult life and I couldn't take steps forward … There were many things in my life I could not take ownership of … because I didn't have the self-identity to carry myself. I didn't have the realness, the core … the power to hold this life, to do things in this life that are good for me and will take me where I need to go. I needed to develop access to my own mind and my mind's access to the outside …. I had to trust so that I could see things around me and trust it is real. This meant learning how – meant not taking cues from others about what is going on, and not being an understudy to everyone around me, and having my own voice and opinions and boundaries.

Telling me about her theory of her recovery, she said:

> I think what I learned in therapy and my practising it out in the world is what really did it. I think a lot of it was using my voice and trusting my own interpretation of reality and taking everything happening to me now and not saying that it is because of my mom that I can't do this or that … connecting

her to my future ... I learned in therapy that I don't have to do that. I think I knew that ... It was a survival technique but it doesn't work for me as an adult.

In many instances, psychotic symptomatology is trying to meet developmental demands. Symptoms may include healthy aspects of the patient that appear aberrant but are the best the person can do from the position he or she is in, an idea suggested by Anna Freud (1958). She prompts us to wonder if behaviour that looks pathological may be a healthy, necessary effort that has become exaggerated. This distinction is critical because it suggests a different intervention than one based on the assumption that symptoms are like cancers needing to be eradicated. To the extent that symptoms are a response to stage-specific developmental pressures, the psychotic adolescent is positioned to face difficulties of self-experience and identity that are normal. He or she merely employs different resources to address them. A functional model demands that psychotic resources be judged by how they work and what they are working at, not by comparisons to other states of mind and norms.

If we assume that the psychotic adolescent is demonstrating typical reactions of normal adolescence but in a more exposed (less repressed) fashion, then the difficulty experienced in recognizing psychotic developmental efforts may be related to what we don't know about normal adolescent development. The challenge may be first to appreciate these normal developmental strivings. I am proposing that psychotic patients may reveal aspects of the transition between adolescence and adulthood that typically go unnoticed. The successful achievement of separation, individuation and identity formation relies on the maturation of relational, emotional and reasoning capacities in ways particular to the adolescent transition (Anthony, 1982). These changes happen in a context of an ongoing conversation between children, parents and cultural authorities that is also in transition. Parents are challenged to reshape their own roles, identities and values, to move beyond acting in the role of parents of young children to become skilled in their new roles as parents of adolescents and young adults (Blos, 1967, 1979; Prosen, Toews and Martin, 1981).

This functional model is the product of a collaborative research effort with six patients. Observations come from direct experience, process notes, contact with parents, psychological testing and the timelines created by patients describing their experience from psychotic episode to recovery. All six patients presented between the ages of 18 and 23. Five began intensive psychoanalytic treatment in a residential setting for three months to five years, followed by outpatient work. One patient was seen only as an outpatient one to two times weekly. Treatments and follow-up lasted between three and seventeen years. Because they hid psychotic symptoms, initial evaluation misdiagnosed all these patients. For one to two years before coming into treatment they had symptoms that would have met full criteria for schizophrenia in five cases and Psychotic Disorder Not Otherwise Specified (NOS) for one.

All patients negotiated adolescent demands in their own ways subsequent to intensive psychoanalytically oriented psychotherapy organized around the functional model. Five of six patients have no psychotic symptoms at present. Three have finished college or advanced degrees. Two are enrolled full time in work or university. One is in a stable, healthy marriage. All experience residual symptoms periodically; these arise transiently and in the context of new developmental stressors. After the acute phase of psychosis resolved, none exhibited the chronically deteriorating course predicted for schizophrenia. I will use examples from my work with three patients, though the principles described are relevant to the entire sample.

What do adolescents need to learn to function in an adult world?

To respond to developmental demands, adolescents need the capacity to reflect on and trust their personal experience. This requires skills and emotional capacities implicit in the use of reason. Refinement of reality testing skills is a developmental achievement of adolescence and a concern for those who have psychosis. Reasoning skills crucial to reality testing undergo shifts during adolescence in ways that parallel changing role expectations. The capacity for reason is dependent on role development. If you destabilize roles, you destabilize emotions, because emotions only make sense in context; roles define that context. Emotional stability, affect competency and adult forms of reasoning and reality testing are attained upon meeting tasks central to the adolescent transition – identity, ability to trust in and interpret personal experience, maturing relation to authority, and capacity to commit oneself to usable ideals and earn membership in a stable community through cultivation and maintenance of one's reputation.

Reality testing: what is it really?

Reality testing defined as the ability to conform to accepted norms is inadequate. Reality testing is the capacity to learn from experience and to apply that learning, gathered from very different contexts, in an effective way, to specific situations in the present. It requires the ability to tolerate the anxiety of not knowing for sure, then to trust in one's mind, to use intuition and scepticism effectively, and to tolerate emotions that come from learning things one does not expect or wish. This learning includes the capacity to reflect on personal experience and to describe it through a model or hypothesis that is then tested out with respect to its relevance to what happens. From this, individuals can calculate the truth-value of their model and hypothesis. They must be able to think in terms of probability when they try to apply past experience to future situations. They must be able to make judgements about the quality of evidence used to draw conclusions. This capacity will be critically important in evaluating the legitimacy of truth claims of others who suggest what they think is true and try to get the individual to validate what they perceive to be reality and comply with how they think the individual should think. The adolescent is trying to interpret impulses within him or herself that press him or her to action and yet also to relate these impulses to what others think (Casey, Jones and Somerville, 2011). Many forces surround the adolescent, pressuring him or her about how to think, telling him or her what is true and what is not (Piaget, 1975).

One of the advantages of this conception of reality testing is that improvement during a psychotic illness can be tracked differently. Rather than recovery being defined as the absence of symptoms, it can be traced in the acquisition of skills and capacities that promote reality testing as defined above. Rather than absence of symptoms, we look for improved functional capacity.

A woman moved from somatic delusion to metaphor: 'I have used my own arm pain to represent for me a whole host of things that are not in my arm ... relationships, friendships, things that really happened to me.'

Reflecting on how therapy was useful, two patients said nearly the same thing: they developed a capacity to listen to themselves. As one put it: 'I think that the tool you gave me is how to listen. What it will mean in terms of my career is that when I interview I can hear what people are saying, not saying, and can put significance on them relative to each other.' The psychotic problem she faced was: 'What do I do when I am looking at something that isn't what it seems to be ... How do you tell what about the picture is accurate and what is true?' Her answer was an example of an application of psychoanalytic listening:

> As I speak I am using one of the tools you gave me – the idea that this thing that is distorted also means something. If you look at something that is distorted but powerful and holds an attraction that almost always means this is hiding something. For me it has been about what to do when I am being lied to.

This patient's personal articulation of the psychotic problem and her ability to link it to her unique developmental concerns is what she identifies as progress and the key to her current functional successes.

The therapeutic approach I am describing addresses the function of psychotic symptoms with respect to current developmental priorities. One considers the efforts behind symptoms to be a way part of the self is working at a developmental problem of concern to the patient. These are not assumed to be conscious or the only meanings of symptoms. This approach invites patients, as part of a collaborative effort with the therapist, to wonder how symptoms solve a problem, how they function.[1]

In being curious with the therapist, patients learn to think about both internal and external aspects of experience and the relationship between the two. Recalibration of experience happens in this collaborative interaction, comparing ideas about what should or might happen with what actually happens between two people that neither of them controls completely, thereby introducing a limit to psychotic omnipotence.

Patients learn that they have more than one role for another person and about how the role they are in affects what they see and feel. With this experience and the knowledge deriving from it, they can explore how to choose which roles are relevant to what they want to accomplish.

This collaborative process produces appreciation for how one's mind works in relation to other minds. Patients learn to recognize patterns of behaviour unique to them, deriving from their choices in the context of a unique personal and psychological history. They become skilled at translating emotions and symptoms into terms that give them perspective on choices and dilemmas, that is, problems of living they face currently. When this occurs successfully, symptoms recede because there is something to replace them, namely articulation of concerns and conflicts. This substitution of articulation of a conflict for the symptom is, I propose, better evidence of recovery than decreasing psychotic symptoms.

A young woman with schizophrenia, asymptomatic for eight years, had a recurrence of paranoia, delusions and hallucinations at a specific moment in her professional development that once again made relevant a problematic aspect of her relationship with her mother. She heard the whisperings of the 'people from the other side' calling her to join them at a time in her career when social and professional forces put pressure on her to change herself to be who others wished her to be. This situation repeated the role she had for her mother growing up, when her mother could not *see* her, but demanded she be what mother needed her to be. The patient's feelings about this situation were expressed in her delusions about the people 'on the other side' who, like her, could not be seen but, unlike her, could talk about it.

She believed she could not be 'mad' about the current situation with her professional colleagues without becoming crazy or destructive. In therapy she could *play* with the idea that she might feel 'mad' and decide how she wanted to respond to those feelings.

I wondered what her mind was referencing about her experience with her mother using the delusions as a tool. Exploration of her anger and curiosity about what personal learning the delusion might contain brought her to awareness that the pattern she was repeating was evoked as a response to current social pressures. The push to take up the old, hated roles triggered an application of old learning that made sense in the context of her family relationships but was inconsistent with the present situation. Recall the proposed definition of reality testing as the ability to access information from the past and apply it to current problems as appropriate to their specific context. Her inquiry into the delusion's possible function brought her to an appreciation of past experiential learning that she was referencing in relation to her current context. From there she could begin to work at what response was appropriate to her current desires and goals.

When she reached this understanding, it made sense why she feared that her anger at colleagues would result in killing them; a concern that someone might get killed was the feeling she had as a child when she felt angry at her mother. This conscious articulation of the conflict enabled her to feel angry at her mother, then think more clearly about how she wanted to direct her anger toward her professional colleagues. This was a developmental achievement after which the 'people on the other side' disappeared once more. Able to express anger at her mother, she did not need the delusion to represent functionally an alternative to over-identifying with who her mother wished her to be at the expense of what she needed to be.

Now she could be a separate self, responsible to goals and tasks that extended beyond her mother's wishes. The capacity for reality testing is in part a product of differentiation and is inhibited by such over-identifications. In saying 'No' to mother's desire, the self that is beyond mother's wishes established a boundary around itself. This is a skill the patient practised with her mother and a skill she needs in order to negotiate a similar problem in the social world, namely how to respond to pressures to gratify others' wishes.

From identification to identity

That last example demonstrates a curious overlap between a universal developmental question of adolescence – how to move from identification to identity – and the specific difficulties faced by persons responding to adolescent developmental demands in a psychotic state. Each patient in my sample prioritized questions of identity: *Who am I? How do I know what to believe?* One said it takes 'bravery to step out into the future not knowing if there will be ground under my feet. It is easier to fall back into old patterns of what my mother made me be for her. That is at least known to me.' This developmental problem may take on delusional proportions in young persons with psychosis.

Adolescents are confronted with the need to survive the emotional disillusionment that accompanies separation and individuation: I trusted some things I was told to be true, but my experience tells me they are not. What does that mean about what I thought I knew? What do I believe about what they say? What ideals do I wish to devote myself to, and why? Who do my parents want me to be? Does my family role and my social role match my inner sense of who I am, or who I want to be for others? What can I believe in? How do I discriminate between various knowledge claims? (That is, what claims about truth do I give authority to?) How do I take into consideration my knowledge of how people camouflage their true intentions, misrepresenting themselves for various reasons (Erikson, 1956)? Paranoia as a symptom functionally asks these same questions, testing what can be trusted performatively in social interactions.

The functional model asks: how does each particular symptom function as part of an organized social and uniquely personal effort to address current developmental priorities? I propose that psychotic symptoms function to research and clarify these and similar questions. In this model the priority is the capacity for 'learning from experience'. The key question is: How do I learn what I need to know?

Two principles follow. The first is that symptoms can be used in the service of a basic drive to grow and adapt to new social roles in response to developmental pressures and social expectations. The second is that prescriptive efforts to change the patient either by instructing him or by challenging the validity of his experience and presuming to know what is in his mind both undermine his ability to trust his mind and his ability to learn how to learn from his experience. Telling him what he should think interferes with his ability to address adolescent tasks (including learning to think independently) and can deepen the split between a false self (created to protect the psychotic self) and the nascent self of a person in the process of creating his identity. One consequence is that the person will feel more isolated, further crippling his capacity to meet developmental demands.

Externally, psychotic adolescents face the loss of vital, necessary, social links. This loss is the product of dismissive expectations created by projections on to him that he is 'crazy' and doesn't make sense. Judging the patient as crazy transfers the difficulty a non-psychotic person may have relating to psychotic states of mind. Crazy becomes a disruptive reference point in identity formation. Efforts to destroy parts of the mind that seem to cause shame at not being able to be like peers was present in the active phase of the psychosis in each person I treated.

Because of current social prejudices about the illness, adolescents diagnosed with psychosis are in danger of losing the guiding pressures of external, age-appropriate expectations and also the availability of an accurate, attuned social mirror to reflect back to them a coherent image of what feels like a fragmented, disorganizing experience of self. These shifting images of themselves reflect the shifting roles and expectations they are reacting to and anticipating. Shifting images of self are present in normal adolescents, too. In psychotic young people, however, external prejudice interprets these shifts as indicative of disease. Categorized and objectified as 'pathological', their discredited experience is less usable as a referent on which to base decisions or as a tool for learning about self and environment.

Adolescents are asking questions about how the mind works. Psychotic adolescents face these challenging questions after having experiences of 'losing' their minds. They bring different resources to the exploration of their minds while also, perhaps, feeling afraid of them. They are trying to make sense of the experience of a radical disruption in what they thought they could trust about their minds and emotions. Like other adolescents, they feel a need for a sense of self-coherence, but their ability to make sense of experience is limited by the aftereffects of disruption. In question is the ability to trust mind as a tool that can be relied on to evaluate and learn from experience.

Able to trust mind, adolescents can access resources in their families and social fields, noting how others solve problems similarly and differently. They need to draw on the examples of others for answers and models for to how to live in the world. Likewise, they need to trust their minds to gain an accurate reflection of how their actions affect others so they can judge for themselves how they match their ethical loyalties. From this lens, what these adolescents who have psychosis are highlighting are mechanisms that promote the transition from childhood identifications to identity.

Psychotic communication in the transition from identification to identity

The form that adolescent communication takes is part of the problematic of the transition from identification to identity. Because of the developmental tasks confronting them, adolescents communicate differently. Actions and identifications become more important. The status and authority of words are being questioned. If adolescents are to move from unquestioned identifications to identity, they must differentiate sufficiently from parental identifications to take their parents as reference points. From that position, they can begin to evaluate those reference points and come to their own judgements based on active comparisons between parents' claims, the adolescent's own experience and claims of cultural norms in which the adolescent is embedded. From these evaluations, adolescents may form their own distinct judgements about values and priorities to which they will commit themselves. This new reference point (their own distinct judgement) gives adolescents the ability to enter new situations, to explore social opportunities and roles outside the family without the overwhelming anxiety of identity diffusion. Relationship to these reference points provides feelings of continuity.

Adolescent experience is mediated by action, identifications and words. Words alone are not sufficient to represent or to describe key aspects of adolescent transition to adulthood. Adolescents are tuned into this. Most of the time, the symbolic meaning of action is in dialectic with whatever words are spoken. There is what people say and what they do. The back-and-forth process between words and action represents the adolescent's efforts to understand the differences between what people say and what they do. Internally, they will develop capacities to grapple with their own ability to follow their intentions through to conclusions and to become familiar with conflicts that make that difficult. What their words mean to them and what other people's words mean to them are areas of active investigation. In some contexts, one's word is meant to be taken as an oath or commitment. Discrepancies can reflect a betrayal of that oath or the vast differences in how words are used and what they are used to describe. Faith in promises and the reliability of an oath is relevant to trust and the ability to reasonably predict one's impact on others. When actions speak louder than words, dissonance can be created that can destabilize the reliability of using words for self-understanding.

When ideas about whom a parent feels himself to be are contradicted by how he behaves, it creates a need in the adolescent to understand why. Unacknowledged fantasies that define the family culture sometimes describe better what parents do as opposed to what they say they do. This situation interferes with the development of usable reference points. Adolescents are often in the predicament of finding themselves defined by, and needing to differentiate from, powerful fantasies and beliefs operating in families. This transition is impeded when parents cannot be spoken to in meaningful ways. Clarification of these points of confusion and defensive distortion is central to the unique developmental conversation marking the separation between adolescents and their parents that is so central to the transition to adulthood. That conversation is the mechanism by which separation and individuation occurs.

To answer the questions of identity (Who am I? What kind of a future do I want to cultivate for myself?), adolescents need to decide which aspects of family to identify with and which to reject. They must develop a base from which they can make those choices. Learning to trust and use their own experience, to understand how to read their experience as information about themselves and about the actions, needs, and purposes of others, is necessary to create that base. Adolescents must gradually create a place for reflection from which the work of adolescence can proceed. From that base, it becomes possible to grapple with institutions of the adult world to understand what they can be trusted for and what they cannot. Adolescents must understand where hypocrisy, overstatements and underestimates blur and confuse reality in the service of defensive purposes of their families and various cultural voices that purport to tell them who they are, what reality is and how they fit into it. Understanding parents' mistakes, as well as the survival lessons they believe have made them successful, prepares young persons to take a place in the world outside their families while maintaining some continuity with where they came from (Jacobson 1961; Erikson, 1975; Will, 1987).

A developmental perspective on how learning about self and world ordinarily proceeds in adolescence helps us form ideas for how we might expect learning in psychosis to proceed. The important function of interactions, of explorations that happen through 'trying it out' as opposed to thinking it out, may sometimes be underestimated in both adolescence and psychosis. Learning happens in a stepwise fashion, where actions may function to practise something as the individual learns to substitute increasingly mature responses to experienced needs. As mentioned previously, action may also function as a prosthesis, holding the place for future actions that advance and mature by substituting one for the next, much as a teddy bear may substitute for the pacifier that has substituted for a breast.

For one patient, a delusion of being Jesus 'the lion of God' held the place for an actual role model, an American football player for the Detroit Lions. This individual had tried to be *like* the football hero before he became psychotic. The symbol of a lion and the number on the football player's jersey became images this boy was obsessed with in his psychosis. Many delusions elaborated from it. In the heat of psychosis, he began to act and look lion-like, and many said he looked like Jesus. During the acute phase, he would *be* him and get lost in that 'hyper-identification' – the word he used to describe his psychosis after his mind was clear of it. At other times he believed he had a special relationship to the lion. The animal and the number 32 were talismans embodying the powers he felt he lacked and knew he needed, qualities like strength and bravery.

One step in recovery from psychosis involves a shift away from identification by abstracting what is of value from it and representing that to oneself as a set of principles or examples useful for solving life problems. After the acute psychosis passed, this patient could represent the principles he associated with the lion, the football player role model and Jesus by picturing one or the other of them in his mind. When afraid, he could think about Jesus. When he felt rejected, he could imagine how by being like Jesus he would gain the respect of people whom he loved and wanted to be close to.

In normal adolescence, teens over-identify with their role models in attempts to embody ideals, qualities and opportunities that appear to be workable solutions to their own life situation and aspirations. This over-identification is one form of learning. The same process applies to adolescents who also have psychosis.

For psychotic adolescents, interest in how their mind works can help them begin to form models for their mind and emotions that facilitate the transitions just described. During the acute psychosis, the lion had magical powers to control situations and feelings. In the early phases of treatment the emphasis was on how his mind worked. The lion's magic was the earliest model of his mind he could discuss with me. Over time, we began to be curious about what feelings might be affected by the lion's magic and Jesus' power. As his relationship to feelings changed, becoming something inside him that he assumed was of potential help, he could tolerate my curiosity about how his mind appeared to be working. He allowed me to make links between his mind and efforts it might be making on his behalf to make sense of things around him. Before, his mind was an enemy; now he could begin to feel curious about his feelings and mind, considering both potentially valuable.

New models evolved, simple models preceding more complex ones. His feelings also moved from simple to more complex. 'Vagabond mind', in which any desire must be immediately gratified, became 'bullet mind', in which feelings were experienced as dangerous because they led immediately to actions, the way a bullet hits a target once released from the gun's chamber. Not wanting to hurt anyone, he consciously made efforts to not feel and to distract himself from dangerous feelings and thoughts. Bullet mind later was replaced by a model of his mind that allowed him to hold feelings in a box in his stomach and look at them from different angles.

In addition to helping him find a position from which to name, admire and work at describing the way his mind worked, the psychoanalytic stance helped him get more comfortable with the feeling of *not knowing* things, which used to paralyze him. Curiosity made doubt possible, softening the claims of certainty that psychosis relies on. The analytic stance assumed and gave reality to the existence of aspects of himself that he could rely on, that were there to support him, but of which he may not be conscious.

Later, his model of his mind included many roles he found himself in, including some he wanted to play for others. As psychosis retreated, he remained faithful to the lion. The image began reappearing in his artwork. When he arrived wearing a T-shirt with the lion on it, I asked him to wonder with me whether his unconscious was bringing something to our attention through the shirt. If he let himself ponder that question, what came into his mind? The capacity to wonder, too dangerous when he operated from bullet mind, was a developmental achievement that allowed experience to become metaphorical, an example or interpretation of reality, not a complete picture of reality itself.

Through wondering about the lion, he became conscious of the link between the psychotic obsession and his pre-psychotic state. The link was made in a moment when he spontaneously recalled that the lion reminded him of an important childhood role model, a football player who made a different choice than the patient's own father had made. The athlete gave up opportunities for greater success, publicly stating his decision to put family above fame, saying he had earned enough money. In my patient's mind, his father made a different choice, leading him to be away a lot.

Over time, through these conversations, my patient's need to *be* Jesus 'the lion of God' (or the athlete) was replaced by the wish to 'be *like* him'. In turn, the identification (that is, the need to be him) was replaced by principles Jesus embodied. These principles then, and even now, served as reference points allowing him to make choices and to judge them as good or bad in relation to an ideal he chose and to which he committed himself. In the acute psychotic state, he had felt lost and could not decide because his own voice was supplanted by others' judgements and decisions about him.

In therapy, we studied how his psychosis functioned. We created a timeline tracing ways in which it was useful and ways in which it was not. When he interviewed for college, he referenced that timeline. Walking into the student union building, he began thinking people were talking about him. He remembered what it had been like to be psychotic. He had stayed away from places like this, believing people were trying to control his thoughts and that he could hear the thoughts of others. He felt a pull to believe he was Jesus, just as he had been when delusional. Then fear jarred him. Fear functioned to remind him of more recent ways he had learned to think of himself in moments like this. He remembered he could think of being Jesus as a role. Borrowing the way of thinking that had been our habit in therapy, he began looking for references in his past experience. He recalled that, when psychotic, he 'hyper-identified' with Jesus in moments like this one because Jesus was 'loved' by everyone. In the logic of the psychotic identifications, if he were Jesus, he would be loved. Identification gave him courage. As he consciously thought of Jesus as a role model, his state of mind changed, and he walked comfortably through the student union building using his behaviour as an ideal model for Jesus's own.

The ability to identify with curiosity and knowledge-seeking is important in this transition. Strategies implicit in psychoanalytic psychotherapy constitute methods for seeking knowledge while tolerating what one does not know, or does not know yet. This method is very different from the absolute knowledge characterizing psychotic states. It also guards against the certainty inherent in some managerial responses to psychosis, and to adolescence more generally, in which the young person is told what is purportedly truth and reality.

Wondering with my patient about the history of times when being Jesus or trying to be the football player came to mind, he remembered being teased by kids. His worries about other peoples' thoughts about him made sense in that historical context. In the student union, his paranoia was unconsciously referencing the time when he was bullied, when others' thoughts about him were hostile. Back then, he began believing the bullies were right about him. The paranoia was right in a way: such things had happened. The paranoia was wrong another way: that past experience was not repeating in his current context.

He began noticing when he 'hyper-identified' with the football player to the point where he feared 'losing' himself. His ability to feel this fear and look for its source was a capacity developed in therapy. His fear gave him the ability to doubt how he was thinking and to access recent learning about himself. The capacity to use fear to connect to learning was a developmental achievement. His fear was followed by the idea that he could be 'like him without being him'. He could take on qualities Jesus or the athlete possessed in his own way, or do what he imagined Jesus or the athlete would do if he were in his current situation.

He made this discovery. I validated that it might be a way to use his delusions as a source of learning, as reference points. Using the special knowledge psychotic symptoms make available, while considering it a kind of learning about the world that he could draw on to solve current problems, allowed him to integrate and value aspects of his psychotic experience and trust his mind and his experience. This integration decreased the shame he felt about having been psychotic. Less at odds with his own experience, he was better able to use it effectively in the present.

If psychosis is a 'sick' experience, it risks becoming a 'not me' experience. Many psychotic patients are characterized by those around them as not being themselves, which is confusing and disorienting at a developmental moment when the self is in transition. He needed to be *like* Jesus (and other identificatory objects) without being him.

The models my patient used to reflect on the way his mind worked underwent further transformations. He observed a further change. The new model suggested a different set of priorities, motivation and greater feeling of choice, but it was still governed by intense emotion. The question of why things happen as they do was being answered differently. He said his thoughts were like sheep he chased around with a wolf. Occupying the place of an internal authority, the wolf is a powerful animal driven by appetite and instinct. He interpreted the wolf as representing momentary fear or guilt. He was not clear what principle lay behind those emotions or if he agreed with the wolf, so to speak. His mind was moving too quickly to determine the underlying emotional logic. In terms of the maturation of his mind, it is important that he now has the ability to notice how his thoughts are being motivated and that he has a choice about it. Functionally, guilt establishes a link to workable authority and guiding ideals. I will elaborate on the changing relationship to authority necessary for separation and individuation in further communications.

Within a month, he moved to a functionally more mature model. He said his mind was like a classroom in which various thoughts, like students, raised their hands for attention. He also noticed he hoped for one solution that would work in all situations – a heroic idea that would fix everything. He wanted this to be the way his mind worked, just as he wanted this to be the way he adopted a role with others. We had for some time noticed he preferred to play heroic roles for others, being the one to save situations. When more complicated ideas 'raised their hands', he ignored them, saying to himself, 'It's all good.' Yet he knew he was creating the appearance of things being good; it was 'all show'. This recognition led to a feeling of conflict. When he was psychotic, he attacked the feeling of conflict, walling off each side to keep them separate. This time he felt it. Just creating the appearance of things made him a 'fraud', made his words not mean anything, he said. Since he wanted his words to mean something to himself and others, he began shifting his priorities.

Prior to this, he had been unable to tolerate conflictual feelings. Now instead of trying to resolve them through the tools of his illness (reversals, delusions, paranoia, acting out emotionally, or 'stopping thoughts'), he dreamed of being able to say to a future boss 'I can do it – here is what I have done to show that I can,' rather than saying 'I think I can do it,' then thinking, 'Shit, I wonder if I can?'

His new model suggests he feels himself to be in a position of authority, like a teacher, performing a task embedded within an institution where consensual validation of ideas can be worked at, where the search for truth takes place. These are developmental achievements that show the structures that are beginning to replace what the psychosis as a prosthesis was doing for him.

Workable ideals in separation and individuation

An adolescent told me the way she thinks about herself is summed up by something a friend wrote in her yearbook: 'If you don't know what you stand for, you don't know where you are going.' Another rephrased it as: 'If you don't know what you stand for, you will fall for anything.' Both adolescent experience and the experience of people in an active state of psychosis are remarkable for questions about what group one belongs to, what the difference is between one's self (who I am) and one's role or place in a group (who I am to them). Adolescents are right to be concerned. One needs to have a sense of this distinction in order to think clearly.

Workable ideals are important because they provide organizing principles that promote self-continuity over time, a sense of where one is heading and how one connects to one's past. Ideals provide a basis on which to refute others' claims of who one is when they conflict with one's needs and goals. One's actions and circumstances may change, but a commitment to ideals can remain steady, providing stability even in the face of failure to live up to them. Workable ideals give an individual life a sustaining sense of purpose and are a living link both to where someone comes from (family and culture) and to where they are going in their efforts to create a future that is theirs, that they want to live in. These are components of resilience.

Ideals are spoken, conceptualized and lived. These options do not always coincide perfectly and may be in conflict. Exploring how psychosis may highlight certain aspects of adolescence that otherwise might go unnoticed, we might consider the way that psychotic symptoms may function as performance – an acted-out version of ideals and conflicts the adolescent cannot speak about. (Adults who cannot speak their concerns may also *show* what they do not say.) Observational learning obtained through what is shown can be more directly relevant than conceptual learning obtained through words. Action as a form of communication is adaptive because observational learning is a powerful way to learn and sometimes can more accurately communicate realities that our concepts preclude us from acknowledging. Children testing their parents employ this method. Getting bad grades and breaking rules is one way to see if parents love the child anyway or if they love their own ideas of who the youngster is more than who the child feels she is.

Each psychotic individual I studied lived out developmental questions as though he or she valued actions more than words as ways of getting others to confirm or disconfirm ideas, comparing the internal experience with what is consensually shared. This process is what family work opens up over and over. Such work helps to highlight the conflict between how parents see the child's actions and the questions the child's actions are bringing to them, so that the conflict between the two can be clarified, put into words and worked through.

In order for this work to be accomplished, parents have their own, parallel developmental work to accomplish: transitioning from being parents of an adolescent to being parents of an adult child. This transition presents a new opportunity for them to engage their relationship to their ideals and identity. A parent who sees herself as primarily a mother who wishes to be good may be challenged when her son apparently fails to live up to all she had hoped for him. Does it mean she is a bad mother? If she is not a good mother, on what does she rest her identity?

Similar to their adolescent children, parents I worked with found themselves caught in patterns of interaction that kept alive concerns about which they could not talk to the child. Instead, they tried to control those concerns through symbolic actions that kept fears unconscious, not available for active or shared problem solving. Since one can never truly control another, and because the task of adolescence is to learn to navigate under one's own control, these types of interactions needed to be highlighted, recognized and spoken about in family work. For example, a child cued to say that he is not angry functions to maintain the myth that 'We do not get angry in this family.' Within the family, his anger is considered 'psychotic'. Some expressions of it may indeed be psychotic in form. On the family system level, the dangerous emotion is attributed to the illness that the doctor and pill are supposed to 'fix'. When his parents say his anger is not 'him', not the son that they had before the psychosis, they instruct him about who he needs to be so as to be considered a member of the family.

One patient's family focused on guilt as a means to 'not pass on the trouble' of the previous generation. The mother took her son's negative feelings as evidence of her failure to be a good mother. This failure put her own identity in crisis because she sacrificed her career to be a good mother. She over-functioned in ways that reflected this. Expressions of upset feelings were evidence that she had failed him, and she spoke to him about it by saying what she had done to cause them.

Whenever her son tried to describe his experience, she took the position that his feelings were 'just like' her own. In the way she spoke to him about her feelings, that mother offered only identification. She put herself in his shoes imaginatively, then referenced her relationship to her parents, claiming it was exactly like his. In this way, stories that might have served as models for her son about how to derive reference points from experience failed because she offered these experiences as something for him to identify with too completely.

From a developmental perspective, her intuition was good. Referencing her experience as the child of her parents was right. It was a necessary step in establishing empathy and in using her experience to understand her child. Due to the pressures she was experiencing and her desire to help, however, it was easy for her to lose her parental role by over-identifying with her son. The parental role organizes itself around the ideal of the child's development. Parents must recognize and communicate the child's developing mind as *similar to but different from* theirs.

This situation was confusing, partly because the son's psychosis put pressure on everyone in the system, including clinicians, to think concretely and in terms of equivalents. In family meetings, mother pressured him to act as if their experiences were exactly the same. His differences from her would be 'reality tested' in the conventional sense. She would argue and contest the facts as he saw them in an effort to change his mind – to show him how he misunderstood his experience of her or got the facts wrong. Her efforts to be responsible inadvertently led to a dynamic between them that made it difficult for him to learn about his feelings, mistakes and the effects they had on others. This dynamic made it difficult to sort out what hurts others and what doesn't.

That dynamic was reflected in the son's psychotic state when he said, with respect to his mother, he felt like empty footsteps filled in by her words, thoughts and feelings (e.g. the way she finished his sentences and the way her feelings replaced his experience through the identifications she connected to him in family meetings). He, like her, felt responsible in an intense, absolute way. Her guilt made her feel responsible for his feelings. His delusion took similar form: he felt responsible for saving the world after the apocalypse. Mother referred to the feelings in the room when they argued as 'apocalyptic'. He agreed. His delusion was not random. It reflected their experience during conflict and efforts at differentiation. He felt obligated to be her saviour. 'Isn't it funny,' he said. 'I am in the saviour/save her role.' This role seemed to be an effort to be for her what she tried to be for him – someone to make things okay.

The dynamic in family meetings matched his descriptions. He could hardly speak without being corrected. He submitted to her redefinition to save her feelings and his place in the relationship. Part of her effort to help him was motivated by a need that had to do with what she did not get as a child – a lack she was ardently trying to make good for her son. This preoccupation sometimes distracted her from what he needed that was different from what she needed in the past. Her reference point for reading the situation was invariably her past. Her experience could be useful and was part of the basis for her empathy, but it also could be problematic when it was overly charged by her own needs.

A shift occurred in a family meeting that signalled achievement of greater separation and individuation for both mother and son. Previously, he complained that he often felt 'erased' by her. He worked in therapy and family meetings to tolerate feelings evoked in him (rather than lashing out at her or becoming shut down), noticing when she was speaking for him and telling her about it in ways she could hear. Using these abilities, he told her he felt something different from what she proposed. He told her he believed she was speaking about her feelings, not his, and this made her feel better, not him, though she said she was trying to make him feel better. The specifics of the example involved her apologizing over and over for changing her mind. He stopped her, saying, 'I told you it was okay. I understand where you were coming from. I think *your* feelings are upset, not mine. Is something else bothering you?' Mother, now able to trust that his observations came from a legitimate place and to be curious about herself and her own unconscious motivations, discovered the truth in what he was saying. Finding an answer to the impasse between them, she felt relieved. It prompted her to notice she was feeling ashamed of him and his behaviour as it was not what she wanted from him and made her feel like a bad mother.

They were able to then solve the problem they were facing – his behaviour and her reaction to it. He recognized his actions as mistakes and said he cared about the effect they had on her. She spoke with him about the kind of mother she wanted to be, her ideals, and how she felt like his behaviour was evidence that she had failed at them. He told her he needed to be able to make mistakes and that he did not feel it made her a bad mother, though he could understand that she felt badly.

This interaction involved a series of steps fostering separation and individuation through engaging conflict in a family meeting. First, mother and son acknowledged a pattern in which she attributed her feelings and wishes to him. He could then authoritatively say what he felt, inviting her to reclaim her feelings. She was able to remain interested and open to his perspective and to the truth he revealed to her about herself. Both were able to clarify their roles in relation to each other as a result, allowing for sharing and recognition of feelings and differentiated responses. Through this interaction, they succeeded in breaking the pattern whereby only one reality at a time could be spoken of. Previously, both their realities could not exist without one surrendering to the other through identification. Hereafter, they referred to this session and practised this new pattern. An improvement in his psychosis followed. This type of transaction can be crucial, enabling adolescent and family to separate and individuate from one another.

Functional significance of symptoms and acting out in social development

From the lens of how symptoms function in families to trigger possible new learning, I noticed that the performance of paranoia asks questions about what can be trusted. These questions are directed to concerns that reflect current developmental interests of parents and child. Clinicians can encourage them in exploring otherwise 'pathological', contentious concerns with one another. Through their shared 'research' about the question paranoia is trying to answer, paranoia becomes neutral ground for discussing what they have learned about who can be trusted for what. This research gives them an opportunity to show what they cannot articulate about the process they use to come to know who and how to trust.

Similarly, grandiosity can performatively make tangible the possibility of a patient's ideals or ethical concerns. Translating from pathological terms to a developmental frame, a boy who believes he is Jesus may be discussing what he believes is key to being a good person. Grandiosity functionally explores the territory of what it takes to live a good life, to be a good man or woman. Likewise, performatively, hallucinations give voice to contradictory points of view, values and roles the young person feels within himself.

Speaking to patients and parents about how symptoms ask important questions addresses healthy aspects of patient and family. It creates a place to sustain and strengthen the conversation around age-appropriate strivings. Such dialogue is a necessary stepping stone toward the patient developing a place from which to view and evaluate experience. Claiming that psychosis contains embedded truth addresses the alienation, guardedness and shame that keep psychotic persons isolated. It also frees the family to address irrationality, illusions and myths that are alive in them. Most families have irrational beliefs influencing their behaviour. Noting links between these beliefs and historical events those irrational beliefs reference can allow them to re-examine beliefs and interpretations of experience derived from them, changing their conclusions if they wish.

This process is important to separation and individuation. A goal of adolescents and young adults is to examine family assumptions and beliefs, to learn how they might apply to new situations and groups they encounter as they begin to establish roles in love, work and play. Inevitably, they will carry some mistaken family beliefs to these contexts. It is part of the work of separation and individuation to learn from the conflicts these beliefs engender with the world outside the family.

Summary and conclusion

Early in the treatment of psychotic adolescents facing the transition to young adulthood, encouraging curiosity about how they intuitively use symptoms to research and learn about age-appropriate goals addresses debilitating effects of shame while building confidence in their mind and the relevance of their experience. Similarities between their developmental struggles and those of others their age functions as a social link. Progress can be expected in terms of achieving those age-appropriate skills.

The development of emotional and cognitive capacities necessary to make appropriate developmental steps is a more robust indicator of growth and a better predictor of improved function than disappearance of psychotic symptoms. Those symptoms may function on a systems level to promote growth or to hold a place open for future developmental achievements. Performatively, they may address current issues of relevance for the dual transitions occurring in the family as adolescents invite parents to participate in a re-examination of beliefs, ideals and roles. Successful negotiation of this developmental moment may precipitate useful identity crisis in parents and adolescents, stimulating redefinition and realignment of resources, beliefs and workable ideals within family members.

Through psychoanalytic therapy, adolescents come to know themselves, learning how to think for themselves and evaluate their experience. Counter to those who suggest that we first fix the psychosis, I argue for the need to prioritize the developmental needs of the adolescent who has psychosis. When development – not symptom reduction – is the focus, resilience is promoted by minimizing attacks against the self and creating the stability that comes from the mastery of conflicts and the development of competencies. This developmental focus emphasizes how the young person is like his or her peers.

Through the development process, a personal model of 'how things work' is created from reflections on experience. For adolescents in general, and psychotic adolescents in particular, ascribing diagnoses says their minds are unreliable, unable to cope with age-appropriate tasks, eroding the necessary base for working on developmental tasks. Diagnosis has dangers.

If we try to predict that certain ideals are unreachable because we believe they are rooted in illness, we may deprive a young adult not only of that particular hope (to be Jesus or at least share his ideals), but also of the developmentally necessary process of moving from disillusionment to hope, from identifications or absolute ideals to workable ideals, to the principles that define an individual and make his or her life uniquely his or her own. We may create an unnatural, dangerous dependency where experts know better than the individual what is or is not 'crazy' in him or her.

The 'crazy' aspect of psychosis needs to be identified in a collaborative way between clinician and patient so the patient's capacity to name it and describe its effects – what it does and does not accomplish well – based on his or her own experience are kept intact. Adult, parental, community and institutional needs to define and take managerial action to prevent one type of harm can act in a direction counter to this developmental need to establish a solid base.

From this position, adolescents can work at identifying and solving life problems in relation to personal experience and ideals that are the product of active, iterative, trial-and-error research. Premature foreclosure of this process has devastating consequences for learning how to use one's mind and emotions to form hypotheses about experience in social situations, and integrate those ideas into models for how the world works and who one wants to commit to oneself to be in it. Decisions about what place one wants to take in the world, what groups one does and does not want to be a part of, derive from this developmental work.

Note

1 See Davoine and Gaudiellere (2004) for a more complete explanation of the connection between psychosis and a broken 'social link'.

References

Anthony, E.J. (1982). Normal adolescent development from a cognitive viewpoint. *Journal of Child Psychiatry*, 21: 318–327.

Blos, P. (1967). The second individuation process of adolescence. *The Psychoanalytic Study of the Child*, 22: 162–186.

—— (1979). *The adolescent passage: developmental issues*. New York: International University Press.

Casey, B.J., Jones, R.M. and Somerville, L.H. (2011). Braking and accelerating of the adolescent brain. *Journal of Research on Adolescence*, 21(1): 21–33.
Davoine, F. and Gaudillière, J.-M. (2004). *History beyond trauma.* New York: Other Press.
Erikson, E.H. (1956). The concept of ego identity. *Journal of the American Psychoanalytic Association*, 4: 56–121.
—— (1975). The problem of ego identity. In A.H. Essman (ed.), *The psychology of adolescence.* New York: International Universities Press, pp. 318–374.
Ewens, T. (1996, unpublished). The other clinic–the theory of mediation and the science of psychoanalysis.
Freud, A. (1958) Adolescence. *Psychoanalytic Study of the Child*, 13: 255–278.
Jacobson, E. (1961) Adolescent moods and the remodeling of psychic structures in adolescence. *Psychoanalytic Study of the Child*, 16: 164–183.
Noble, D. (2008). *The music of life.* New York: Oxford University Press.
Piaget, J. (1975). The intellectual development of the adolescent. In A.H. Essman (ed.), *The psychology of adolescence.* New York: International Universities Press, pp. 104–108.
Polanyi, M. (2015). *Personal knowledge: Towards a post-critical philosophy.* Chicago, IL: University of Chicago Press.
Prosen, H., Toews, J. and Martin, R. (1981). The life cycle of the family: parental midlife crisis and adolescent rebellion, I & II. *Adolescent Psychiatry*, 9: 170–188.
Somerville, L.H., Jones, R.M. and Casey, B.J. (2010). A time of change: behavioral and neural correlates of adolescent sensitivity to appetitive and aversive environmental cues. *Brain and Cognition*, 72(1): 124–133.
Whitehead, A.N. (1978). *Process and Reality: An Essay in Cosmology* edited D.R. Griffin and D.W. Sherbune. New York: The Free Press.
Will, O.A., Jr (1987) Human relatedness and the schizophrenic reaction. In J.L. Sacksteder, D.P. Schwartz and A.Y. Madison (eds), *Attachment and the therapeutic process: essays in honor of Otto Allen Will, Jr.* Madison, CT: International Universities Press, pp. 263–298.

Chapter 4

Neuroticism is the way home

Mark Egit

> What thou lov'st well remains,
> the rest is dross
> What thou lov'st well shall not be reft from thee
> What thou lov'st well is thy true heritage.
> Whose world, or mine or theirs.
> — Ezra Pound, The Pisan Cantos 81

Introduction

Sometimes, sitting at the edge of a body of water, hundreds of birds will suddenly stir and soar in concert, in response to some invisible force of which they have all become aware, but which remains a mystery to observers. Innocent of what just happened, only the watcher is aware of the great organized choreographed disturbance, quelled now, seemingly forgotten by the returned flock. The birds are wired to react, but have no memory; the observer remembers the reaction, but has little insight into its origin. This, at the level of undisciplined metaphor, is how we begin to experience the wonder of the ubiquity of the object. It repeatedly scatters the patient, the therapy, into an organized disarray. This is the nature of transference, of object relations.

I want to situate my sense of this object in the office closer to the 'staggering' bond available to the toddler lost in the supermarket. Separated from the parenting figure (the object), there is a loss of world. With this absence, only abject terror remains. Russell Meares (1990) imagines this loss in *The Fragile Spielraum*. This article provides an insight into an experience of absolute loss of object, equilibrium, of all things and, thus, the experience of reactive terror – the sudden affective realization of the magnitude of the object only in its gaping absence.

I will speak about the ubiquity of the object in the consulting room – that footfall on the beach that scatters the flock in such disciplined, organized patterns – underscoring the massive presence of that object in the clinical space. A presence that sits in the room with us, animating the proceedings. A tempestuous, Shakespearian presence which, like the playwright, informs all things: affects, speech, text. We are written into this life and the object is author.

For the purposes of this chapter, I will claim a robust formulation for the object in the consulting room. Less subtle than transference, more ingrained than habit, it is an entity that will not release. I leave here considerable leeway for the unconscious, for the ricochet of experience, for Bollas' (1987) unthought known. All these, in this formulation, are vibrant and in play. What I will not consider is the genetic, the inherited, the biological. I leave that work to others. The biological is, for us, clinically unavailable; it is the new metapsychology.

Let me reference a case. For some months, I have been seeing a young man who was unable to continue with his out-of-town studies as he felt he was too far from home. He wishes to be, he says laughingly, a prophet, or a rock star, to be recognized, loved, and upheld. He craves and strives for attention. Wearing cologne and model-like clothes, he is attractive! Signing up for yoga classes, he buys $150 worth of beads and a new muscle shirt so he will look good, fully aware of the 'commedia dell'arte' aspect of all this. When he dresses up, when he walks through a crowd, he is only cognizant of the need to be looked at, admired. At parties, he wishes he could be part of the popular crowd, looked at, belonging. Those people, he says, look so tight, so together.

His mother, as a teenager, some years before his birth, was imprisoned. She spent two years in a political 'third world' penal facility, a place where if you didn't die, you wished you had. After two years of unspeakable horrors (others in her situation died and made our newscasts), she was released and left the country. I wondered what would it have been like to have been the mother, a child really, in a world of the 'disappeared'? To where would your mind go? Where would it be when the time came to feed your own child? I said something like that to the patient: that his experience must have been of trying to catch her vacant eye, to get her to 'look' at him. His response was a childhood memory of being in his room with his mother's face turned to the wall and having this feeling, this wish to get her to turn around magically. And so he spends time trying to catch the eye of the other, to turn the other's face, to soothe what is unsoothable, while looking to turn the other's face. The object resides within us, writes the script, and directs the action.

This chapter is an attempt to understand the nature of the impression of the object on us. Through an embedded metaphor, the object asserts its domain. Appropriating that metaphor, we therapists have the opportunity to gain access to the roots of our patients' unhappiness and promote change. The pull of the object invariably and repeatedly drags us into the 'alike'. The repetition is the 'alike'. Being able to have, and ultimately enjoy, a different experience results from treatment. Ongoing therapeutic interactions deposit a new layer of experience which, mixed with the old, creates a 'different', attenuated object, now pulling in a direction less neurotic, less painful.

Vignette

A women's issue of the *New Yorker* featured an article by Daphne Merkin (1996) writing about her lifelong fascination with, and desire for, being spanked while engaging in sex. She explains this as perhaps a memory of the nanny spanking her brother and the affective draw of that memory in a household where affection was lacking, hence the need to duplicate that 'scene'. She finds a man who fulfills that wish. They marry, have a daughter. Subsequently, the seven-year marriage dissolves. She is apparently getting better, less puzzled, and hopes that with therapy she will be able to further address and overcome what has for her become a guilty, now open, secret.

In passing, she reports one other fleeting early memory where, unable to sleep, crying outside her parents' locked bedroom door, she hears mother say, 'Your tears do not move me.' She makes little of this incident; I make more.

'Your tears do not move me.' A compelling memory, yanking her to repeat that moment so that she, in proximity to someone causing, and at the same time unmoved by her tears, brings her 'home' to that moment, that affect, that echo, duplicating that far-off event. The husband, perhaps unable to continue spanking the mother of his child, unable to remain unmoved by her tears, ceases to be 'home' and for this reason, among so many that dehydrate a relationship, the marriage unravels.

What is it in such 'behind the door', 'your tears do not move me' moments that tugs at us throughout life? Pulls at us again and again, such that this and only this is a worthy target of our desire, just as we know it to be distressing. That pull is in the direction of the only possible satisfaction, the direction of what I will call home. It is not that, as with moral masochism, we are merely wedded to pain, but that the profile of that pain is so exquisitely etched on to the plane of our desire. It is so clear, so distinctive, so reflective of that earlier, alike moment, so reflective of home.

Why that moment? Surely there are others? How did that moment, mingling with the memory of the other, so different, so distant, become not merely alike, but became us? How does this memory embed itself and tug at us throughout life? And how does treatment help?

The ubiquity of the object

My understanding of the object concept is best explicated by Hanna Segal (1999) in *What is an object? The role of perception*. In her second paragraph, she begins cautiously: 'The object is something that is cathected by the subject' (p.96). In the third, she allows more latitude: it 'is something or someone who has emotional meaning for the person'. Four lines further, she lets it all go. 'It is almost the totality of our emotional experience.' This is our playing field.

I concur with the cautious, those who posit that we begin neither as exclusively pleasure- nor experience- nor object-seeking. We begin with a combination. We do not seek in general. Rather, we seek a particular combination of satisfactions, a particular mix, a particular object and experience, the culmination and totality of which becomes home.

Consider an arbitrary slice of a developmental sequence. When the infant turns over for the first time, it is likely he or she is uncomfortable. In the plethora of sensations that accompany that turn, the discomfort is alleviated (pleasure). Also, and suddenly, in turning over, the world has twirled, so if I do this again, and again, it's a theme park helicopter ride. The next time I do this, it is in part the discomfort, but also the excitement, and the striving for the remembered experience. While we're pushed by the physical, we're drawn by an expectation. Discomfort and expectation become one. Discomfort, admixed with the search for experience, drives action.

Something in that 'experience' draws us, so we repeat. We learn not only that the helicopter twirl is repeatable, but that we enjoy it. We go back to do this once more ... but every time it changes. The next time, not only is there twirl, but colours; not only colours, but speed; not only speed, but sound ... and here's the start ... not only twirl, colours, speed, and sound, but ... the object. The object knows how to put you on and off speed, colour and sound until everything becomes the experiential negotiation/mediation/fusion with the object and its objects. The object can twirl you even faster or make you go to sleep. It can spank you because you're angry or satisfy your hunger. It can coo in sequence or shout in despair. It can hold on to you, or hold you off. While experiences vary – speed, colour, sound, more stimulation, less nurturance – are all episodic – the negotiator is forever. It mediates all experience, internal and external. It is, it remains, the object. All that appears, disappears, reappears, fulfills and eviscerates – all that is now negotiated through the object. It floods nearly everything. All things are saturated with it. It is the colour of air, yet infuses all experiences, all memories, all thought, (...yes it's blue.. say blue, what is it? Blue, 'atta boy, blue). All is imbued with the object. OK, perhaps not all, but what memory/affective trace is 'object free'? Given part objects, split off objects, internal and external objects, object representations and object loss, how could anything be 'object free'?[1] If not even the colour blue is object free, how much less are affects, memories, passions, longings? Winnicott (1987, p.99) was more succinct. If 'there is no baby' (without a mother), then this is how 'there is no baby'.

When I feel a discomfort (fear, anxiety), I am drenched with the object. When I have a wish (hope, desire), I am saturated with it. I look to the object. I look with fear, desire, longing, disdain, but always I look with, at and for the object. Whether we are pleasure-, experience- or object-seeking, we are inevitably seeking. In seeking we are oriented, 'in transit', on our way home even when we may seem to be heading away from home. The seeking is imbued with the object. Susan Isaacs and Melanie Klein (Greenberg and Mitchell, 1983, p.131)[1] speak about the object of desire being implicit in the desire. Here, the object of the search is implicit in the seeking.

How could it be otherwise? Prior to the act of intentional looking, is the fantasy of looking for. The search is oriented towards union, or the fantasy of disconnection; in either instance, the fantasy of home. What we know of the world, of wish, of desire, of concrete experience and fantasy – all this is object imbued.

Every time you strove for the object, the striving brought the object into view. Strive, there's the object. If you find it, you're with the selfobject experience; if you don't, you've cathected the emptiness left by the absent object. Every time you strove, it's both a different time and it's like every other time. In all instances, this is home. All the striving for home is home; your home. We've been branded. It's always there, this calling, always distorting in the same old way.

Why my home only, and my home always? Because the object is the closest, the first, and the only. When all else is stripped away, it sticks, leached of all else; it is what is left. Let me illustrate with three images, one experiential, one apocryphal and one videotaped.

The first, we have a common experience when visiting the old folks' home. The residents who are furthest gone, but still vocal, call for their mothers. Maybe it's just a short-term memory breakdown product. Maybe, but there they are, with the object.

The second, probably not substantiated but … Kamikaze pilots hurtling to their death. What or whom do they call out for? Not the emperor, not prophanities; they implore the object.

Finally, visual: in an awful corner of the human condition, two Fullerton, California, policemen ordered to stand trial for the July 2011 video-recorded beating of Kelly Thomas, a homeless man, to death. As they beat him, he repeats, 'I'm sorry, I'm sorry' in rhythm with the truncheon. Then he calls out, 'Dad, they're killing me.' It's biblical, this calling for the object. We call on it when all else is gone; we are alone, no other desire, no needs remaining. We call on the object when there is nothing but need of the object. It is the last thing that matters.

The canvas

How do we remember the object? Where does it reside? How do we access and use it? If ubiquitous, if it is the 'totality of emotional experience' (Segal, 1999, p.94), how does it play itself out? If we are individuated, separated and matured, where does the object now reside? How does it make itself known? I will argue that the other makes itself known through our longing to return home.

The object lodges itself in us. Internalized, it becomes isomorphic with an experiential construct – what I view as a psychic canvas. That canvas is the repository of all experiences and inner reactions to experiences as they effect and inform our inner life. The canvas is the raw laying down of traces of all meaningful experiences ranging from the most powerful, to those that seemingly do not register. It is the melding of all relevant interactions, both internal and objective. It is more textured than the ascription of 'a mental state to the child that is ultimately perceived by the child and internalized' (Fonagy, Gergely and Jurist, 2004, p.286). In addition to wrenching and laying down the sense of mind from the other, it is the internalizing of the texture of the affective negotiations, the twirling, sound, colour, timbre of the object and its unconscious ramifications. This canvas documents the nature of the experience with the object, the affective memory of 'home'. This is the tracing out of our experience, our formative life. The object is part of action, activity, affective colouring, emotional valence, the way things are done, felt, understood and acted upon both consciously and otherwise.

This is the canvas of our history and the inner reactions to that history as it traces, effects and informs our inner life. Diagrammatically, it is a Jackson Pollock documenting our experience, splotch by splotch, well ensconced, boldly outlined, or faint and peripheral, hardly there, or even missing. The missing, too, is documented. (See, for example, Guttenplan's [2013] nodding to Derrida with 'a presence of absence' [pp.17–18]). This is the sediment that settles in the bones.

What to do with this canvas? How does it impact us? How does this splattered construction, this sediment, peopled and heavy with history, interact with the world? It is cumbersome, this history of our life with the object, this lifetime of impressions. How can an entire emotional history interact with the particulars of a life? It's too awkward, too unwieldy. We can't apply our entire past life, every discrete historical 'memory' in a one-to-one correspondence to every ongoing interaction? How then are all these impressions marshalled? What happens to them? What happens to those impressions of the other in us? How do they impact our world?

The Embedded Metaphor

A simplification takes place: this trauma, that delight, this disappointment, that surprise. What occurs is a metabolization of these memories, a shorthand which is available for use, a focusing of light. Like a dream, this simplification holds within it the traces of the constituent parts and the tension of the now and the then. This canvas is metabolized into something understandable, something that 'makes sense', which has utility for work in the world. It morphs into a shorthand for the memory and interactions with the object. It is imbued with the object (which is, in part, the search for the object). It is an emotional double helix that stands for and encapsulates the affective sequences. It is how we grasp the world. It searches as it always had, and how we search now for the object, for completion, for home.

This Jackson Pollock is metabolized into an embedded metaphor available to the individual's inner life to do work, to be empirically and clinically available. It intermingles with our ongoing, inner and outer life. Like blots on canvas, it too must reflect the object's valence and so must be pervaded with it. It morphs the Jackson Pollock into a representative, metaphorical Roy Lichtenstein – still blots, but now ordered, accessible: 'I hoped against hope that you would love me again …' This is the distillate with which we work in interacting with the world. This metaphor is clinically available. It is sometimes our formulation. It is the home we strive for, home as we find and re-live it. This is the shape of our ever striving for the object, as it is made available to us. It is the vehicle which bridges past and present. This is the 'your tears do not move me' construct to which we are forever drawn.

Why this one moment? How does that instant, that metaphor, stand for the sediment in the bones? How does it become essential? This metaphoric essence is a developmental accomplishment. It is an emblematic stamp. It provides the underpinning for our yearning, for our dis-ease, for our life. It gives heft to our inexorable, relentless desire to return. It is the longing for home, for rest, and it will not desist. Emblematic of the life lived by the child, the metaphor is the affective experience that occurs throughout the 'interaction with the object'. That is what the metaphor encapsulates.

What makes this 'your tears do not move me' moment emblematic of a life? The experiences alluded to through that metaphor are illustrative of the affective code for interactions with the object, not merely that one time one was locked out of the bedroom. It is a frozen canvas, like Dali's *Still Life En Vivant*, that reveals one's striving, one's life.

If the mother is consistent in locking her door, she will do so in myriad ways. She will offhandedly leave the child with nannies. She will casually prefer the brother. When dressing, she will ask the child to bring her underwear – always the wrong pair: 'I can't get you to do anything right.' All these micro moments have, and will necessarily have, a similar experiential profile. Each will be encapsulated by the 'your tears do not move me' metaphor. This is shorthand for the relationship with the mother – to whom you are the other – who is home. This is how you recognize yourself. This is what you long for, how you walk into the world and find yourself in it. The embedded metaphor's utility is that it fits all the above situations. It stands for your life and is recognizable within it.

This is who we are! When I return to that moment, I am back with the object, the real memory, the real object. Here I recognize myself. This is the distillate of my inner life, standing for the many activities and interactions with the object. While the dream allows for the interaction between inner and outer worlds while asleep, this distillate does this work while awake. It takes the shards, makes them whole and pushes for satisfaction. It makes sense of your life trajectory. It is the profile of the longing for the object made flesh, belonging to the self, recognizable and imbued with all things object, including, of course, the longing for the object.

The metaphor is a moment in time, in phantasy, which collects the affective state of the relationship for the child. It gathers within itself the nature of the object, the affective memory of 'home'. It is the trace of how we experienced our formative life. It is the entity that forces us into the world and animates us in the hope of realizing our desire. That hope, too, is part of that embeddedness. It lurches us in the direction of recapturing the object. Both the desire to recapture and the act of recapturing are pervaded with object. You find the object in looking, in the hope of finding, in the frustration of not finding, and in being abandoned by it. You do not *not* find the object.

I noted Isaacs' observation that the object is implicit in desire. But desire is also implicit in the object; it beckons to us. We've created the object not only to be called out to, but also to call out to us, to beckon. The metaphor, standing for the object, is Odysseus' siren call. It lures us. How could we tolerate existence otherwise? How could we stand the loneliness?

Without home, there is nothing calling out to us. It may of course be missing, but that missing is the lure, the reason, the draw. That missing is home. In an undergraduate class, in response to the assignment of 'Tell me the story of your birth and its impact on your life', a young woman volunteered that, as she had been adopted, she had no story. We are drawn by this object and so, not alone. If we are primarily social beings, then 'not alone' must be the push and pull. When we set our sights for home and 'hone' in on it, whether we control it as projective identification or simply project it, we have something out there which entices and, like the psychotic's mother's voice, beckons.

The pull

Whether we are pleasure-, object- or experience-seeking, and likely a combination, we are invariably seeking. How could it be otherwise? In seeking, we are oriented, 'in transit', imbued with the object.

On a flight, from the back of the plane, a 20-month-old, mom's hand touching the back of her head, rushes forward, peeks around every row of seats, says 'Hi,' giggles, steps back to feel the hand on her head, stamps her feet, picks up her elbows and lurches ahead to the next seat to gales of her own laughter. This is touching base with the object, forging ahead, with the object firmly behind. It is seeking, with the sensation of the palm-print on the skull, and returning to that very sensation. It is an interaction inconceivable without the presence of the object. This is about the excitement of the new, possible only with the sensation of the imprint of the palm.

The object is the memory of the object. Seeking it invigorates the connection, brings the object to life. Seeking it rounds out the selfobject, completes the selfobject experience. It is not merely the memory of the object that is the object – that is merely the form; joined with the search for the object, its essence, it becomes the object incarnate. Once found, however, only the form is available, drained of the search, purpose and vigour. A single 'your tears do not move me' moment cannot suffice; it is merely the shell. It is sought repeatedly and in the seeking is invigorated.

What is this longing for the object? How are we to understand this trajectory, this pull? Why do we aim for that 'closed door', that 'not moved by your tears' experience? The driving force is the craving, the need, to be united with the beckoning object.

This metaphor is clinically available to us. It is this metaphoric essence, this representation of home, of which the clinician is pre-consciously aware. It is, in treatment, the profile of the recurring, dystonic, painful behaviour. It is why patients return, session after session, to therapy.

When this psychic canvas is forged, designed, ingested, when it is framed, each component is imbued with the object, but not a static object. Each component is itself comprised of being sought. It is animated, propelled by the search. You can no more remove the search for the object from the object than hydrogen from water. Without the search, it has little valence. This is the difference between the lady you visit on Sunday and the memory of the motivating object. The object is charged. Like walking home through a storm, we lean towards it.

We know that infants recognize mother's face. What does 'recognize' in this context mean? Orient, put out arms to, grasp, rattle the crib for and ignore/dismiss/be frightened by others. Object seeking is the adult version.

The object within us is dynamic. A shard of it is its beckoning. We only need to look at psychotics where this beckoning is visible. The metaphor, too, is dynamic. It will lean toward the beckoning object for completion. The metaphor is and will search for home. It reveals the trajectory of our longing, and finds it. Consequently: 'your tears do not move me'; repeat visits to the woman's shelter; the same husband three times running, the same unhappiness with each. These are things we know about object seeking. And object seeking, we know, is not an option.

The pull for the beckoning object is ubiquitous. For the neurotic, there is no delight, only the dull drumbeat of the inexorable force for completion. That fulfilment is possible only 'at this home'. For those otherwise blessed, it is a pull in the direction of the accepted, the unruffled, the normal. The pull is every bit as strong, but it pulls into objects that don't hurt, so it seems those in that fortunate situation aren't pulled but, of course, the pull remains, only the pain is absent. It is absent in the object, therefore is absent in the metaphoric pull. It is absent across psychological and social modalities, hence invisible. Let me provide some examples of this pull, and some of clinical change.

A woman living with, and ambivalent about, a partner whose farmhouse is insulated with newspapers remembers and hates the memory of her mother's home. There she swore she would never live in another newspaper-insulated home.

A man, at the age of 12 months, lost his 43-year-old father. His mother's beleaguered face turned away from him. At age 43, he breaks his ankle in an accident. Unable for three years and all medical intervention to stop the pain, he retires to his room. His wife and children want to engage, are unable to, and finally turn away. He is bereft, alone, no one understanding his pain. He has found home. He is reunited with the object.

A man, parents from a rural, religious background, his mother much later to identify herself as gay, but then without a language for it, not understanding, unknowing. The father, more aware, understanding something. Patient's childhood spent in an intergenerational household he calls 'a house of shame'. Parents distant, each for their own reasons dismissive of their progeny. A house where loneliness mixed with shame encapsulated the generalized affect. His presenting issue is that in spite of a long-term relationship, whenever he feels lonely or dismissed, he acts out the all-consuming need, one or more times daily, to visit massage parlours, steam baths, parks. When done, he can't dismiss the other party quickly enough, then feels, as he is religious, all his ancestors looking down to shame him for his behaviour. 'Oh doc,' he says, 'they all know. I'm gonna burn in hell.' In his suffering, he is reunited with his dismissive object.

What does therapy accomplish in this schema? Following Markson's (1993) explanation of therapeutic action, if we experience someone (the therapist) who will not lock the door between himself or herself and us, who, this time, is not shaming, whose face is not turned away, then we may allow ourselves to be beckoned by someone who *is* 'moved by our tears' – a new object.

Therapy is the incremental laying down of a new layer of sediment – a mixture of the old and a plethora of minute, therapeutic interactions. This is why it takes so long. As the original sediment is attenuated, so will the metaphoric essence, so will the beckoning object, so will the way home. Two examples:

A member of a religious order – graduate degree from an Ivy League school, Irish born, father stern, dour, siblings all away at residential school, his mom, quiescent, devout – presented with an unusual situation. When living in his community's houses around town (regular houses, undistinguished except for maybe a small cross on the front brick), his housemates would go elsewhere, so, inevitably, he would be left alone. This happened a number of times. Sometimes he would be so angry when he went into his room he would want to slam the door, again and again. In the consulting room I, too, often felt like a worm in the beak of a pigeon slammed against a brick wall. We worked together for nine years. When it was over, he left for Rome, charged with organizing the order's world congress. When therapy began, he had centrifugally flung everyone away. With treatment, he brought them all together again – a different essence, a different home.

A young woman presented with post-partum depression, always serving, always servicing, in a false self sort of way. This baby was one service too many. She just couldn't do it. She could do nothing for this child. Blackness descended. In treatment, the object of the search shifted. After a year, she said, 'When I came here, I had had a child. I've become a mother.'

The sediment sifts. Another beckons. What thou lov'st, alters. Alike and different. Where the perennial old object was, there the new object shall be. An easier way home.

Note

1 The historical development of the concept of 'object' within analytic theory is articulated by Greenberg and Mitchell (1983).

References

Bollas, C. (1987). *The shadow of the object*. New York: Columbia University Press.
Fonagy, P. and Target, M. (2003). *Psychoanalytic theories: perspectives from developmental psychopathology*. London, New York: Routledge.
——, Gergely, Y.G., Jurist, E. and Target, M. (2004). *Affect regulation, mentalization, and the development of the self*. New York: Other Press.
Greenberg, J.R. and Mitchell, S.A. (1983). *Object relations in psychoanalytic theory*. Cambridge, MA and London: Harvard University Press.

Guttenplan, D.D. (2013). Lincoln. *The Times Literary Supplement*, 25 January, pp.17–18.

Markson, E.R. (1993). Depression and moral masochism. *International Journal of Psycho-Analysis*, 74: 931–940.

Meares, R. (1990). The fragile spielraum: an approach to transmuting internalization. *Progress in Self Psychology*, 6: 69–89.

Merkin, D. (1996). Unlikely obsession. *The New Yorker*, 26 February, pp.96–115.

Segal, H. (1999). What is an object? The role of perception. In P. Fonagy, A.M. Cooper and R.S. Wallerstein (eds), *Psychoanalysis on the move: the work of Joseph Sandler*. London and New York: Routledge, pp.96–104.

Winnicott, D. (1987). Anxiety associated with insecurity. In D.W. Winnicott, *Pediatrics to psycho-analysis*. London: The Hogarth Press, pp.97–117.

Chapter 5

An unpublishable paper

Harriette Kaley

In this chapter I have the unenviable task of explaining why a paper I presented at a conference on a theme pertaining to the topic of this book cannot be published as planned. The paper was a clinical study of a young patient whom I called Lee. In the course of treatment, Lee shifted from defining himself as a gay man to defining herself as a woman. Amidst much anguished soul-searching and complex negotiations with his family, he began the process known as transitioning. My paper described Lee and his history, the course of the treatment and a consideration of whether any process could bridge one of our most ingrained dichotomies: that between male and female. Was Lee fated always to be different from the gender he felt was his, or was he able to become just like a woman? If he became a woman, would she be like or different from other women? What was it like to accompany this very appealing, deeply yearning person on his/her journey?

Lee and I had been working for about two years, meeting generally twice a week, when the conference announcement came out. I had been taking detailed therapy notes as part of a consultation/supervisory process and I believed they could form the backdrop for an interesting, professionally illuminating paper. In what I considered standard fashion, I told Lee I was thinking of writing about him and our work for a presentation and, in accord with the usual ethical requirements, I asked his permission. To the best of my recollection, in a fairly simple and straightforward exchange, he agreed, and I proceeded to write. When I finished the paper, about three weeks before the conference, again following what I understood to be the ethically appropriate procedure, I offered it to him to read. He accepted. That's when the difficulties began.

To the distress of both of us, Lee was very upset about the paper. He had pretty much forgotten that it was being written. Now, having read it, he was floored by it. As nearly as I can tell what his objections were, he had expected an abstract, theoretical piece about – about what? Being transgender? Transitioning? A critique of the society in which he was trying to live as a 'transwoman'? What he got instead was what I had intended all along: a case study as a vehicle for considering questions of likeness and difference as they arose in working with a transgender person. I had carefully disguised many clinically non-essential aspects of Lee's history and all identifying details of place, employment, education and other such items, but the paper also included clinically salient facts, such as aspects of his childhood history and his young-adult relationships to his family. Lee's objections were initially inchoate and hard to articulate, but eventually it came to seem that he felt exposed by that material, misunderstood in some general overarching way, and missed what he had hoped would be a presentation to mental health professionals that would turn them into advocates for his view of transgenderism. While he could not have said – or at least he did not say in advance – what he expected, it came to seem that what he expected was an impersonal didactic presentation, and what he got was a clinical study and the professional musings it occasioned. The warmly sympathetic tone seemed not to have mattered to him. Lee was, I think, sideswiped by the paper. Though it was a traditional kind of presentation, albeit on a topic that was then relatively unusual, Lee simply had no experience, no context for it, and felt betrayed by its failure to be simply an advocacy statement.

The danger to the therapy was the immediate problem. There was also the practical problem it posed for me: I had a commitment to deliver a paper, but now I had to rewrite it so that my patient could accept it, without doing violence to its substance. How was I to handle this?

What I did was give Lee an electronic file of the paper. I asked him to review and comment on it in general and at every point where he had reservations or objections. He agreed, and e-mailed me a sheaf of corrections, deletions, additions, criticisms and comments. We went back and forth a bit, but eventually, in one way or another, I incorporated pretty much all of what he wrote. I dropped some background information that he felt was too close to the actual facts and corrected some historical material. Most of all, I went to some lengths to include the perspectives that he wanted to impart to mental health professionals. For example, he wanted to make it clear that the well-known description of transgender people as having felt all their lives trapped in the wrong body was too narrow and confining, and that it did a major disservice to transgender people because there are other routes, including his own, that eventuate in transgenderism. One of his major additions, and to me the most poignant, was his objection to the implication that his journey was somehow a difficult struggle. He wrote that, for him, it was a necessary and fulfilling process and that if he thought of it as a struggle he might never have the courage to undertake it. He wanted it seen not as the end result of a tortured process and the beginning of a fraught transition, but as a homecoming of the true self. The interesting thing is that the paper ended up, I am convinced, significantly better.

When in the course of the therapy it became clear that Lee's presenting problem – a break-up with his boyfriend – was just the tip of the iceberg, I had begun to immerse myself in the transgender literature. I attended transgender meetings, professional panels, workshops and continuing education activities of all sorts. I consulted colleagues knowledgeable in the field, watched movies (including ones that Lee recommended), read books and articles, newspapers and newsletters, and generally tried to keep up with the burgeoning conversation, within and outside of the professions, about transgender lives. By far the most immediately valuable of all these was my continuing weekly consultation with a highly respected, openly gay psychoanalyst. While we had known each other casually for years, it wasn't until I took a continuing education course of his on sexual variation that we began a closer association. At the time of the class, as a heterosexual woman, I was concerned with sharpening my work with the several homosexual men I was then treating. After the class ended, I continued in private consultation with my colleague, so by the time I began seeing Lee we already had an established productive working relationship. I presented my work with Lee in consultation for many months, and that proved invaluable to me when the contretemps developed over the paper.

The consultation served many functions: checking with a colleague about what had transpired to be sure that I had behaved ethically and professionally; reviewing the clinical material to try to preserve the therapy and protect Lee's interests; providing support as I wrestled with what might have become a therapeutic disaster. When it became time to prepare the paper for publication and a second chapter opened in the story, it was imperative to have a colleague with whom to discuss all developments and to reach the wrenching decision not to publish the paper as written.

How did it happen that the paper actually got delivered? Prior to the conference, there were several intense sessions with Lee over a period of two weeks or so, including a meeting devoted specifically to the paper.[1] We reviewed his comments and went over the revised presentation. We discussed the changes in detail, hammering out our differences in perspective, in tone, in focus. In the end, Lee announced I could deliver it. He had realized, he said, that it was my paper, not his.

At the conference, I delivered the paper with some satisfaction, noting how much Lee had hated the first version, how much input he had had into the final edition and describing how we had resolved a very delicate situation. It was, as he said, my paper, not his, but at the same time I felt it represented him as he would have wanted. It was a much better paper than the original: richer, more nuanced and more deeply reflective. It was very well received.

Some months later, when I learned that a book related to the conference theme was being created, I prepared my paper for that volume. I have been advised that I needn't have shown it to Lee again, but, because it was modified very slightly for publication, and because I wanted to be scrupulous, I showed it to her. (By then she was much further along in the transition process. She was living as a woman – with many painful incidents when she did not 'pass' – and was militant about being addressed with the proper pronouns.) She vociferously objected to the paper. Her reasons were again diffuse, but highly emotionally charged: it was an invasion of her privacy, it didn't say what she wanted it to say, it served no useful purpose, and so on. She remembered that she had acknowledged that it was my paper, not hers, but still objected to it in a global sense.

Taken aback, I conferred with several colleagues, including my consultant. They helped me frame conversations with Lee in which I attempted to describe to her that new clinical areas like transgender studies often proceed from individual stories like hers, and that the paper had the potential of being useful to other transgender people through the simple fact of becoming a part of the burgeoning professional literature. Of course, I also tried to explore with her the psychoanalytic implications of our exchange. All in vain: Lee did not want the paper published.

It took some serious reflection on my part and considerable discussion with my consultant to accept fully what I suspected from the very first: I simply could not publish the paper. Lee and I had had, I thought, an effective, close therapeutic relationship, with warm feelings on both sides, and I recall astonishment that she would reverse herself in this way. Apparently, truly informed consent is a very hard thing to make happen.[2] In the end, there was no alternative: given Lee's objections, I had to withdraw the paper from publication.

Some time thereafter, though Lee insisted she valued the work we had done and wanted to continue therapy, she now wanted a trans therapist. More than three years after we had begun, we stopped working together.

The editors of this volume asked me to consider writing a chapter whose usefulness would be in delineating what had happened. I thought that there might be something productive about that, and I was interested in salvaging something from the considerable work already done, so I agreed. You have that chapter before you.

If there is value in this story, it is not just in its cautionary tale. It is not even in what it illuminates about the rocky arena of informed consent. It is in what became clear were the issues Lee was grappling with and that caught my paper in the line of fire.

Lee and I had forged a tolerable resolution at the time of the conference that allowed the paper to be presented. But by the time the paper was ready for publication, Lee's commitment to the therapy had significantly changed. She was not where she had been at the time of her earlier objection to the paper. While her struggle for self-definition was active even then, afterwards it progressed rapidly, if not always visibly, consciously and in articulated form. This is important in thinking about what transpired, and in some ways I think it may be the most important thing I learned from the whole experience. By that time, almost a year after the conference, Lee's transition had progressed quite far. She was on hormones, had long hair, breasts, extensive facial and body hair removal, and was using the feminine form of her name. More important, she had become acquainted with leaders in the transgender movement, and had found in these remarkable transwomen the role models for successful transition for which she had longed. She was no longer a young gay man transitioning to female; she was a transwoman wanting to associate with others like her, to learn from them, to model herself on them, to believe as they believed in their identity. She wanted to consolidate her gains, and create and belong to a community of people like herself. She had found a peer group.

Lee began therapy with an almost crippling passivity, which was the focus of a lot of our work. I comfort myself as a therapist with the recognition that treatment had borne fruit; clearly, excessive passivity had not gotten in her way when it came to ending her therapy. I comfort myself even more, though, in thinking that the therapy process had taken her a very long way. She had overcome her anxieties and doubts, had chosen a path, had undertaken the demands that path placed on her and had embraced her place in a world of people who validated her. I think it was a significant next step for her to move on in her therapy to someone to whom she did not feel, rightly or wrongly, she had to justify or explain herself. It took a while to come to terms with that simple idea, to resolve my own feelings of having been unfairly treated by her, to halt the smarting from the whole painful and professionally awkward position that had been created. I was sorry to see her go and I am sure she knew that. But I came to acknowledge, in my own mind, that it was, in fact, time for her to move on.

From a psychoanalytic perspective, there remain unanswered questions and unexplored issues. Was there some significant transference that was not explored? With her delayed opposition to what I had imagined was a resolution, was Lee expressing anger towards me in the guise of righteous indignation? Were there specifically transgender dynamics at work, as, for example, Lee's feelings about me as a ciswoman[3] or mine about her as a transwoman? Envy perhaps, or hostility? Was she feeling exploited, or perhaps simply trying out an emergent sense of power? Were there classical psychodynamics at work about mothering? For that matter, what counter-transferences were operating to muddy the waters? For all my sense of being reconciled to her initial objections to the paper and to her later blockage of it, were there feelings on my part that leaked through and damaged our work? Did either of us feel, in some way we could not express, that we could not restore a working relationship? Was the interpersonal field too sullied to be revived? For that matter, did the very process of obtaining 'informed' consent significantly change the psychoanalytic relationship? Do we as psychoanalysts need to wonder more about the breakage of the analytic frame that inevitably accompanies our request for permission to discuss our work with colleagues? These and other knotty matters deserve consideration in another essay.

Despite all these possible subterranean currents, Lee's treatment ended, I think, reasonably well. She had wrested a considerable sense of personal identity and self-worth from the work as well as from her life and even, perhaps even especially, from the back-and-forth tussle over the paper. In the end, my final contribution to Lee was, I think, that I let her go. Once I recognized her sense of having found a community, I did not struggle against her. While I could not have stopped her, I could have made it harder. Initially, I might have done so; I had psychoanalytically rooted sorts of suspicions about what was going on, and listened only grudgingly to her plan. Soon, however, I came to respect that her decision emanated from her newly stabilized self-definition and sense of an appropriate future path for herself. Of course during the sessions we gave to termination we explored analytically what was happening; we examined it as much as her determination to move on permitted. Of course I worried over whether I was reinforcing resistance. Of course I questioned her motives and mine, reviewed our process in my mind as well as with her to the extent that she permitted, and wondered about enactments. But I did not keep up a fight with her over wanting, needing, a trans therapist. Her commitment to our work had changed, though her commitment to therapy had not, and I thought it could be a good time, as she insisted, for her to move on in that way. I hope she knows that I was and am cheering her on.

Coda

The passage of time sometimes permits thoughts, feelings, ideas that were previously vague crystallizing, matters once considered unthinkable surfacing, and positions modifying with the addition of new information, social changes and professional shifts. Something of that sort has happened in my musings about Lee and about likeness and difference in the time since the conference, more than two years ago.

Primarily, it seems to me now that Lee's decision to see a therapist who was herself a transwoman reveals the complexity of the question of likenesses and differences between transwomen and ciswomen. Lee made it quite clear that she wanted to see a therapist like herself, someone who understood her experience by virtue of having lived through some such experience herself. What does that mean about how alike transwomen are to ciswomen? It certainly suggests some difference, such that a transwoman has experiences of being a woman that a ciswoman does not, and vice versa. Lee was quite militant in her stated belief that she is as much a woman as any other, as like a woman as any other: at one point, she dismissed the experiences of menstruation and issues around pregnancy by noting that many ciswomen did not menstruate and many could not become pregnant. That might have been a matter of politics rather than a conviction that there is no difference, for her choice suggests she has something in common with transwomen that does not exist between her and ciswomen.

What does it imply that transwomen share experiences around being women that ciswomen do not (e.g., experiences of coming to womanhood)? What does it imply that Lee apparently felt that her relationship with me as a ciswoman would not be as helpful to her in transitioning as a relationship with another transwoman? In what ways would it not be? Because of the differences in our experiences as women? Because she did not want to or could not identify adequately with a ciswoman? Because of a plethora of other transferential matters? These questions develop central importance because of the politics of transgender, which claim equality for trans and cis people, and in my opinion quite rightly do so as a matter of civil liberties. Does that make them actually alike? It appears that Lee herself, in some way, on some level, did not think so. Despite her militancy, it now seems to me, more clearly than it did then, that she understood in some not-quite-conscious way that the process of becoming a woman is distinctive for transwomen and that this difference matters.[4]

The recent shift in societal and professional attitudes towards transgender – and towards gayness and albeit to a slightly lesser extent bisexuality, cross-dressing and queerness – has been dramatic. One thing that seems to have greatly assisted this process is the public stature of several well-known transwomen.[5] They raise the question of what it means to be 'like'. Their stereotypical female good look lends verisimilitude to the position that they are women; indeed, they are convincingly attractive as women, and that argues for their being like (cis)women (at least like attractive ciswomen). Their equally public insistence on being known to be transwomen retains the awareness of difference.[6] While I applaud the part of this that becomes a victory for equality, I note that it is an argument for 'alike but different'.

What I have come to in the end about Lee and transwomen is that the question is no longer 'alike or different', but rather both. Knotty social and cultural problems are thus created, and a tension is set up between the politics of equality and subtler issues involved. Nevertheless, a most welcome clarification is also created; for once and for all, the binary of male and female is revealed as a limiting – and historically too often damaging – concept. Clearly, there are men and women. But just as clearly there is a range of genders in-between. Furthermore, not only is there a range along a continuum, but the range does not move in a straight line. There are offshoots from the continuum. As Anne Fasteau-Sterling (2000) has felicitously put it, sex and gender are points in a 'multidimensional space'[7]; there are genderqueer people, transvestites, cross-dressers (both heterosexual and homosexual in orientation), intersexed people and undoubtedly many other variations whose existence will come to be known only as people become more and more open to recognizing and acknowledging the constricting limitations of the binary. And, of course, in this context, there are also transgender people, like Lee.

As general awareness opens up to these realities, it expands to do more than embrace larger and larger groups of hitherto marginalized people. It also makes sense of myths, legends, rumours, stories and historical anomalies of all sorts, understanding that what was whispered about, mythologized, transformed into fantastic stories and shapes, were often manifestations of the differences among people that the binary thinking of the past simply could not encompass or comprehend. This seems to me a significant enhancement of our grasp of reality. It also seems to me that the evolution in our times of such awareness will eventually dissolve the binary-relevant implications of this book's somewhat dichotomous theme: Alike/Different.[8] Why can't someone like Lee be both? Why can't she be a woman, a certain kind of woman, and ciswomen be another certain kind of woman, alike in some ways, different in others? Since that's the truth of it, why not?

Notes

1 For obvious reasons, there was no charge for this session.
2 A special issue of the journal *Psychotherapy: Official Journal of APA Division 29* on Ethical Issues in Clinical Writing explores this problem in some depth. One conclusion I draw from the discussion therein is that the concept of patients' informed consent to use of their material in clinical writing needs to be far more fully articulated than it currently is. What does a patient have to know in order to be able to give reasonably informed

consent? At what level, conscious and unconscious, does this 'knowledge' have to occur? If a patient withholds consent, is there any format in which a therapist can nevertheless move forward or 'is the therapist then to avoid writing about the patient'? (Woodhouse, 2012, p.24).
3 'Cis' is a prefix, derived from Latin, identifying people who have a match between the gender assigned them at birth, their bodies, and their personal identities. Intended as a non-evaluative term, it is the complement of 'trans'.
4 While I suspect that similar issues arise for transmen, the transition process for female-to-male is significantly different (purportedly easier and quicker) than for male-to-female. I am confining my remarks to transwomen.
5 It is also true that many transwomen do not want to be identified as such; they prefer to be known simply as women. Because they are not self-identified as trans, it is hard to know how they understand themselves and their gender. Still, though they function in the world as women, they are in some ways different from non-transwomen, if only by virtue of their distinctive journey to femaleness. Are we not all marked by our journeys to maturity?
6 In a profile of the transgender model Andreja Pejic (*New York Times*, 7 September 2014, Styles, p. 1), she is quoted as saying, 'I identify as a woman but I am also proudly trans.' Later in the article she is also quoted as saying, 'I'm asking for the same equal treatment and equal respect as any other female model.' To me this means she understands herself to be a woman both like other women and different from some, but that fairness requires that she be treated equally with all women. I agree.
7 Fasteau-Sterling is primarily interested in biologically intersexed people and the damage done to them by the constraints of a culturally ordained belief in a binary, dichotomous set of categories. Her recommendations for enlarging the conception of gender and sex nevertheless apply equally to transsexuals.
8 Even the subtitle, *Navigating the Divide*, loses its intended conciliatory value when the 'divide' no longer exists.

References

Fasteau-Sterling, A. (1993). The five sexes: why male and female? *The Sciences*, 33(2): 20–24.
—— (2000). The five sexes, revisited. *The Sciences*, 40(4): 18–23.
Woodhouse, S. (2012). Clinical writing: additional ethical and practical issues. *Psychotherapy*, 49(1), Special section: Ethical issues in clinical writing: 22–25.

Part II

The work of the therapist to find him or herself in the patient

Chapter 6

Reluctance to finding myself in the other
Treating an alleged paedophile

Susan Kolod

I received a call from a man I will call Frank,[1] obviously in great distress. Arrested for sexually molesting his seven-year-old granddaughter, he was taken from his home in handcuffs, incarcerated, and fired from his job as a substance abuse counsellor at the Veterans Administration because of the arrest. Charges were dropped when his granddaughter recanted, but at the time Frank recalled his file was still open in the Administration for Children's Services (ACS) and he was only permitted supervised visitation with her.

Frank was not mandated for therapy – he was seeking treatment for two reasons. First, he was suffering and traumatized by the arrest, incarceration and job loss. Profoundly depressed, he cried constantly, unable to enjoy anything in his life. The second reason Frank sought therapy was because his lawyer told him a letter from a therapist saying he did not fit the profile of a paedophile would help get his ACS file sealed.

Somewhat fascinated by the thought of working with an alleged paedophile, I agreed to meet. I encountered a normal-looking, visibly suffering, 68-year-old man. We began psychotherapy on the condition that Frank not ask me to advocate for him with the ACS, with his family or in any court-related hearings. My reason: there was no way for me to know that he did not, in fact, molest his granddaughter.

The accusation

The granddaughter, whom I will call Esther, complained to her father, Frank's son, that, 'Grandpa lifted my skirt.' Frank vehemently denied having molested her and, in fact, told me she frequently flipped up her skirt and he told her not to do that. He also told me the two of them often played in his bedroom. She insisted on locking the door, according to Frank. She liked to play a game in which he tied her hands with a belt and she escaped. When I commented that this was an odd and someone suggestive game, Frank agreed. He had been uncomfortable with it, but Esther insisted.

Esther's parents were divorced. She lived with her mother, whom Frank described as 'borderline'. Esther was in therapy for emotional problems. When she complained about Frank lifting her skirt, her father told her mother, who told Esther's therapist. The story grew into one in which Frank was depicted as touching Esther's vagina while masturbating.

Frank and I worked together for two and a half years. During this time, his symptoms of Post-Traumatic Stress Disorder (PTSD) abated significantly. He became less depressed and more able to enjoy his life without ruminating constantly on the arrest, accusations and revenge fantasies. In many ways, he was a model patient willing to explore inner experience, dreams and fantasies. I was never completely sure whether or not something inappropriate had gone on between Frank and his granddaughter, but, as I hope to show, this mattered less and less as we worked together. In fact, in order for the treatment to be therapeutic, it became clear to me that I needed to maintain neutrality on this issue.

Countertransference

As this chapter's title suggests, I was reluctant, at first, to identify or empathize with Frank. Over the course of the treatment, it became increasingly more possible for me to find myself in him. I will try to give a sense of how this was accomplished.

Maintaining neutrality about whether or not Frank was a paedophile was much more difficult than I thought it would be. There were times, particularly at the beginning, when I experienced rather strong negative feelings towards him – disgust and apprehension in particular. Did I feel negatively about him because there was something bad about him, or was it just that he had been accused unfairly of doing something that disgusted me? Frank himself expressed disgust at the idea that he could have molested his granddaughter.

There was, as well, that feeling of fascination. Combined apprehension and fascination made me very uncomfortable. Never sure whether I could trust my gut instincts, I was more distant with Frank than I usually am with patients – more suspicious and less likely to ask pertinent questions. For example, I was unusually reluctant to enquire into his sexual life and fantasies, a clearly relevant subject. I often experienced a distinct 'not me' reaction to him. In short, I was uncomfortable with the idea of finding myself in him.

In an attempt to overcome this countertransference problem, I did something very unorthodox: I consulted with Tom O'Carroll,[2] who is himself an unapologetic paedophile and expert on the subject. He has written several books: *Paedophilia: The Radical Case* and, under the pen-name Carl Toms, *Michael Jackson's Dangerous Liaisons*. In retrospect, I believe I contacted him rather than a clinical supervisor because I wanted to discuss the issues with someone who would not be disgusted, fascinated or suspicious. I was attempting to bridge the gap between 'us' and 'them'. Tom's reactions and advice were very matter-of-fact and helpful. I will quote some excerpts from our dialogue.

My e-mail exchange with Tom O'Carroll

SK: I've read several chapters in your book, Paedophilia: The Radical Case, which is very interesting and well written. Clearly, your paedophilic interests are completely ego-syntonic. I cannot agree that it is OK to have sex with children and am not interested in debating this with you. Neither of us will convince the other. I do have a clinical question. [I summarized the case for him, then told him that my patient seemed to be looking for a therapist willing to testify on his behalf that he 'didn't do it'. I had told the patient that under no circumstances would I be willing to testify in court, but if he wanted psychotherapy I could provide that.] We've been working together for close to a year and Frank's depression and PTSD symptoms have abated quite a bit. However, he spends a great deal of each session talking about how he didn't do it. I think there might have been some sexual activity, possibly initiated by the granddaughter. He has said some things, vaguely, that make me think that. How can I help this person?

TO: Hi Sue. Thanks for your very interesting question, which reminds me that therapists have the hugely responsible job of dealing with real people and their difficult problems. I am pleased you apparently feel I might have something useful to say. I am not sure that I do, but I am very happy to give it a try.

First, though, you say: 'I cannot agree that it is OK to have sex with children but am not interested in debating this with you.' That's fine by me and very understandable. I can tell you, though, that I am by no means convinced that 'it is OK to have sex with children' in present circumstances. I do maintain there is nothing intrinsically harmful in it, but the extrinsic sources of harm are immense in the present state of our culture, and cannot be ignored.

That said, let me turn to your question: 'How can I help this person?' This phrasing contains the optimistic assumption that you can indeed help, but that is not necessarily the case. He might be in greater need of a lawyer than a therapist: someone willing and able to fight his corner in court against the child protection people. The guy was found not guilty, after all. Why should a citizen who has never been convicted of a sexual offence (I presume this is the case) have to prove his innocence? Proving a negative is notoriously difficult.

Your client has a huge stake in convincing you of his innocence, and that may be the only reason he is continuing in therapy. Although you have told him you will not testify in court, it sounds as though he has not given up hope that you will. Or he may hope for some sort of endorsement from you that will enable him to regain the respect of his family and community – and restored relations with his granddaughter.

If the guy was 'fessing up to paedophilic interests I'd probably be suggesting you could introduce him to certain literature, and perhaps to an organization such as B4U-ACT. But that is not the case.

SK: Hi Tom. To hone my question a bit, I keep wondering if he'd feel better if he could speak openly to me about what really happened. This may be very naive on my part – he seems genuinely horrified at the accusation.

TO: Hi again Sue. He might [feel better], but perhaps that would put you in a difficult position in the long term. It might also make him permanently nervous about what you could eventually reveal [not that you would]. Of course you want to know the full picture, but I'm not sure it would be wise to press for this.

SK: Hi Tom. You've been extremely helpful. I'm convinced that it might do more harm than good to press.

Subsequent to this e-mail exchange, I stopped trying to get Frank to confess to anything. Once I relinquished that responsibility, I found I was able to empathize with him. I stopped feeling apprehension, disgust or fascination towards him and was able to experience him as a fellow suffering human being. My exchange with Tom O'Carroll helped me to 'defetishize' my patient. The consultation gave me the possibility of bridging the 'alike/different' divide, of seeing Frank as 'more simply human than otherwise' (Sullivan, 1947).

Although it still seemed relevant to explore whether or not Frank was innocent, particularly since he spent a good part of each session attempting to convince me, I found that I was more effective with him when I was able to set that question aside. In a sense, a preoccupation with the accusation was a red herring in terms of his psychotherapy with me. His status as the 'other' made it seem as if there were special issues we needed to address. When I set that aside, I was able to work with him as I would with any depressed, traumatized patient.

Despite my change in attitude, Frank continued to plead his innocence. Leaving aside the question of whether or not he had actually molested his granddaughter, I found myself focusing more often on how it might feel to be accused of something so repulsive if, in fact, one was innocent. In that way, I began to find myself in him.

Dream

Frank often brought in dreams full of interesting imagery and emotion. He reported the following one two years into treatment. Many of the transference and countertransference elements described above are explicitly stated both in the dream and in our analysis of it.

> I'm working again but I'm marginalized and now it's even to the point where I was working in a place that was actually a bar. They gave me a little office in the back of the bar, which of course, is ridiculous since, you know, I was a substance abuse counsellor – and I felt really pissed off that they would put me in that environment to work in but I was glad I still had my job. Then I walked down the street to where I usually go to take a break or visit somebody. There were bars all over the place. It seemed like base had become just one big bar or drinking establishment. It was like I found everything that I did in terms of prevention as well as the treatment part of the programme was gone. They told me, 'We don't use that kind of programme anymore, so if you want

to work here you'll just have to go along with the programme.' [*Which would mean what?*] A lot of drinking and don't hold people accountable. It's a new world and the old ideals were down the tubes.

In this session we explored, through Frank's associations, the many ways in which he felt marginalized by the accusation, arrest, loss of job and reputation, even though the charges had been dropped.

Frank: I'm feeling, I'm still feeling very much marginalized by everything that happened and I think that's what I'm working on.
SK: So it's a dream about being marginalized.
Frank: Feeling helpless, powerless, manipulated.

As he enumerated all the ways he felt marginalized, I finally asked:

SK: Well, it's also a dream about being a therapist, so do you think it could have anything to do with how you're feeling about what we're doing? Do you feel marginalized by me?

At first he denied feeling this way, but eventually he responded:

Frank: I felt in the beginning that you thought that I might have done this. And that I couldn't convince you as I can't convince anybody that I never did this. I don't have any proof that I didn't do it. So I always wondered, does Susan think I did this? Does she believe, by anything she sees in my personality, that I could be a paedophile? That stayed in my mind as a question mark. It wasn't reassuring to have that unknown question, in my mind, about what you think.

That's how I look at everybody in the world. How much and at what level do they believe me or do they question me? Even after I was exonerated by everybody.

I sometimes wondered whether Frank had noticed the shift in my attitude towards the question of innocence or guilt. Perhaps he felt he had lost the opportunity to prove his innocence with me. If he struggled with my attitudinal shift, he never said so, nor even indicated that he noticed it.

Termination

In the last six months of the treatment, I finally confronted my own resistance to enquiring about Frank's sexuality. What was I afraid of? He was quite attached to me and I sensed the beginning of an erotic transference, which I was uncomfortable about exploring. This discomfort with and avoidance of exploring an eroticized transference was a new experience for me that I believe had to do with vestigial fears that I would uncover some perversity in Frank or that he was fetishizing *me*. At one point he brought in a picture of himself when he was in his thirties. He was quite handsome. He mentioned several times that he really enjoyed our sessions and, although he was feeling a lot better, he knew it would be difficult to say goodbye. Through dreams and associations, he expressed closeness and even romantic feelings towards me. He reported this dream:

> I have a younger girlfriend. I'm infatuated with her. I'm still married to Marcia and am leading a double life. Her friend says, you have to either make a commitment to her or give her up. [*Feel?*] She made me feel good, young. The dream was mixed good and bad feelings.

Of course, as with many things Frank-related, this could also refer to romantic/sexual feelings about his granddaughter. That was the kind of ambiguity inherent in this treatment. Mostly we talked about this dream in terms of his feelings of closeness and aliveness in relation to me and the treatment.

We had been working together for almost two and a half years. Frank was no longer depressed. His PTSD symptoms had abated. He was able to enjoy the things in his life that he had enjoyed before the arrest. He now had two more grandchildren and loved spending time with them. He still was only able to see Esther very infrequently, under supervision, but the terms of the supervision had relaxed considerably. He even had a sense of humour about the situation. We agreed to terminate in one month.

In the last month of treatment, Frank expressed gratitude for the work we did. He also referred frequently to his continued puzzlement over whether or not I believed in his innocence. Whenever this question arose, I validated his sense that there was some ambiguity in my mind. Despite this, we both felt quite warm and loving toward each other. I told him the door was always open if he wanted to come back.

Discussion

In terms of working with 'the other', there is no patient more 'other' than a paedophile. Although Frank did not come to me as a paedophile, but as someone accused of paedophilia, the stigma attached to this accusation creates powerful countertransference reactions that made it difficult to identify or empathize with him. Much of his communication (his insistence that he was innocent, dreams of being sullied and dramatic pronouncements about his love for Esther) could be seen either as indirect confession or as the tortured expression of someone unjustly accused. Although I tried to maintain neutrality on the question of whether Frank could possibly be a paedophile, this was not easy.

In her 2011 paper 'The sex monster' Abby Stein makes the point that we all have disowned part of ourselves that wish to do harm. These disowned parts are easily projected on to the alleged perpetrator, who is experienced as repellent and alien. 'In the presence of perpetration we may be repelled but we are also excited. In an odd way, people who have done awful lurid sexual things to others [or in the case of

Frank, alleged to have done these things] are not just interesting – they are downright sexy' (pp. 512–513). These twin countertransference reactions, disgust and fascination, are disturbing. They can result in attempts on the part of the therapist to distance herself, see the patient in black and white terms and/or become moralistic.

Although clinical supervision probably could have helped me to deal with my intense countertransference, I was concerned that a supervisor might get caught up in questions of guilt and innocence and would have the same difficulty seeing Frank as a suffering human being rather than the 'exotic other' as I had. I consulted with Tom O'Carroll because I believed he would look at the issues in a more neutral, less emotionally charged manner than most people, since he would most likely be neither horrified nor fascinated by details of the case. This turned out to be true. Tom's reactions and advice were down to earth and practical. He helped me attain the neutrality for which I was aiming. After that very helpful consultation, I stopped trying to get Frank to own up to any wrongdoing and things moved forward.

Treating a person who comes in expressing paedophilic interests would present a completely different set of issues for a therapist. Treating adult sexual abusers of children is very difficult; research on the effectiveness of various treatment modalities is inconclusive; recidivism among adult offenders is common (Langstrom et al., 2013). The single most important factor in the recovery of a sexual transgressor is his/her attitude towards the transgression and openness to and capacity for rehabilitation (Celenza, 2007). However, this is a separate topic.

My work with Frank, where the charges against him had been dismissed, was focused on helping him recover from the trauma of being accused and the trauma caused by changes to his life due to the accusation. I hoped to show how difficult it can be to empathize and identify with a patient whose paedophilic interests are just alleged. This challenging topic deserves more attention and guidance for therapists.

Notes

1 I want to thank 'Frank' for allowing me to use verbatim material from his treatment.
2 I want to thank Tom O'Carroll, who gave me permission to quote him.

References

Celenza, A. (2007). *Sexual boundary violations: therapeutic, supervisory and academic contexts.* New York: Jason Aronson.

Langstrom, N., Enebrink, P., Lauren, E., Lindblom, J., Werko, S. and Hanson, R. (2013). Preventing sexual abusers of children from reoffending: systematic review of medical and psychological interventions. *British Medical Journal*, 347: f4630.

O'Carroll, T. (1980). *Paedophilia: the radical case.* London: Peter Owen.

—— (2010). *Michael Jackson's dangerous liaisons.* Leicester: Troubador.

Stein, A. (2011). The sex monster: dissociations as parallel process in the response to sex offenders. *Contemporary Psychoanalysis*, 47: 497–518.

Sullivan, H.S. (1947). *Conceptions of modern psychiatry.* New York: The William Alanson White Psychiatric Foundation.

Chapter 7

On intersubjective firsts in the analytic third
Becoming a subject in the presence of the other

Ionas Sapountzis

Looking back at the case of an anxious boy with a diagnosis of gender identity disorder, I still recall the unspoken *Now what?* feeling that hung over early sessions like a cloud. I had experienced it many times in the few months I had been seeing him – the feeling of not knowing what I was offering and what he was finding in our work. Despite many promising starts, sessions felt incomplete, as if something were missing, like when he brought and assembled his French horn and tried to blow some notes. It was a laborious, frustrating process that produced only a few not really melodious sounds that left both of us unsure as to what to say to each other. A few weeks later, he brought a stack of pictures from a recent family trip, but became disinterested after looking at a few. Invariably, when the time was up, I felt, as I watched him exit in a hurry, that I had expelled him, as if he had not performed to my expectations.

These experiences of mine remained unchanged even as he started bringing with him copies of foreign language alphabets he had printed from the internet and proceeded to copy them carefully in his 'language' notebook. His interest in 'distant' foreign languages (Russian, Korean, Sanskrit, Cantonese, Japanese, Urdu, Greek) and his desire to show me what he found and learned felt genuine and, also, an acknowledgement of me. I was intrigued and impressed by his persistence in copying the characters, including Greek, then attempting to make words with them. But the few spontaneous moments he generated when he pointed to the distinct features of different characters would soon fizzle out as he became increasingly absorbed with the copying task. Seeing him pull away into solitary activity, I had the palpable feeling of having failed to maintain his interest, and, more importantly, of having failed to make something out of his acts, out of his desire to show me what he found meaning in.

It was only when I decided to let the awkward and persecutory feelings be, and allowed for things to come without looking for anything to say or do, that the effort he was putting in copying characters correctly finally registered with me. As I watched him meticulously transcribing Japanese characters and writing the corresponding English sound next to them, I found myself drifting back to the image of me at pretty much the same age, sitting alone in my room, struggling with German homework, having to copy, much like him, sentences in my language notebook, but, unlike him, having no interest whatsoever in what I had to do. These images were followed by the thought that at that age I never felt I did anything 'quite right'. This was not an unexpected realization, for I had never liked German lessons, which I had to take in preparation for the entrance exam to the German School of Athens. I had often been castigated for my lack of motivation. What surprised me was realizing that I had never thought of my experience of myself in this manner before. I had never thought of myself as 'not good enough', even though I knew very well that I was not a good enough candidate for the German school. This realization quickly led me to one about the little boy. He, like me, did not feel quite right. He felt different and not-good-enough despite his obvious skills and impressive persistence. These readily comprehensible realizations – after all, this was a boy who expressed his identity in the not-me, and I never forgot my discomfort as a student of German – contributed to a shift in my experiencing of him. I found myself regarding him not as a difficult to engage boy with whom I was not sure what to do and say. Instead, I found myself becoming increasingly fond of this very expressive but fleeting boy who could not express himself with words, but immersed himself in languages no one around him could communicate in; a boy who was eager to show me who he was and what he could do, but felt very self-conscious of his need and unsure of what else I might see in him.

It is still a bit of a surprise to me how this moment of resonance with him, which emerged as I watched him immerse himself in foreign languages and was reminded of a particularly lonely period of my life, changed how I experienced our sessions and made me feel more connected to him. I began to see him as a boy who was looking for something he could not articulate verbally, a boy who generated experiences that, though noticed, left people unsure as to how else to respond.

There were no dramatic statements and no incisive interpretations on my part. I found myself looking not at the possible meaning of the symbols he created but at how he made himself present and what he generated for himself through the desire and fear reflected in his acts, conflicting emotions that left him unsure in what he did and wished for. I found myself comfortable making comments as they came or watching him in silence without feeling left out and without making him feel as if he had damaged me. More important, I let myself 'be' (Winnicott, 1971a) without feeling this was the correct therapeutic stance, letting the sessions unfold any way they did. Over time, the little boy found himself feeling less ambivalent in his desires and less persecuted for his acts.

A precondition for therapy, Winnicott (1971b) reminds us, is the capacity to play, a capacity that needs to be displayed and experienced by both participants in order for something to be created out of the seemingly ordinary. The experience of playing, with pleasure first, before it was understood and became a subject to possible interpretations, contributed to a space where me/not me and engaging/not engaging experiences could be experienced by both of us, not as polar opposites but as expressions of his being that corresponded to each other.

As sessions continued, I noticed myself waiting for his arrival, looking forward to what he was going to do. By the anxious knock at the door, notebook and copies of different alphabets tightly clutched under his arm, and by his eagerness to show me what else he had come up with, I could discern his growing fondness of me which he could not communicate verbally. So we proceeded, with him showing me with growing excitement his discovery of words in Urdu or Greek, then progressively becoming absorbed in correctly copying the words without waiting for me to join in, and me acknowledging what he had discovered, not feeling left out when he ceased seeking my attention and concentrated on what was very meaningful to him.

Our sessions continued without either of us ever uttering a word related to gender identity issues, his sense of aloneness in the world and his feeling of being different, not quite like the other boys in school. Instead, we focused on his desire to find meaning in other languages and cultures. I concentrated in preserving and validating what mattered to him. A year and a half later, after he had successfully transitioned to middle school, had formed a group of friends and was not displaying the behaviours that had marked him as 'odd', we ended our sessions and I was left with the satisfied feeling of a job well enough done, and a folder containing symbols and copies of my name in Korean, Urdu, Sanskrit, Japanese, Russian, Hebrew and Greek.

Looking back, I can argue that this case is not unlike many others when, in the course of treatment, therapists find a lot that resonates with their patients' experiences and the treatment atmosphere changes as a result. There are many accounts in the literature that describe therapeutic exchanges in the course of which therapists come to sudden realizations that change their perspective and understanding of what is happening and what to make of their patients' acts and projections. It is my impression, however, that most of these accounts are rather unidirectional, focusing almost exclusively on the therapist's understanding of the patient. That is to be expected, of course, since in the patient–therapist dyad it is the patient who seeks the therapist's assistance in understanding him or herself and feeling understood. But apart from the insight the therapist generates about the patient from whatever is communicated in sessions and whatever associations or reactions the therapist might have, there is also the insight the therapist often reaches about him or herself. Such moments, when the therapist in the context of interactions with the patient realizes aspects about him or herself he or she was not as conscious or aware of before, contribute to lessening the distance between therapist and patient and in changing how the patient's statements and acts are registered. As Billow (2004) pointed out, his capacity to experience himself differently through interactions with his patient and to modify, as a result of these experiences, his therapeutic stance, contributed to exchanges led him to be experienced as a 'trustworthy' and 'thinking object' (p.1061).

In the contemporary psychoanalytic literature, moments of understanding emerging from patient–therapist interactions, including therapists' realizations about themselves, are increasingly regarded as psychic events in the shared space between them. Baranger and Baranger (2008) were among the first to postulate, back in 1961, that analysts and patients form a bi-personal field within which it is not at first possible or even useful to distinguish what belongs to one and what to the other. Matte Blanco (1988) proposed a zone of indivisibility between subjective and objective experiences. For him, analysts' experiences cannot be differentiated from their patients'. They constitute parts of an indivisible whole that becomes the focal point of the treatment. In the analytic/bi-personal field, associations, reactions and experiences are not understood as independent events but as dependent on the interaction between the two participants (Ferro and Basile, 2009).

Elements of these views can also be found in Stern (2004, 2009). He argued that the therapist's understanding is always influenced by the patient's participation and, therefore, is always dependent on the patient's projections and mode of engagement. His metapsychological frame differs considerably from the notions of a therapeutic field and an indivisible whole postulated by the Barangers and Matte Blanco, but his emphasis on the therapist's unwilling immersion in enactments does remind us how coloured the therapist's understanding is by the patient's acts and modes of engagement.

Reflecting not on the patient's role in the therapist's understanding, but on the meaning and implications of the therapist's associations, Ogden (1994, 2004) articulated the position that even the analyst's seemingly random thoughts in sessions are not self-generated, but represent psychic elements that belong in the shared space between both participants. Even seemingly incomprehensible drifts, like the therapist becoming preoccupied with his or her pulse or noticing and reacting to the postage rate of a letter from overseas, are created by the interaction of the two subjectivities. These 'analytic objects' point to a shared psychic reality.

Conceptualizing the analyst's experiences as manifestations of an interpersonal field acknowledges how interwoven the analytic process can be and how linked or resonant each participant's experiences and reactions are to those of the other. Conceptualizing incidents like the one between me and the young boy as belonging in the analytic third moves such experiences outside the analyst and locates them in the space between analyst and patient. Though such a view is consistent with current metapsychological frames for decoding what is happening in treatment, an unfortunate corollary is that it may inadvertently divert attention from the personal, from what is located 'within' (Fiscalini, 2006, p.445), what the analyst brings into the treatment. What is not emphasized enough in current musings on the analytic third and the patient's effect on the therapist is how linked the therapist's reveries, associations and random drifts are with core aspects of his own life history and psychic make up. Therapy, Ogden (2004) argued, is an interpersonal event and therefore never exclusively an aspect of the patient's or analyst's experience. But therapy is also a deeply personal event that is experienced at a deeply personal level. Treating the therapist's experiences as phenomena primarily generated in an analytic field tends to downplay the therapist's contribution to the patient's projections and may result in practices that, as Sopena (2009) pointed out, register interpersonal exchanges along standardized roles and devote less attention to the specificity of each participant's contribution. Equally important, such a stance does not acknowledge the journey the therapist finds himself involved in, a voyage that often requires becoming a subject to him or herself first so that he or she can experience the patient as a subject. This is particularly the case, I believe, for therapists who work with deeply traumatized and/or disturbed patients who demonstrate a failure of meaning at a fundamental level. With such patients, Levine (2012) argues, to facilitate the interactive process, the therapist often needs to create or approximate something 'that may not yet have achieved sufficient presence in a figured form' (p.368). Levine's point is echoed by Frank (1997), who, a decade earlier, argued that the analyst's affective involvement and personal contribution is not only inevitable, but also crucial to the treatment's unfolding.

In her recent commentary on psychoanalytic activism, Gerson (2012) drew attention to how much therapists change as a result of their work. She referred to a well-known saying in the interpersonal tradition: 'If a treatment has not changed us, it has not really been psychoanalytic treatment' (p.329). In the case of the little boy, the point is not just how much I changed in my interaction with him, but also what I found about myself in what was enacted in the room that enabled me to pay more attention to the experiences to which his acts alluded. The little boy's immersion in different languages triggered my associations about my experiences at that age. What is important is that his immersion and my reactions became a shared experience only when I found the personal and private in what he evoked in me. It was only then, when I found myself responding to him as a subject, that what was created in the room began to feel like a shared experience between us and his Japanese characters and, by extension, he became 'of consequence to me' (Truckle, 2004) and, as a result, I and our sessions became of consequence to him.

Locating the personal in the interpersonal, finding the first in the intersubjective third, is an experience that expands one's sense of presence in a session and contributes to the creation of a space that allows other experiences to emerge and become subjects of attention. In *The Patient as the Therapist to the Therapist*, Searles (1979) presents several examples in which he realized that his experiences and associations to his patients' projections were not simply indicative of their conflicts projected onto him and of his ability to understand and contain them, but also suggestive of core experiences from his life of which he had been unaware. In the case of Miss B (p.387), Searles describes how her 'outrageous and obstreperous behavior which involved sexual provocativeness as well as physical onslaughts of various kinds' eventually succeeded in fostering in him a degree of 'decisiveness and firmness' that were expressed in 'masterful kinds of limit-setting' that he had not achieved with anyone else in his life. With Mrs C (p.388), Searles realized that her provocative behaviours and intensely erotic, rageful and murderous feelings towards him were not simply attempts to incite in the transference her abusive and vigorous father. They were also expressions of her strivings to rejuvenate Searles, to transform him from the aging, impotent, helpless father-figure he experienced himself as to someone who would eschew his professional neutrality and assume a more active stance. In another case (p.389), Searles felt Mr D was not only responding in the transference to a depressed mother, but also striving on behalf of his depressed mother, as personified by Searles, to create an enthusiastic response, to feel excited and experience the other as exciting and alive. On a less conscious level, Searles came to realize this patient was also alluding to Searles' own characterological inability 'to express undisguised and unambivalent enthusiasm for the contribution the other person has made or is making' (p.389), to marvel at his own and others' productions and expressions.

The value of Searles' paper, in my opinion, lies not in his proclamation of an innate diathesis for psychotherapy in all humans, nor on his awareness of how patient and therapist can influence each other, something with which most contemporary analysts would fully agree. It lies on his willingness to 'personalize' his experience, to claim the personal in the shared space between the patient and the therapist. More important, his cases point to a larger clinical context that might not be discerned if one focuses only on linear epistemological frames of understanding – what was projected and enacted and what was metabolized and reflected back. Searles' sudden realizations, just like my associations as I watched the young boy trace Japanese characters on a notebook, point to exchanges where the line between subjective and objective is blurred. The experiences that emerge alert one to how much else is there 'waiting to be found' (Winnicott, 1963, p.181) and engaged with. For Matte Blanco, such incidents represent a symmetrical mode of experiencing each other that is incompatible with linear concepts of time, space, causality and subject/object distinction. They allude to psychic events that transcend polarities and point to an apprehension of reality where the subjective and objective are both present (Wilner, 1998). In such moments, what becomes important is not what belongs to whom and how one influences another, but what one finds in what is created, *when it is created* and how one's perception and experience of self and other is changed as a result.

Following this line of thinking a bit further, I would like to argue (yet again) that in such moments it is not just that a part of a client's psychic state becomes known – a subject – to us, but that we become subjects to ourselves as well. True, as Wilner (2005) remarked, one's subjective experience is always part of one's private domain and, therefore, never fully subject to someone else's understanding. What is important, however, and what is typically ignored when we muse about our work, is not how correct we are in understanding the other – in fact, there would always be a part that is incorrect – but what we understand about ourselves as we seek to understand the other. As Wilner (2012) put it, understanding one's sense of 'I' is an experience that involves the singular and unique in the context of subject–object dualisms. One can therefore argue that as long as one's understanding takes place in the presence of the other or is facilitated by another, then the other is not simply understood as a subject but becomes part of one's understanding of one's own subjective experience. Our understanding, in other words, is never independent of who we are and what we make of ourselves and the other. More important, it is always linked to what we understand about ourselves while involved in the act of understanding the other.

For instance, when I understand the psychic state my son is in at a given moment, it is not just an aspect of my son that I understand but also an aspect of myself as a father. Likewise, when I resonate with my wife's anguish as she senses from another continent her mother fading away, it is not just my wife's subjective state I understand, or her relationship to her mother, but myself as a husband and us as a couple at this stage of our lives. In the same vein, when I understand something about myself as a supervisor, therapist or colleague, my understanding is never independent of the other, but emerges, whether I am aware of it or not, in the context of the other and becomes part of how I understand myself. It is often in this space, a space that cannot easily be accounted for, where the subjective and the objective overlap and distinctions between self and other become blurred, that one's experience of the other and of self becomes more resonant.

What matters most in our exchanges with others and in our realizations about ourselves, as therapists, parents, partners or friends, is not our ability to grasp an objective reality, for the latter is always subject to our psychic states and, therefore, always elusive, nor our level of knowledge and expertise per se. What matters most is the unfolding that takes place when we allow ourselves to wander away and wonder off in the presence of, and in response to another, so that other realities and possibilities can emerge. Looking at the cases in the literature that involve patients who don't dare (or simply cannot) process their own subjective states, what is clear, whatever the theoretical frame the therapists rely on to make sense of their patients, is how deeply present the therapists are in the unfolding that takes place and also, how concordant their associations are to their patients' psychic states. Therapists may rely on different theories to guide themselves, but in every session, as Mathelin (1999) remarked, and one can add, in every case, what matters most is the therapists' capacity to listen to patients according to their own deeply personal and therefore deeply resonant, unconscious. Extending Mathelin's view a bit further, I will venture to say that most of us do not work exclusively with an objective insight, but with what we make of it, what becomes part of us, and what we find in ourselves and the other. Understanding our countertransferential reactions and making sense of projective and introjective matrixes are not just technical skills that reflect our development and level of sophistication as therapists, but also depend on our psychic state and are very much a reflection of our own psychic uniqueness (Wolstein, 2000).

With patients who are present, engaging and can articulate their psychic experience, our task of making sense and locating the other is easier, for we do not have to search as actively for our pulse, as Ogden did, to feel the patient and remain alive in his presence. But with patients who exist in the 'not' and seem lost in themselves, like the little boy with the Japanese scribblings, the therapist often needs to become a subject first, a subject who senses the 'me' underneath the 'not', so the patient's 'not-me' expressions won't feel as distant and foreclosed. With such patients the therapist needs to generate meaning not just to interpret the patient, but, more importantly, to represent his or her own state of mind and to be able to move from 'unrepresented to represented mental states' (Levine, 2012, p.393).

Present in the maternal gaze that allows one to see in it a reflection of oneself is not just the mother's empathy but also, as Likierman (1988) pointed out, *what* the mother finds for herself in that exchange, the meaning and identity she finds in being the mother of *that* child. The words of my son at the age of six, when he was struggling with himself, convey the point well: 'Dad,' he asked as I was saying goodnight to him, 'Dad, do you like me?' Before I had a moment to reply, he hurried to expand his question, 'No, Dad, I'm not asking you if you love me, I know you do, but do you like me?' This six year old, who was struggling with language delays that made him feel not good enough, was asking a very sophisticated question, one he had to express precisely and to insist on before it would finally sink in for me. In his question, and in the urgency with which he asked it, I came face to face with how he experienced himself in the world and, more importantly, what he saw reflected back in my gaze – my own ambivalence and difficulty to see past his learning difficulties and be a father to him, a father not preoccupied by his language difficulties but by his potential.

Ten, fifteen years later, I hear again the anguish and plight of my son's words as I watch a ten-year-old boy who displays symptoms associated with severe ADHD move incessantly from item to item without ever settling on anything for too long and without creating any continuity between acts. He asks questions without being interested in the answers I attempt to articulate. His incessant movement and seeming lack of interest in anything he engages in generate, I am sure, states of senselessness and confusion that make him feel more agitated and restless as time goes by. It is an experience I never had myself, that of not being able to find something to hold on to and make something from what is around me. This insight gives me a glimpse of the unthinkable state this boy finds himself in, time and time again. Once I look at him not from the prism of his 'objective' deficits but from the loneliness and emptiness he finds in whatever he attempts to do, I find myself moved by the discontinuities he experiences in his interactions and I sense the same desire, however disowned, to feel liked, to feel that he matters and has an effect on someone else. It is then that I become a subject in his presence and I step in and invite him to try different things with me, reassuring him that we can find something else to do and settle in, if he and I look for it. Whether he picks a box full of Lego to build something that has no discernible form, or goes to the blackboard to draw something that is hard to figure out, what I see is not just a blob or a formless something but a beginning, the beginning of a beginning, and I find myself a subject again, a therapist who is interested not in interpreting him but in discovering him and in finding what the two of us can create with each other and for each other.

References

Baranger, M. and Baranger, W. (2008). The analytic situation as a dynamic field. *International Journal of Psychoanalysis*, 89: 795–826.
Billow, R. M. (2004). A falsifying adolescent. *Psychoanalytic Quarterly*, 73: 1041–1078.
Ferro, A. and Basile, R. (2009). *The analytic field: a clinical concept*. London: Karnac.
Fiscalini, J. (2006). Coparticipant inquiry: analysis as personal encounter. *Contemporary Psychoanalysis*, 42: 437–451.

Frank, K.A. (1997). The role of the analyst's inadvertent self-revelations. *Psychoanalytic Dialogues*, 7: 281–314.
Gerson, M. (2012). Psychoanalytic activism: historical perspective and subjective conundrums. *Psychoanalytic Psychology* 29(3): 325–329.
Levine, H.B. (2012). The colourless canvas: representation, therapeutic action and the creation of mind. *International Journal of Psychoanalysis*, 93: 363–385.
Likierman, M. (1988). Maternal love and positive projective identification. *Journal of Child Psychotherapy*, 14(2): 29–46.
Mathelin, K. (1999). *The broken piano: Lacanial psychotherapy with children*. New York: Other Press.
Matte Blanco, I. (1988). *Thinking, feeling and being*. New York: Routledge.
Ogden, T.H. (1994). The analytic third: working with intersubjective clinical facts. *International Journal of Psychoanalysis*, 75: 3–20.
—— (2004). The analytic third: implications for psychoanalytic theory and technique. *Psychoanalytic Quarterly*, 73: 167–195.
Searles, H.F. (1979). The patient as a therapist to his analyst. In *Countertransference and related subjects: selected papers*. Madison, CT: International Universities Press, 1999, pp.380–459.
Sopena, C. (2009). The dynamic field of psychoanalysis: a turning point in the theories of the unconscious. In A. Ferro and R. Basile (eds), *The analytic field: a clinical concept*. London: Karnac.
Stern, D.B. (2004). The eye sees itself: dissociation, enactment and the achievement of conflict. *Contemporary Psychoanalysis*, 40: 197–237.
—— (2009). *Partners in thought: working with unformulated experience, dissociation, and enactment*. New York: Routledge.
Truckle, B. (2004). On becoming of consequence. In M. Rhode and T. Klauber (eds), *The many faces of Asperger Syndrome*. London: Karnac.
Wilner, W. (1998). The un-consciousing of awareness in psychoanalytic therapy. *Contemporary Psychoanalysis*, 35: 617–628.
—— (2005). Dissociation as disassociating from one's associations: an experiential perspective on the issues of dissociation and enactment in psychoanalytic therapy. *Psychoanalytic Perspectives*, 3: 87–95.
—— (2012). Personal communication, 9 October.
Winnicott, D.W. (1963). Communicating and not communicating leading to a study of certain opposites. In D.W. Winnicott, *The maturational process and the facilitating environment*. Madison, CT: International Universities Press, 1965, pp. 179–192.
—— (1971a). Creativity and its origins. In D.W. Winnicott, *Playing and reality*. London: Routledge, pp.65–85.
—— (1971b). Playing: a theoretical statement. In D.W. Winnicott, *Playing and reality*, London: Routledge, pp.38–52.
Wolstein, B. (2000). An interview with Benjamin Wolstein, conducted by Irwin Hirsch. *Contemporary Psychoanalysis*, 36: 187–232.

Part III

Cultural, racial and cognitive/emotional divides

Chapter 8

Our not-so-hidden shame

Lack of ethnic diversity in the field of psychoanalysis

John V. O'Leary

> Look – I open my 'store' every day. I will serve anyone who comes in. If they don't come in, they don't get served – period. I'm not turning anyone away. It's their choice not to come. I will not go begging.

At a recent psychoanalytic conference, the topic of racial and ethnic diversity was aired and debated. One psychologist participant referred to his practice in the manner quoted above. His words rang in my ears all the way home. The sense of fulfilled responsibility and the rather tepid welcome candidly expressed a position even many liberal-minded members of the profession appear to maintain. Interest in exploring such attitudes and seeking open dialogue about them had motivated me to prepare that conference paper in the first place. I felt some hesitation, not being a person of colour, never having spoken to the issue before, and with nothing particular on my curriculum vitae to back me up. There was and still remains, however, a sense of urgency. While the subject of race and ethnic diversity is politically sensitive and highly charged, the time is long overdue for psychoanalysts to confront the vague uneasiness we feel – perhaps embarrassment – whenever it is raised. Responses like the one above confirm that it behoves us to approach the subject with curiosity and humility, and approach it we must, even if we tend to feel more comfortable if it does not come up at all.

In the later 1980s Robert M. Young referred to 'the loud silence' (1987, p.1) in our profession and its literature regarding race. He sought to explain this dismissiveness. 'A racist society will have a racist science,' (p.3) he stated. A professional group's values are shaped by its members' social identity. They 'will determine the questions that get asked, what counts as an acceptable answer, what research is prestigious, what work gets funded and published' (p.3). Young attributed professional complacency on race to the fact that our institutions, incomes and careers had not been put on the line by failure to address it. Those days are over.

National census figures project that by 2042 more than 50 per cent of the USA will be non-white. Some major cities have already passed that benchmark. The unprecedented participation of non-white voters in the recent election of an

African American to second term as president is proof of fundamental change that can no longer be dismissed by any political or professional group. As ethnic diversity increases, it is common to hear therapists complain that their practices are dwindling. Psychoanalytic treatment reaches only a small percentage of this ethnically diverse population (U.S. Department of Health and Human Services, 2001). What holds us back from coming to grips with such an important bread-and-butter issue? Writers invite us to consider: why do we refrain from dealing with our failure to attract and train a proportionate cohort of ethnically diverse psychotherapists (Sue and Sue, 2002)? When will we begin to support more thorough, balanced research into diversity within the profession (Watkins, 2012)? Finding answers to questions such as these requires us to look inward at attitudes that have become 'deeply – unconsciously – sedimented' (Young, 1987, p.3).

A recent survey at the William Alanson White Institute asked 100 graduates what percentage of their practices are made up of people of colour. The modal response, between 0 and 10 per cent, is probably typical in psychoanalysis. It would be absurd to suggest minorities are simply healthier or less in need of help than others. On the contrary, the U.S. Surgeon General's Report found that 'racial and ethnic minorities bear a greater burden from unmet mental health needs and thus suffer a greater loss to their overall health and productivity' (U.S. Department of Health and Human Services, 2001, p.3). Why fewer patients when there is greater need?

Ample research since the early 1980s has shown that minority clients prefer treatment with members of their race and tend to mistrust therapists from other racial or ethnic groups (Wierzbicki and Pekarik, 1993). Study after study reveals the misgivings African American patients have about white, Anglo-American therapists, whom they perceive as racially biased (Sanders-Thompson et al., 2004). While this is surely not categorically the case, such perceptions are powerful deterrents. An early study reported that 'White therapists generally rated their clients, and especially their black clients, as psychologically more impaired than did black therapists' (Jones, 1982, p.724). However, these same patients did not necessarily do worse in therapy. In spite of more recent efforts to dispel such views, they may linger:

> Members of disadvantaged ethnic groups in the United States do not have an increased risk for psychiatric disorders. Members of these groups, however, do tend to have more persistent disorders. Future research should focus on explanations for these findings, including the possibility that these comparisons are biased.
>
> (Breslau et al., 2005, p.319)

Other studies point to the relatively rare occasions when patients of different ethnicities do seek psychoanalytic treatment and are generally found to be less engaged and more likely to terminate sooner (Sue & Sue, 2002; Vasquez, 2007). Such findings raise the question whether the problem is with patient or therapist. Subtle forms of profiling might be inherent in the studies themselves.

It's not surprising that potential clients of colour cannot find a match with which they feel comfortable. With basic mistrust combined with so few psychoanalysts of their ethnicity, countless needy patients never engage the system at all. Practices suffer from the inability of white psychotherapists to attract a culturally diverse clientele and from our failure to train ethnically diverse practitioners. Something is terribly wrong.

A visit to almost any American psychoanalytic institute will quickly highlight the paucity of African, Hispanic, Asian, Native American or mixed race professionals. Attendance at any large conference might evoke surprise at the number of women – clearly a triumph, since they historically have been seriously underrepresented. When Marvin Margolis (2001), past president of the American Psychoanalytic Association, wrote about psychoanalysis entering its second century, the numbers of female candidates for psychoanalytic certificates had risen to 50 per cent. Noting only marginal representation of Asian, Black and Hispanic groups, 'communities *we have ignored or insulted* in the past' (p.18), he anticipated substantial improvement within 25 years. He was wrong. 'Psychoanalysis remains a profession that is overwhelmingly white and the socioeconomic diversity among those who teach, train, or who are treated psychoanalytically is limited,' according to a female African American psychologist who has written extensively on race issues (Leary, 2012). Were it not for the vast numbers of social workers among us, it would be difficult to find non-white practicing psychoanalysts.

Powerful factors contribute to deficits in professional and patient representation. These domains are inextricably bound up with one another and with the third focus of this discussion, research. In a remarkable study in *Psychoanalytic Psychology* with the subtitle 'How "white" are the data?" Watkins (2012) asked: 'To what extent do our studies ... reflect attention to and inclusion of minority group members as research participants? And how might that inclusion have changed over the years?' (p.296). The 104 studies analysed covered a period of 50 years, encompassing 9,000 subjects. While age and sex of all participants were reported, no race–ethnicity variables were reported in 75 per cent of the studies. Data on socioeconomic status was similarly ignored. It may be that so few people of colour were being seen by analysts that it did not seem important to count them. Absence of information might be construed as indifference to whether a patient was identified as minority or not. Depending on the time at which a study was done, this omission might reflect concern for 'political correctness'. When gathered, the single category of 'non-white' is often the only box to check for African, Latino, Asian and American Indians. Some 'non-whites', objecting to this catch-all identity, might decline to participate. Among the 25 per cent of studies in which some information on race and ethnicity was collected, the research focus had something to do with drug use.

Psychoanalytic research seems selectively, deliberately white. The failure to include thousands of minorities and to document differences and universalities among subgroups is shocking and inexcusable. A massive amount of data is lost, unavailable to help us build a narrative about minorities and their unique sensibilities.

Psychoanalysis has a long history of selective representation. Originated by Ashkenazi Jewish males, its early contributions were nourished on their scholarship and that of their mentees and offspring. Some have argued there is a good fit between the cultural personality of Ashkenazi Jews and qualities valued in the discipline, like introspection and ease with uncertainty (Ostow, 1982). Nevertheless, psychoanalysis has undergone dramatic membership changes. Witness the current representation of women in what was once a man's field. Note, too, the strides of gay psychoanalysts. Our history reflects occasional strivings to bring new populations into the field. Freud convinced a generation of psychoanalysts to open free clinics in Vienna, Berlin and other European cities. They succeeded until the beginning of World War II (Danto, 2007; Altman, 2010). The most universally accepted formulations of race dynamics have been provided by psychoanalytic theory. We are all familiar with the conceptualization that one unconsciously projects undesirable aspects of self onto the other, allowing a prejudiced person to deny a negative characteristic (such as aggression) while at the same time justifying the release of aggression toward the despised other.

We are not a bad lot. We consider ourselves models of inclusiveness and progressive thinking. We take pleasure in teasing out reasons why negative, unproductive attitudes and behaviours persist. We are a sophisticated group. There is no endemic reason we cannot move progressively on matters of minority representation. What gets in our way? Certainly not malice. To judge the disproportionate representation of race in our field as proof of prejudice and hatred would be simplistic and counterproductive. It would also be false to say there has been no progress. For example, I wrote the following e-mail to our institute in New York last spring after attending a conference at the New School titled 'Black psychoanalysts speak'.

> The Saturday event was stunning because of the extraordinary caliber of the speakers, and powerful because it confirmed that there are so many talented and articulate black analysts with new ideas. I have argued that psychoanalysis is a wasteland when it comes to both treating people of color and encouraging them to join the profession. Largely, this is still true. But there are beginnings and this event was certainly one of them. It was heartening to hear from so many who had a deep love for psychoanalysis, how it changed their lives, how it continues to inspire them. The audience was at least 60% people of color. New and refreshing voices all over …

I'm sure others are witnessing change, but one swallow does not make a summer. For the greater part of our history, we have chosen not to deal with racial diversity.

Many fine articles are being written on the process of treating people of colour or the treatment of whites by non-whites. These works are rich, deep and sensitively tuned. However, they tend to probe individual cases with no broad demographic context. With the exception of Watkins, searches of the psychoanalytic literature yield so few studies on the topic of professional and patient demographics it suggests collective denial.

The American Psychological Association examined minority representation in preparation for the profession. The picture is bleak. At the doctoral level, we're stuck at about 15 per cent, and the great majority of candidates for this degree do not choose to practise psychoanalysis (Maton et al., 2006). Studies of the minority composition of university faculties across all disciplines in the United States are also discouraging. A summary of 252 high-quality studies found minority representation among academics with PhDs to be roughly 17 per cent (Sotrillo et al., 2008). As low as this percentage is – half of what it ought to be – it far exceeds that for psychoanalysis. Other prestigious professions with demanding requirements have come to grips with their minority problems in ways that psychoanalysis has not. These data belie the commonly held belief that minority representation must await the arrival of a more robust middle class and more educated people of colour, the idea being that a rising tide will lift all boats. Many minorities have arrived in the educated middle class, but they are choosing other professions. Why are they overlooking us?

Psychoanalysis has experienced a loss of prestige and influence in the world. We long for renewal. Clinical doctoral programs in the U.S. largely skip over analytic theory as outdated, less practical and useful in today's world. Cognitive behavioural and pharmacological theories are favoured. It is difficult to get insurance reimbursement for psychoanalytic treatment. Few of us practise it in pure form. We have everything to gain and nothing to lose from an infusion of new ideas, experiences and sensibilities that diverse peoples could bring.

Many hard questions can and must be posed. Are we so ashamed of the demographic results that we try to cover them over? Is there some secret rule that keeps studies from being done and articles published? Is the data so hidden (in the name of confidentiality) that researchers cannot access it? Do we naïvely suppose that nothing more needs to be done now that we have a black president? Do we dismiss the poor, among whom are to be found significant percentages of people of colour, because they cannot afford our fees? I have seen too many acts of generosity (analysts offering reduced fees) to believe this is true.

What is the unconscious dynamic that supports complacency about inadequate racial and ethnic diversity in our profession – especially for the many among us who have vigorously championed racial integration and for the many among us who understand the tragedy of exclusion and marginalization from a personal perspective? Perhaps we need to consider a possibility raised by writers, like Helen Block Lewis (1987), who describe a shame so deep and painful that it must be disassociated from conscious experience. Do we fail to face our deficiency with regard to racial exploration because it brings up feelings too unpleasant to bear, resulting in broad denial that there is a problem. A kinder formulation is what Leary calls an 'adaptive challenge' in relation to an ideal that we fall far short of in everyday practice. These gaps have different meanings to different constituencies (e.g. white analysts) who have different stakes in the outcomes. Gaps can seem like a mere crack in the overall system or the size of the Grand Canyon, depending on one's perspective.

Some have argued that our models of analytic therapy are a poor fit for people of different cultural backgrounds. Models based on examining personal history may be inadequate to deal with the effects of generational social oppression, especially with Afro- and Native Americans whose historical legacy includes serious long-term violation of personhood. O'Loughlin (2008) described an analogous situation with Australian Aborigines. His insights regarding genocidal policies remind us that subsequent generations do worse if they cannot articulate generational horrors. (This has been widely observed with Holocaust and rape victims.) Past abuse must be made conscious and a narrative generated for real healing to take place and to avoid perpetuating abuse. This issue cannot be compartmentalized and considered not directly relevant to the psychoanalytic process. How can a new generation of therapists address this concern?

Our cultural ideal is often defined in terms advancing the individual autonomous self and undermining dependencies. Other cultural orientations may view those same dependencies as strengths. Our culture tends toward spiritual neutrality. Others see the universe as more spiritually infused. Some data suggest Afro-American and Hispanic patients do better in treatments that underscore religion's importance (Vasquez, 2007; Mishna, Luksted et al., 2009). They may also do better in treatments that acknowledge and deal with the pervasiveness of racial and ethnic bias (Sue and Sue, 2002; Vasquez, 2007; Altman, 2010). Our models are not built to embrace such cultural differences. We tend to deny, ignore or even belittle them. Even more dangerous is the tendency to feel justified in these operations. It is well worth a little soul-searching to root these propensities out.

We may need to use more imagination in presenting psychoanalytic theory. Perhaps we should build a more inclusive one. The result might be a multiplicity of theories, each with limited relevance and no claims towards universality – anathema for some of us. I am sanguine. Fortunately, I subscribe to a theory where, because it prioritizes notions like 'co-construction', the interpersonal dyad is always shifting and renewing itself. I accept that no therapy is like any other. Reaching across the professional 'aisle', I find enrichment and increased relevance. I see this as the path to a kind of renaissance in the field, but we will never know until we begin a thorough, unflinching conversation on the topic of ethnic diversity.

There is surely a will for this change among a great many psychoanalysts. Some may be resigned or even comfortable with the status quo, but let us not underestimate the power and possibility of change. Certain concrete actions could support it simply by raising the topic's visibility. The current president of the American Psychoanalytic Association could make his views known through the many channels open to him, such as newsletters and the *Journal of the American Psychoanalytic Association*. At the annual APA convention, tables could be set up to recruit volunteers interested in making racial diversity a priority. Workshops could be offered. The APA could use its considerable weight to put every member institute on notice that their efforts to address the issue would be part of any evaluation process.

At the institute level, we need more debate within governing bodies. In this writer's five years' experience as a member of one such body, the issue never came up. (I am told this no longer the case.) Another area to look for ideas about outreach is institutions and professions with better track records for attracting minorities. For example, psychology has produced far more minority PhDs, especially in recent years. A recent article entitled 'Exemplary efforts in psychology to recruit and retain graduate students of color' identified eleven departments that were way above average in this regard (Rogers and Moline, 2006). The strategies that seemed to work best were: offering attractive financial aid; engaging current minority faculty members in recruitment; having faculty make personal contact with prospective students; creating linkages with historical institutions for people of colour; offering diversity issues courses; and having students do research on diversity issues. Mentoring was also mentioned. This example demonstrates what can happen when the topic is finally brought to the table.

Looking back on the conference that prompted this chapter, and the man who said his store is always open, it is clear we have work to do. We must reach out to those who will not set foot in the place even though the store is well stocked and eager for business. Our storekeeper must understand that, while the door looks open to him, it may still appear closed and uninviting to many others. We need new storekeepers with greater sensitivity to the demands of a broadened, invigorated clientele. I am reminded of Edwin Markham's poem 'Outwitted'.

> He drew a circle to shut me out.
> Heretic, rebel, a thing to flout.
> But love and I had the wit to win
> I drew a circle that took him in.

Can we draw that larger circle? Yes, especially if we can own our shared, imperfect history. I hope this chapter takes a small step in that direction.

References

Altman, N. (2010). *The analyst in the inner city: race, class, and culture through a psychoanalytic lens*. New York: Routledge.

Breslau, J. (2005). Lifetime risks and persistence of psychiatric disorders across ethnic groups in the United States. *Psychological Medicine*, 35(3): 317–327.

Danto, E. (2007). *Freud's free clinics: psychoanalysis and social justice, 1918–1938*. New York: Columbia University Press.

Jones, E. (1982). Psychotherapists' impressions of treatment outcomes as a function of race. *Journal of Clinical Psychology*, 38: 722–731.

Leary, K. (2012). Race as an adaptive challenge: working with diversity in the clinical consulting room. *Psychoanalytic Psychology*, 29(3): 279–281.

Lewis, H. (1987). Introduction: shame – the 'sleeper' in psychopathology. In H.B. Lewis (ed.), *The role of shame in symptom formation*. Hillsdale, NJ: Laurence Erlbaum Associates.

Margolis, M. (2001). The American Psychoanalytic Association: a decade of change. *Journal of the American Psychoanalytic Association*, 49: 11–23.

Maton, K., Kohut, J., Wicherski, H., Leary, G. and Vinokurov, A. (2006). Minority students of color and the psychology graduate pipeline: discouraging and encouraging trends, 1989–2003. *American Psychologist*, 61: 117–131.

Mishra, S., Lucksted, A., Gioia, D., Barnet, B. and Baquet, C. (2009). Needs and preferences for receiving mental health services in an African American focus group sample. *Community Mental Health Journal*, 45: 117–126.

O'Laughlin, M. (2008). Radical hope or death by a thousand cuts? The future for indigenous Australians. *Arena Journal*, 29: 175–202.

Ostow, M. (ed.) (1982). *Judaism and psychoanalysis*. London: Karnac.

Rogers, M. and Moline, L. (2006). Exemplary efforts in psychology to recruit and retain graduate students of color. *American Psychologist* 61(5): 395.

Sanders-Thompson, V., Bazile, A. and Akbar, M. (2004). African Americans' perception of psychotherapy and psychotherapists. *Professional Psychology: Research and Practice*, 35(1): 19–26.

Sue, D.W. and Sue, D. (2002). *Counseling the culturally diverse: theory and practice*. New York: John Wiley & Sons.

U.S. Department of Health and Human Services. (2001). *Mental health: culture, race and ethnicity – a supplement to 'Mental health: a report of the Surgeon General'*. Rockville, MD: U.S. Department of Health and Human Services, Substance Abuse and Mental Health Services Administration, Center for Mental Health Services.

Vasquez, M. (2007). Cultural difference and the therapeutic alliance: an evidence based analysis. *American Psychologist* 62(8): 878–885.

Watkins, C. (2012). Race/ethnicity in short-term and long-term psychodynamic psychotherapy treatment research: how 'white' are the data? *Psychoanalytic Psychotherapy*, 29(3): 293–307.

Wierzbicki, M. and Pekarik, G. (1993). A meta-analysis of psychotherapy dropout. *Professional Psychology: Research and Practice*, 24: 190–195.

Young, R. (1987). Psychoanalysis and racism: a loud silence. Revised version of a talk given to a conference on Psychoanalysis and Racism, sponsored by the Association of Child Psychotherapists, London, October. Available online at http://human-nature.com/rmyoung/papers/loud.html [accessed 24 June 2016].

Chapter 9

Finding their way home
The struggle of the Australian Aboriginal people to become one people within one nation

Janice A. Walters

Beginnings: likeness and difference – crossing the racial and cultural divide

Sullivan believed that humans are more alike than they are different (1953). The question raised in this chapter is to what extent likeness and difference applies to the Australian Aboriginal people as they struggle to reclaim their place within their country of origin.

My introduction to racial and cultural difference came when, as a child, I listened to adult conversations about removing Aboriginal children from their families that were perceived as incapable of childrearing. The philosophy was to place them in institutions where they could be socialized into the white culture. I was aware of the words and that something did not feel right, but my young age did not allow me to put meaning to these words. In my child's mind, the question these conversations raised was whether this could also be my fate, especially since my home did not feel stable due to constant parental conflict. This is a terrifying thought that causes anxiety and dread for a vulnerable child. For those who were taken, the terror was, and for many still is, unspeakable.

At university, I became passionate about the Aboriginal people's fight for land rights. Another event that created great passion in me occurred while I was living in a homogenous Brisbane suburb. A woman screaming outside my home awakened me in the middle of the night. I felt fearful of the unknown terror as someone pounded on my door. Opening it, I found a young Aboriginal woman in great distress. The man who lived next door had taken her there and, after engaging in sexual activity, threw her into the street. She was terrified and isolated from any familiar environment. This encounter provided me an opportunity to learn about her culture as she told stories through the early hours of the morning. It also brought the realization that he regarded her as less than human, someone to satisfy his needs, but to be discarded at will.

History: connectedness, belonging and identity

Land was critical for survival for both Aboriginal people and colonists. Their different perceptions of land utilization created conflict. *Kanyini*, an Aboriginal word describing the belief that everything is connected, brings them responsibility and pride. Australian Aborigines' core identity, their belief concerning the interconnectedness of land, spirituality and family, is illustrated in the following passage (Knight 1996):

> We don't own the land, the land owns us. The land is my mother, my mother is the land. Land is the starting point to where it all began. It's like picking up a piece of dirt and saying this is where I started and this is where I'll go. The land is our food, our culture, our spirit and identity.

The health of land and water is central within Aboriginal culture. Home is where you are. The land is both home and mother. Aborigines feel that it is their responsibility to take care of it and leave it unspoiled. In contrast, colonists focused on their need to cultivate for survival and profit. Based on Darwinian (1784) ideas, they believed cultivation indicated higher intelligence. The Aboriginal people's refusal to use the land this way resulted in their being assigned status as inferior in the chain of human evolution, thus not deserving survival. Social Darwinism also justified refusal to make land treaties and forced removal of Aboriginal people from their land (Roberts, 1978).

Cultural clashes: paranoid-schizoid splitting, racism and genocide

Klein's (1946) paranoid-schizoid position and projective identification contribute to understanding racism and genocide. In 1788, the first fleet brought 1,000 people, more than 700 of whom were convicts from Britain's fast-growing urban underclass. They were deemed inferior citizens and expelled to relieve growing pressure on the prison system. New South Wales became a penal colony. These persecuted, dehumanized settlers likely departed with anxiety and arrived in a harsh, hostile, threatening land, creating intolerable anxiety and causing flight to an idealized internal object, with a need to keep ideal and persecutory objects separated and under control (Klein, 1946). Real and perceived fears of persecution and annihilation led hatred and destruction to govern their relationships and promoted splitting of their internal and external worlds based on culture and race (Walters, 2012). Previously persecuted colonizers became persecutors.

Freud (1920) proposed that the cultural superego might mobilize individual aggression and punitive behaviours. Idealism and patriotism might facilitate the release of this hostility (Freud, 1930). Individual idealized superegos may merge with the cultural superego (Volkan, 1988). The psychology of the Nation justified systematic acts of physical and cultural genocide.

The Aboriginal people's refusal to assimilate and cultivate was used to justify their dehumanization and inferior status. They were removed from their land and placed on mission stations, where they were closely supervised. Disconnection from their beliefs, land, spirituality and family resulted in loss of their languages, culture, identity, self-worth and human dignity. This psychic death had enormous consequences.

The goal was to eliminate the Aboriginal race. Acts of physical genocide occurred from the beginning of colonization throughout these years. What could not be achieved with a flawed survival of the fittest theory, the dominant culture tried to accomplish by socializing the children to be white. They aimed to eliminate the race through cultural change. Cultural genocide reached its worst between 1883 and 1969, when Aboriginal children were removed from their families and communities and placed within white families or institutions (Read, 1981). They experienced the unspeakable terror of abrupt removal, then often suffered physical, emotional and sexual abuse by caretakers. They were told they were orphans: their parents either were dead or had abandoned them. They were led to believe contact with their families and culture would cause them destruction and shame. Messages of shame negatively impacted Aboriginal people's capacity to exert power. Identifying with an idealized, saving, yet punishing white culture, the Stolen Children lost their Aboriginality. Once they became of childbearing age, their white custodians often raped them. They – especially the women – were expected to think and act white so that they would become desirable for marriage to white men, with the goal of breeding out the Aboriginal race by making it unacceptable and fearful for them to choose Aboriginal men as fathers for their children. When released, the Stolen Generations found themselves caught between both cultures, not belonging to either. They lived in a state of nothingness as a lost people.

The Stolen Generations

In 2010, I began a longitudinal ethnographic study in the western suburbs of Sydney where many of the Stolen Generations reside. I visit participating families yearly. They have an Elder member who was taken as a child, or whose children were taken. Aboriginal Elders must be respected and often mentor for younger generations. They, and subsequent generations, are experiencing the consequences of intergenerational trauma. I will speak about some of these families and their struggle to become one people within one nation.

Tara

Tara, an elderly woman, gave birth to nine children, eight from her marriage to a white man and one from a sexual assault by a white man. She lost her five oldest children after her husband beat her, leaving her with a broken leg and in a government condemned house. Christian volunteers offered to care for her children until she found another home. Desperate, she agreed. When she tried to visit her children, she was refused, and told they were better off without her. They were told the same. White Australia's perception of Aboriginal people led these caretakers to believe they were saving the children. Over the years, Tara cared for her remaining children, and made many attempts to get her others back. She described the anguish she felt on being separated from them. When she found out that one son fostered by a white family had drowned in their care, she found that she could not cope and became a murderously enraged deadened mother (Green, 1986). She directed her hatred, anger and rage toward herself and others, became depressed and drank heavily. Inhabiting a state of persecutory fear, she believed violent intruders were plotting to break into her home. Boarding her windows, she locked herself inside. A son climbed through a window to encourage her to leave. She was hospitalized. When she returned home, she received support from the Aboriginal community. Ultimately, she was able to integrate her experience, forgiving herself and those who had wronged her. Her taken children returned home, but the relationships were strained. Today, Tara has a relationship with most of her children and has reconciled past abuses and betrayals. Her children struggle with various problems including depression, anxiety, alcohol and drug abuse, and inability to mother their own children.

Alice

Tara's youngest daughter grew up believing Tara's deceased husband was her father. Alice married her white childhood sweetheart and they lived in a home with their two children. This changed when she visited a government office with her mother and was handed a paper that revealed she was conceived from the aforementioned assault. The trauma was unspeakable, and knowing her life came from such destructive forces appears to have caused her to engage paranoid-schizoid defences. She began struggling with the potential goodness and destructiveness of her internal and external worlds. When I met her, she believed her presence could only bring destruction to her children, so she left her home and children in the care of her husband. She moved into her mother's house because she could not sustain herself. Further, she feared separation from mother, even to sleep, would leave them both unprotected and cause their destruction. Like Tara, she refused to leave the house. She reacted to her paranoid thoughts and feelings by lashing out at others. I suspect the majority of these persons were white.

Struggling with depression, anger, rage and paranoia, Alice engaged in self-destructive behaviours. She wishes to be a 'good mum', but her demons cause her to fear she will destroy all she touches. Her presence causes financial and emotional stress for Tara. On my most recent visit, Alice had moved into her own home with her children. Now older, I suspect they have become her caretakers. Tara was happy to have her peace and privacy back. Alice struggles with being a silent recipient of her mother and her siblings' trauma as well as the shock of finding out how her life began. Unknowingly, she passes this trauma on to her children.

Lila and Bertha

Taken from their parents as infants, Lila and Bertha were placed in Cootamundra Girls' Home. Told they were orphans, they were forbidden contact with Aboriginal people. They internalized messages that culturally they were white and that Aboriginals were undesirables who were to be feared, especially the men. When released from the home, they found themselves rejected by the white community they were forced to identify with, while also struggling to be accepted by Aboriginals.

Along with many other Stolen Children, Lila and Bertha were deprived of the mother–infant attachment bond that researchers (e.g. Ainsworth, Blehar, Waters and Wall, 1978) have shown to be so important. They were terrorized from abrupt separation from their mother and placement with caretakers who were often abusive. As adults, they live with the conflict of their desire for love and goodness and their fear of annihilation from hate and destructiveness from themselves and those around them (Klein, 1946), especially white people. They married white men and gave birth to several children. Because of their trauma, they were unable to provide integrated selves for their infants. Trauma experienced in one generation has profound effects on the emotional lives not only of the next generation, but even six to ten generations hence (Fraiberg, Adelson and Shapiro, 1975).

Children of the Stolen Generations are suffering from the consequences of their parents' trauma as well as their own traumatic experiences. Their trauma has now been passed on to their children. The Aboriginal community, especially the male members, is at risk of losing yet another generation. Many have become perpetrators or victims of homicide, together with drug and alcohol abuse. Many are imprisoned. Other problems include poor health, premature death, domestic violence, family dysfunction, abandonment and abuse of children, psychological disorders and high rates of suicide. The Elders, especially the women, struggle to reclaim their traditional status as leaders and cultural messengers for younger generations, yet these women are very active within the community and hold the future of the next generations in their hands.

Transference and counter-transference

I have had many emotional reactions to each of these women's lives.

Tara

Elderly Tara waits at home for her pension cheque every two weeks to buy necessities. She was a go-getter in her early years, but has become frail. After years as a welfare recipient, she has learned helplessness. My mother, a fiercely independent woman, also became frail and helpless with age. Women from their generation were expected to be helpless but, by necessity, had to be independent.

One afternoon I sat in my car waiting for Tara outside a medical office. I was overwhelmed, feeling I had been in this place before. I became aware that I was responding to Tara's needs as I had to my mother's during her later years when I flew home and found she was too afraid to leave the house. Her basic needs were being neglected. While I was drawn to my mother and Tara's life-giving goodness, my role was to protect and save them. When I drove Tara to purchase things she needed, I struggled with desires to be the good, life-preserving object and guilt and fear that I would soon become the bad, withholding object when I returned to my home and work in New York. In Tara's case, I was painfully aware that I did not want to be like the destructive white people who had abandoned her in dire circumstances. Playing the role of protector, I felt guilty at the prospect of not being there to meet her needs. Yet I knew Tara would get her needs met because she elicited similar responses from others. I was reliving my guilt and anxiety when my mother's dependency assigned me the role of persecutor each time I left her in a helpless state.

Alice

When I met Alice, her anxiety, depression and paranoia were so severe she could not dress and leave home. She feared any separation from Tara would lead to her or Tara's destruction. As I listened to her hope that I might save her from her psychological trauma so she could be a good mother, I found myself conflicted between my role as researcher and psychoanalyst. She saw me as having the ability to relieve her pain and suffering. I began to see myself the same way. I shared her anger and helplessness as I witnessed the repeated failure of the healthcare system to help her. Each time I saw her at Tara's, I experienced her pain and my helplessness. To become her analyst, then leave in a few weeks, would make me one of those destructive, abandoning others and increase my guilt about not being able to save her from her demons. I continually walked a fine line between researcher and analyst and was happy when she agreed, once again, to seek medical care.

Lila and Bertha

Bertha agreed to tell me her story. She suggested I drive to her house and we go meet with Lila. When I arrived, Bertha's paranoid-schizoid need for separation and distance from me, the potentially destructive white person, was evident. Bertha greeted me. She, Lila and several other family members were seated around the kitchen table playing cards. My first response was that I had the day and time wrong but Bertha reassured me and invited me in. I felt like an intruder, questioning my right to be a voyeur within their inner world of pain and suffering. Was I just another white person using them for selfish gains? Their brother, also taken as a child, was known for his dislike of white people and his belief that they only wanted 'a piece of him'.

As I sat among them, Bertha and Lila shared their stories with me. The ongoing card game was not the setting I had anticipated, but I came to appreciate their need for self-preservation in the face of my intrusion into their past. I was reminded of when I have been in public places with Aboriginal friends, with eyes focused on them as outsiders in a white world. I was now the outsider in Lila and Bertha's world – one they carefully guarded from intrusion by potentially destructive white people. My initial discomfort soon passed, as I believe theirs did. They enthusiastically told their stories between rounds of cards until it was time to terminate both the card game and the storytelling. I left feeling very clear that my place in their lives would always be separated by race and culture.

Working with likeness and difference

I struggle with my view that the Aboriginal people I spend time with are not different from me and my need to recognize the differences that define their place within the community and nation. To not recognize their experiential and cultural differences is to do them an injustice. Their daily struggle to belong and be accepted and respected within white Australia is apparent.

When I first visited these women, it was evident that while each approached me differently all did so with anxiety and mistrust. I experienced my own apprehension, not knowing how they would react to my intrusion into their lives. In each case, as our anxiety lessened and trust developed, we began establishing a space in which mutual, respectful participation based on trust and respect could take place. I feel much gratitude for having been invited to participate in many aspects of their lives. I have been referred to as Aunty, a title of respect and inclusion into the mob (an Aboriginal term for the extended family). Despite racial and cultural differences, I feel our likeness. I resonated with their pain as I re-experienced my own growing up with domestic violence and feelings that come with it, especially when others' eyes are focused on your family as the troubled one.

During one visit, I found myself without accommodation due to unexpected circumstances. I struggled with my childhood experience of being homeless because of domestic violence. I now felt marginalized in the country I call home. I was in another part of Australia, far from my childhood home and family. I entered into the experience of these families, all victims of violence, displacement and marginalization. I was also aware of our differences. I could not feel their terror and unresolved losses. I could only feel empathy. I was a member of the other group, a great grandchild of white settlers. As I struggled with my pain and feelings of homelessness, I was reminded of my ability to change my situation. If I could not find alternative accommodation, I could return to the comforts of my home. The Aboriginal people I would leave behind did not have that choice. Living from welfare or pensions, they often do not have enough money for basic needs.

Could I bear the guilt of not being able to change the circumstances of my mother, my country, my powerless Aboriginal friends? Intergenerational trauma for Aboriginals is not the same for whites. We are similarly human, yet forced to be different because of the country's institutional separation based on culture and race. I was and am not different, yet I am painfully aware of our difference, especially when I leave my early childhood experiences behind and return to New York. Because of my race and culture, I have been able through hard work to avail myself of opportunities. Hard work is not enough for them. They did and still do not have the same opportunities. We are alike in so many ways, yet so different. To work with Aboriginal people one must navigate the divide between likeness and difference while also finding a space in which mutual participation can provide a holding environment for their pain and suffering as well as the continued development of hopefulness within a mutually trusting relationship.

Obstacles to truth and reconciliation

Conflict exists within the Nation between paranoid-schizoid splitting that maintains racial and cultural division versus desire for reparation and integration, making one people and one nation (Walters, 2012). Obstacles impede progress.

Alford (1989) helps us understand how paranoid-schizoid anxiety prevents emotional development. He argues that when it is assigned an objective focus, groups legitimate and reinforce paranoid-schizoid defences, such as splitting and idealization. Individuals in the group are made to feel less anxious, at the cost of emotional development.

I believe the cultural and racial split that exists within Australia impedes emotional growth and stands in the way of truth and reconciliation. To be Aboriginal means assignment to dependency, inferiority and shame, while white culture is represented by independence, superiority and pride. This division is reinforced by using welfare as payment for suffering, marginalizing Aboriginal people who have been forced to or have chosen to live on urban fringes. Welfare becomes a means of control, encouraging the cycle of intergenerational helplessness. Reconciliation requires recognition and acceptance that both white and Aboriginal Australians are Australians, regardless of race, cultural beliefs and practices. Despite our differences, we are all more human than otherwise.

Aboriginal people believe the land is one mother for both white and black Australians. They want to be acknowledged and valued as Australians who share the same country, while retaining pride in their identity and belief systems. They want the right to determine their best interests as equal citizens. They want to be free to live according to their meaning of home within the country that was originally theirs. Caught between two cultures, they cannot go back because the old culture no longer exists. They need to accept and mourn its loss. The philosophy of assimilation requires that, to be accepted, they give up their Aboriginal identity and blend into mainstream culture. To do this, they must live with an internal void, a lost identity. Loss of *kanyini* leads to many problems. There is a need to incorporate the traditional within the new culture to allow for rebuilding pride, dignity and responsibility. White Australians need to genuinely acknowledge Aboriginal people's beliefs, spirituality, family and culture. Both cultures need to learn from each other.

There is hope among many Australians for reparation and integration with recognition and acceptance that both white and Aboriginal people are part of one nation, sharing mutual love of being Australian. While we are all more human than otherwise, there needs to be mutual recognition and respect that all people, regardless of race, have the right to practise freely cultural traditions that highlight their differences. While the optimist within me likes to believe truth and reconciliation are close, much work needs to be done before that can occur.

In the words of Mick Dobson (1997), an Aboriginal:

> We have extended our hand to other Australians. Those who take our hand are those who dare to dream of an Australia that could be in true reconciliation. Through the remembering, the grieving and the healing we become as one in the dreaming of this land. This is about us, our country, not about petty deliberations and politics. We must join hands and forge our future. Will you take our hand? Will you dare to share our dream?

One people, one land

The following song speaks to the quest to find one people within one land. It is relevant for all people who experience the effects of discrimination, trauma and displacement from their home and country.

> There is a land, an ancient land. It bears a vast and rugged face.
> Its spirits deep, haunting and free.
> It calls to you, it calls to me.
> Come find your soul, within my depths.
> Come make of me, your homeland true.
>
> This is our land, we are its people.
> A nation that's free to realise its dream.
> A dream that's for all who dwell in this land.
> To live as one people, one people one land.
>
> There is a people, an ancient people.
> Their spirits rest deep in this land.
> Their dreamtime myth, story and faith.
> Make this land a sacred place.
> They seek of all a true embrace.
> That reconciles all that we are.
>
> And from distant shores many have come.
> To find their home in this great southern land.
> Where the spirit yearns and seeks to unite us all.[1]

Note

1 From the song 'One people, one land'. All rights reserved, copyright 2001. Used with special permission from Monica Brown and Emmaus Productions.

References

Ainsworth, M.D.S., Blehar, M.C., Waters, E. and Wall, S. (1978). *Patterns of attachment: a psychological study of the strange situation*. Hillsdale, NJ: Erlbaum.

Alford, F.C. (1989). *Melanie Klein and social theory: an account of political, art, and reason based on her psychoanalytic theory*. New Haven, CT: Yale University Press.

Darwin, C. (1874). *The descent of man*, 2nd edition. New York: A.L. Burt.

Dobson, M. 1997. Retrieved from http://peacejustice.wikispaces.com (accessed 30 June 2016).

Fraiberg, S., Adelson, E. and Shapiro, V. (1975). Ghosts in the nursery. *Journal of the American Academy of Child Psychiatry*, 14: 387–421.

Freud, S. (1920). Beyond the pleasure principle. *The standard edition of the complete works of Sigmund Freud*, vol. 18. London: Hogarth Press, pp.1–64.

—— (1930). Civilisation and its discontents. *The standard edition of the complete works of Sigmund Freud*, vol. 21. London: Hogarth Press, pp.64–145.

Green, A. (1986). The dead mother. *On private madness*. London: Hogarth Press.

Klein, M. (1946). Notes on some schizoid mechanisms. *International Journal of Psycho-Analysis*, 27: 99–110.

Knight, S. (1996). What is Aboriginal spirituality? Online at http://www.creativespirits.info (accessed 27 June 2016).

Read, P. (1981). *The Stolen Generations: the removal of Aboriginal children in New South Wales 1883 to 1969*. NSW Government Human Services Aboriginal Affairs, NSW.

Roberts, J. (1978). *From massacres to mining: the colonization of Aboriginal Australia*. Impact Investigative Media Productions.

Sullivan, H.S. (1953). *The interpersonal theory of psychiatry*. New York: Norton.

Volkan, V.D. (1988). *The need to have enemies and allies*. New York: Jason Aronson.

Walters, J. (2012). The psychological and social consequences of trauma and race relations on the Australian indigenous people. *The International Journal of the Humanities*, 9(8): 149–164.

Chapter 10

The autistic core in Aboriginal trauma

Breaking down or breaking out of the autistic defence

Norma Tracey

This chapter attempts to give understanding of the catastrophe resulting from dislocation from culture and loss of continuity through Stolen Children, community and land. The ensuing tragedy leaves these people devoid of protection from the current world they live in and from within their own psyche.

The Dreaming and *Dadirri* were cultural phenomena of early Australian Aboriginals. From them we gain ideas of how trauma was treated and the roots of how it is treated today. Can psychoanalytic therapy, with its focus on the symbolic, with its use of ancient forms of *Dadirri* and the Dreaming, help restore their internal world?

This chapter is predicated on these two significant gifts from ancient Aboriginal peoples: the concept of the Dreaming and the most ancient form of treating trauma known to every Aboriginal group as *Dadirri*, or, for modern Aboriginal people, 'healing circle'. In the ancient contents of the Dreaming, Aboriginal people imbued their external world and events with meaning from their internal world. They created boundaries and symbols for this meaning. This chapter attempts to understand the way meaning is stripped away by trauma. Ancient Aboriginal culture healed trauma through *Dadirri*, a ritualized form of 'deep listening'. This was not an ordinary witnessing but an empathic psychic action, now known to the modern world as psychotherapy.[1]

I want to show how the Aboriginal people have been cut off from access to aspects of their culture that might have helped them to accommodate and recover from traumatic aspects of current culture. After fourteen years of working with young Aboriginal mothers and their infants, I dare to hope that psychoanalytic thinking may approach a new way of repairing this loss. My co-workers and I observe psychoanalytic therapy symbolizing in much the same way as the Dreaming.

Breakdown in trauma

I propose that 'autistic cut-out' is a normal primitive defence that protects people from over-stimulus. In extreme cases of infant, childhood or severe adult trauma, if the defence becomes concretized, an autistic 'pocket' or core internal mind-state may result. Emotion cannot be experienced. Pain cannot be suffered. Meaning is lost. 'Thingifying' (concretization) causes loss of internal reverie and empathy. This may have happened to Aboriginal people when they were cut off from their culture, community, earth place. Meaning became lost for them. Far more seriously, they also lost ancient ritualistic and customary ways of dealing with trauma.

At the other extreme, for some the autistic defence does not hold and 'breakdown' results. Chaos, envy and rage overflow. Primitive enactment ensues and may include criminality. Perhaps in efforts to quell the nightmare of such mad emotions, Aboriginal people may turn to addiction, violence, rape, murder, suicide. These individuals have no internal holding boundaries to protect themselves or others from this primitive overflow.

'Trauma breakout' is quite different from what I have just described. It allows movement out of what may be a psychotic autistic defence, sometimes expressed as a scream of existence, or a suffering of the suffering in the suffering. This is more of a recovery from trauma. As part of the recovery process, there is no return to a 'normal' way of being, but rather an explosion of primitive emotions that could not be accessed because of the strength of the autistic defence (Tracey, 2000). Holding this 'breakout', very different from 'breakdown', allows restoration of health. After this initial 'flood' of trauma breakout, dosage and timing of responses are extremely relevant, requiring empathic awareness on the part of the therapist.

In ancient Australian Aboriginal tribes, a process took place between person and group. The collective presence allowed pain to be expressed, empathized with and suffered in a way that processed it. This is *Dadirri*. It embodies the most ancient and most important form of healing. Elders gather around the traumatized one and listen for hours in deep silence while the troubled person talks and talks. (This is his/her scream.) It is the opposite of 'thingifying'. Recovering in psychotherapy is similar, requiring a space where suffering the suffering in the suffering can occur, where careful monitoring and negotiating of how much the ego can tolerate, use and process in terms of timing and dosage can take place.

> We sit in a circle around the person. We hear, in the depth of our inner spring. We do not talk, we own his story, his pain. The owning makes us one with him, it heals. This is Dadirri. A big part of Dadirri is listening. Throughout the years, we have listened to our stories. They are told over and over, as the seasons go by. When a relation dies, we wait a long time in sorrow. We own our grief, we share our grief, our group owns our grief and their owning of it allows it to heal slowly.
>
> (Ungunmerr-Baumann, 1993, p.34)

This presence is similar to what a mother does for her infant in reverie. The central psychosis of terror is neutralized; that terror of being, or of being annihilated, is dispelled by psychic holding. The mother does that; the healing circle of *Dadirri* does that; the good-enough psychotherapist does that. Like *Dadirri*, psychoanalytic therapy liberates, through the therapeutic encounter, the capacity to dream, creating a renewed womb, as a new foetus begins to evolve from the therapeutic couple.

In establishing our centre in Gunawirra House, we did not dare imagine that young Aboriginal mothers would by choice come to psychoanalytic therapy. Was this 'new' form of therapy actually a form of the *Dadirri* that was lost to the Aboriginal people when they lost their culture? An Aboriginal health worker described it best: 'I thought this psychoanalytic stuff was a lot of shit. Now I listen to it carefully and it fits so perfectly for our people. It is in the same place as our dreaming.'

From this capacity to dream evolves meaning. Wisdom is transmitted through generations by Aboriginal Elders in oral and cave art forms. This ancient spirituality gives historic continuity to the inner self. Providing links to ancestors and elders in the past, it gives a sense of belonging in the present living community. It links internal to external world, giving meaning to the relationship between person and nature, and inner person and environment. It gives value to selfhood, community and culture. The rules or laws that bind these meanings become sacred, and the symbols born from them are precious, creating a boundary within which to contain and hold meaning. From here all sense of internal and external chaos and disharmony can be tolerated until a self in harmony within and without is experienced.

Does dislocation from this dreaming, this spiritual cultural base, affect the way a people experience themselves? I propose that the trauma of dislocation for Aboriginals as a people kills meaning, nullifies the internal illusion, destroys the capacity to sublimate into art and story, and destroys the psychic binding that symbol formation gives. It denudes the experience of a living self. The person experiences themselves as a no-person, an autistic defence that protects against overwhelming internal chaos. Dreams become real, concrete. The Dreaming is lost, replaced by a nightmare.

In the beginning, before the Dreaming: precreative space

At the core of personality is a particular psychic space, which I describe as the precreative, primordial abyss. It is the nothingness, the no-where space, appearing in most religions as the primary abyss: 'the earth was without form, and void' (Genesis 1:2). This space was there before all creative experiencing, before all ambivalence. In the Tao, 'It is before is and is not' (Mitchell, 1992, p.21). In Hebrew, it is known as *tehom* – the abyss, or 'bottomless sea'. It is not a static space, for there is dialectical movement to and from it in every living experience. Patterns of being are surrendered to allow return to the abyss, yet, paradoxically, for the first time. From there emerges potential to be born psychically anew. This dynamic constitutes a continuum from birth to death, from womb to tomb (Tracey, 2009, p.1025). Miriam Rose Ungunmerr-Baumann, an Aboriginal Elder, writes, 'It is the place before we were born, before we were in our mother's womb' (Farrelly, 2003, p.viii).

There is another psychic space – the dark abyss resulting from unresolved trauma. It has no growth, no movement. There, death becomes more active than life, annihilating life. At the centre is terror. The mind closes down even in a physical sense as the amygdala is closed down from the hippocampus. This creates the autistic-like space, the nothing space where nothing grows. The Aboriginal understood this dead 'no-faith' space. In the Kimberly Region of Western Australia, paintings by the Wandjina tribe are retouched. An Elder says,

> I don't know all what happened to you, but all your spirit has gone out of you. No men or women watch over you, for the people who belong to this place – my aunties, sisters, fathers and grannies – they are all dead now. Only I, who belong to another place came to visit you, but you are lonely for all those people who died and your spirit has gone away now. Because you are looking all dull – you are not looking bright – I'll try and draw you. I will try and put new paint on you people ... Don't get wild! Don't send rain! You must be very glad because I will make your eyes like new. My eye it has life, and your eye has life too, because I make it new.
> (Isaacs, 2005, p.71)

The Dreaming

In the Red Centre, the name given to the central Australian 'red' desert area, the mythic landscape has existed for countless millennia. 'These people have sought to reconcile themselves to an outwardly barren environment by living a rich imaginal life inspired by the power of the myth' (Cowan, 1994, p.22). The Dreaming network of tribal boundaries, languages, sacred songs, rituals and ceremonies held their culture together, Cowan states. He tells that in the Northern Region of Australia a sacred cult known as *Kunapipi* still preserves the mythogenic reality of the Sacred Mother, the perpetually pregnant woman. This fertility figure is linked to the Rainbow Serpent, a symbol of abundance and renewal. To talk of her is to engage in a dialogue with all mothers. Her form may be the many-breasted Diana of Ephesus, a plump effigy vessel from Minoan Crete or the Egyptian goddess Nut overreaching the sky. She may be Kali, Rati or Venus. Whatever her image, *Kunapipi* embodies a principle of fecundity that transcends her many manifestations. She is female in her creative, nurturing phase, and male in her seminal, ordering phase. Combining mysteriously with the Rainbow Serpent, vulva and phallus merge into one generative organ in her being. 'She is Sophia, the "spirit and the bride" of the Apocalypse, the process by which all things are spiritualized by the "living waters" that she represents' (Cowan, 1994, p.22).

> The Australian continent is crisscrossed with the tracts of The Dreaming: walking, slithering, crawling, flying, chasing, hunting, dying, giving birth, performing rituals, establishing things in their own places, the land forms and water, making relationships between one place and another, changing languages, changing songs, changing skin.
> (Daly River Aboriginal artist Miriam Rose Ungunmerr-Baumann, quoted in Atkinson, 2002, pp.35–36)

What results when the mythology, the spiritual culture of a race, is lost, when people are dislocated from their culture, community and earth 'place'? That sense of the sacred in which meaning is symbolized and embedded is thingified. The loss of ritual and boundaries results in the enactment of a psychotic world of lust and criminality.

Gidegal the Moon Man

When the Moon Man was on Earth he was a great lover of women. He created many songs to make them fall in love with him. He gave the sacred ceremony of *Djarada* so that a man could sing a woman to be his wife. In *Australian Dreaming* (2005), Isaacs tells the story of such a ceremony, which may be still practised in remote areas. When a man sees a woman he would like to have, all his close male relatives help him. They go out into the bush and create a sacred piece of ground with a big circle. In the centre is an oval shape painted with red ochre and white pipe clay. The red centre represents the woman's vagina. A tall pole decorated with paint and feathers is stuck in the ground in front of the oval to represent the man's penis. Strings covered with white bird dung are hung from the top of the pole to represent seminal flow. Men decorate their bodies with red and white paint and ochre bird dung. When everything is ready, the *Djarada* man stands before the feathered pole with legs spread, knees bent, hands on thighs. His grandfather and uncle kneel at the side and begin singing love songs. They sway their hips back and forth in rhythmic motions of love-making. In the first song the dream is that the man will be strong and attractive to the woman he has chosen. In the second, the dream is that she will think sweet things of him in her own dreaming. In the third song, the dream is that she will dream of making love to him. He then sings a fourth song to make himself more attractive to her and rubs juice from roots of a special bush over his body. He sings all day and all the next night, repeating the song cycle over and over. These songs never fail. The woman can't help falling in love with the singer even if she didn't like him before.

Clinical vignette

Presented now is a narrative from late in the first year of a young Aboriginal woman called Kirra's therapy.

> I'd been down at the pub with my girlfriends and my cousin Kylie. They seemed to be having a good time but I was bored and I wanted to go home. I had never been with the bloke and I had no thought of being with one at that time.
> On the way home Anthony Crowl was coming along the road behind me. I knew he was a 'bad' one and I was very uncomfortable about the way he seemed to be following me. Next he gets close enough and he drags me down the passageway between the buildings. I try to scream. He put his hand over

my mouth and he rips off my pants as he puts his hand up between my legs. I scream again and he bashes my head really hard against the bricks. My mouth starts to bleed. My jaw is broken. I hear a crack. I can't see from two black eyes from the bang against the bricks. Only that my cousin saw my shoe sticking out from behind the building. He could have killed me because I knew who he was. My cousin yelled for help and dragged him off me. I don't remember anything else. I woke up in hospital two days later. My mum was sitting by the bed. You wanna know what she said? She said, 'Daughter you been raped. It's okay because we gonna get a lot of money from this.' There I was, nearly dying, and she was thinking about money for drugs.

She pinched my jacket while I was unconscious. It was a beaut leather jacket I bought with my first pay that day. She took my wages out of the pocket. I was so low I didn't care. I just went home. After, when I said 'Hey, I want my jacket back,' [she said] 'Love! I was bursting to do a pee, so I got down in the gutter outside the Cop Shop in Botany Road where I was tellin' 'em about Anthony Crowl doin' you and I got pee all over the jacket. It ain't any good anymore.'

What happened between the *Djarada* narrative, full of meaning, and this one stripped of meaning?

Absence and loss

Absence and loss are central to the Aboriginal race – loss of land, family, community, spirituality and culture.

> To be born Aboriginal is to be born into an ongoing, unfolding catastrophe. For each individual the disorientation is particularly awful because they have no way to process that catastrophe. Their culture and identity no longer give a sense of who they are or who they could become.
> (Jeff Eaton, personal communication, 2010)

The loss of mother played an important part in Kirra's story, re-evoking that loss with its unbearable pain. This double traumatization explains why we so often fail in our therapeutic work with these young women.

'The patient feels the pain of an absence of fulfilment of his desires. The absent fulfilment is felt as a "no thing"' (Bion, 1977, p.20). Bion adds: 'Non-existence becomes an object that is immensely hostile and filled with murderous envy towards the quality or function of existence wherever it is to be found.' Could this help make sense of the suicide, assaults and domestic violence that are so prevalent in Aboriginal groups?

When a certain threshold is crossed, this destructiveness is total. It is despair in which there is a sense of being destroyed and having no hope of finding life again, of self ever being reconstituted. Bion speaks of 'the awful superego, so cruel, so powerful, so destructive, that it denudes it [the self] of any right or will to live' (p.21). Is this what happened to Kirra?

Eigen (2006) describes it this way:

> We may or may not know all the details about our annihilated selves. But we know such things exist, even if we don't know what to say of them. Annihilation processes are part of the way we are constituted. We live with dead areas. My hope is that making room for our annihilated self will enable us to be less destructive. We often injure, even destroy each other, in order to reach the realness of our annihilated beings. How much destructiveness aims at 'showing' how destroyed we feel! Therapy is one place to try to contact the annihilated self without destroying ourselves. Speaking, sensing, and imagining is a less costly method of discovery than giving in to the compulsion to destroy.
>
> (p.28)

As Kirra's therapy progressed, she began to complain of terrible stomach pain. Worsening, it moved further up towards her chest each session. She understood when I talked about the pain of being alive as the deadness was received by us both. She told me about other traumas. Her mother left her with a strict but caring Irish grandmother at age three. In adolescence she looked for her mother and was excited to find her in a Redfern squat. Mother wooed her with ideas of their living together; then mother took her money and threw her out abusively so she could go buy drugs. Kirra swore she would never return, yet a few weeks later the desperate pain to find her mother returned. She spoke of the pain of being lied to, betrayed, but being so desperate she had to go back with mother.

Kirra stopped going to work and ceased attending therapy. I had a massive urge to seek her. She called a year later. She was on drugs and wanted receipts from her therapy so she could claim it in her tax return. She had lost her job and boyfriend. She told me she was now fat and misshapen and I would be shocked when I saw her. She arranged to pick the receipts up the next morning, but never came.

Was once a week insufficient to hold her against the tide of pain? The force to numb the pain was greater. Perhaps she was already set on that other road of self-destruction when she came to see me. I had not understood why the local doctor was continually writing scripts for medicines and sickness forms for her to miss work.

The whole process of attachment is lost through the generational gap. A person whose internal protection is thus lost is psychically experienced by the other as 'no person'. To the perverted, such people present as available victims, objects for use and abuse. Transgenerational tragedy continues.

Many Aboriginal infants are sexually abused. In some communities, reports state that up to two-thirds of children do not reach puberty unmolested. The predator at some level senses the prey and often has himself been prey. The schizophrenic terror of disintegration of the ego from persecution by bad internal objects is a reality in external life for many Aboriginal people.

Loss of self

Central trauma is a deadened, deadening internal mother. The internalized good mother's containing womb was shattered. That internal holding psychic womb becomes sterile, deadening all emotion. That which holds the unknown, unknowable, 'core self' part of us is violated and ruptured in a horrifying way, aborting the foetal self. The central core becomes a 'non-person'. The sense of self is fragmented, like a foetus being suctioned out in parts in an abortion. Negative fears exceed positive hopes. There is no creative space. The inner world becomes a dark, frightening abyss instead of a safe, protective place. Life is rooted in abject fear and terror, freezing all emotion and joy. Sometimes bits of emotional breakthroughs present in the form of flashbacks, dark daydreaming or nightmares. For a subjugated people killed like animals, taken from their mothers at birth, all this is passed on to the next generation with terrible consequences, because the mother, not having her own core self, cannot hold the child in a way that sustains the child's core self (La Mothe, 2006, p.450).

Dadirri perverted

Saturday night at the park, a dozen Aboriginals sit in a circle. This is not the traditional sacred *Dadirri* circle where pain is shared, held, and transformed. Not this circle! They drink until Sunday night or until the police come. Some do drugs. Pain is not suffered. It is numbed. Too many have suffered too much already. This is what happens when people lose that which is meaningful and sacred. Men neglect their partners, leave, are absent during pregnancy. They move through a nightmare world of drugs and petrol sniffing that does not give true dreaming, but is better than the nightmare that reality has become.

How akin is murder to all this? You will hear in Ursula's narrative how loss from death, suicide, murder, sexual abuse, being taken by social services and miscarriage are all seen as part of the same events. Death, mourning, loss, murder, suicide, miscarriage, spirituality and evil all mix.

Where are all the men gone? They are hiding in shame, numbed by drugs and alcohol – two suicides in one family, six months apart, at exactly the same place in the same dark lane. An Elder, Ursula, calls me the day of the funeral. She talks and cries for an hour. I cannot hang up. I have to let her cry. I have to take the pain. She tries at first to escape the truth, saying, 'Foul play at hand and I will get those murderers who gave him {?} the drugs'. She finishes by saying, sadly now, and quietly resigned, 'He is his own murderer. Why?' She comes to see me.

Here is Ursula's narrative: 'Like something inside me froze – I froze.' She begins to speak very fast, as if overwhelmed, free-associating, hard to understand because of the speed.

> When my little girl was abused I had to switch off or I would go down; I tell her now, if she goes down she will take me down with her. [Her daughter is

now a mother with four children, each to different men who abandoned her. Time is tangled up as if it is all right now.] It's killing me, but I am saved because I have faith – the dear Lord works in mysterious ways ... Charlie died down the block in the lane at the back of Edward Street. You have to lift layers, pull back the blankets to see what is underneath. He was no saint, but he never deserved how she cornered him for one attack of DV [domestic violence]. He was up there for this funeral and they had a wake and he was so drunk, and he had this young woman and he had conked out from the grog with her. She must have got up out of the bed where they were lying and went partying. He woke up and went to wake her up and there she was on the floor. He thought she fell out of bed because she was drunk and then he found she was dead. She had been stabbed and they had wiped her and cleaned her up and then brought her in and put her near the bed. They even washed her because the blood and stuff you can find [with] the florescent light they use. They couldn't find anything. Of course they blamed him. Any 'Abo' would do. He done himself in, killed himself in Redfern Lane the Police reckoned, but we didn't believe it. Maybe they killed him, who knows. Then six months later there was Charlie, this really handsome man. He was my mum's sister's boy. He came to Sydney bless him because he needed his family. He worked at the Annan Reconciliation garden bridge and he slept in a room in the pub there. He must have come to Redfern to see his family – a man found him lying unconscious on the ground. They rushed him to hospital and we all went to hospital to see him. They turned off the life support on his birthday. [Her face is ashen, her voice quivers. You cannot help but see years of wear and pain on her face, weather-beaten.] It was just six months before our nephew Lizzy's son died in exactly the same spot and they reckoned he killed himself too. This week's been so bad. Out of the blue Jeannie died. Bill her husband had his heart attack. I was with him and then I was going to see Cathy and Rob died so I had to go to his funeral. I got back and got Louleine [granddaughter who lives with her] and I was going to take her and go and see Cathy and I get a call – Cathy is dead.

Strange about Charlie, [when] they found him in the lane way there was a suspicious hit on the head, could have been from the fall the police said and they just were not interested. They said, he killed himself, he died of an overdose. That is funny because none of us even knew he took drugs. His girlfriend was pregnant. You would kill yourself while your girlfriend was pregnant? She freaked out completely. Same place!!

Aunty Judy she was another one. She was in Cootamundra girls' home. See, my grandmother had abscesses on her legs and couldn't walk, so when my aunt and her husband split, the children were taken, the boys to Kinsella and Aunty Judy to Cootamundra. She was abused there and she attacked the matron, in fact she nearly killed her, and she ended up in Parramatta girls' home didn't she. She was such a beautiful woman, but from there she began the self-destruction. She had a razor and she would cut and cut at herself. Her face was so cut it was just a heap of scars and the same for her arms and hands. No clean flesh left anywhere. Then she killed herself and they came and took 'baby Colin'. A white woman came and grandma was sittin' in a rockin' chair on the veranda and she just wrapped him up, this white woman, and she took him out of her arms. I can still remember the tears rolling down her cheeks. We never saw him again, but I always wondered what happened to baby Colin. When I was working in legal aid I decided to find him. I found him alright he was in Lithgow jail. Too late I was; he had just become another death in custody. He had been fostered with a family in north Sydney in 1975. We got baby Colin alright. We brought him back home too, but in a wooden coffin. We buried him. So many tragic, meaningless deaths!

Counter-transference

It was like I was somewhere I should not be. I had done something I should not have done. I would stand accused and all good things and all good people would desert me. Bad would happen to me. It was catching, contaminating, touching an area inside my psyche I had not touched before. Guilt, yes, but worse, a total disbelief in forgiveness and atonement for a sin I had not committed. I had opened Pandora's box and could not get away from the black, terrible things inside.

Time and time again I tell myself I am not affected by the lives these people narrate to me and time and time again I have an outburst in another area of my life that I know is the result of material I have not, cannot process. How can *they* process it?

The dynamic of regression and progression for a people who dare not, cannot, struggle to be born as a result of core foetal terror matches so much of what I am writing and thinking. For many Aboriginal people 'the relation to the primary good object is one of a fear-enforced infantile dependence that is experienced as being smothered' (Guntrip, 1968, p.82). This may explain why 80 per cent of young Aboriginals who suicide do so by a slow smothering wrongly called hanging. For them, a good internal object involves fear of loss of their active ego by imprisonment in smothering passivity (Guntrip, pp.84–85).

A young Aboriginal girl's dream

Martha is 15 years old when I first meet her. Fostered at age 5 to an Aboriginal family, she was already given to self-harm and attacking the foster family. She had no speech and became violent when frustrated. Her biological mother is diagnosed as paranoid-schizophrenic. Drugs and alcohol play a large part. She has access to her daughter, but rejects this right. Martha never knew her father. He could be any Aboriginal man wandering the inner city.

Foster mother is angry, finding it harder to cope every day. She has diabetes, high blood pressure and is constantly exhausted. Martha, diagnosed as mildly retarded and traumatized, is in year nine in a special class. She can read and write certain words. Since age 13, she is intensely rebellious. When a boy at school teased her, Martha raced out and sat in the middle of the road with traffic swerving around her. Her lack of awareness of danger is frightening.

Martha describes her biological mother to me.

> Her face looked like stone. She looked poor and sick. She can't give me anything because she needs all her money to buy food. Don't want to see her anymore. I want to catch a bus and go anywhere. I will never be able to work because I am dumb and slow in the head and I can't read. I'm no good at any stuff! I hate school, I hate all teachers. I hate it because I'm no good at it.

She brightens up, saying, 'I can play any sports though! I'm really good at sports. I'm very good at soccer, swimming, running and football.' Her smile fades as she says, 'I lose the words I want to say and everyone picks on me because of that. You know I lose the words in my head. I'm dumb so I'm not any good. You some sort of a psych person?' she asks.

'Sort of!' I reply. 'Why?'

'Because I have this dream!'

Every night Martha has the same dream, sometimes twice. She is being chased by she does not know what or who. It is terrifying. There are many pursuers. She reaches the edge of a cliff. Realizing there is nowhere else to go, she throws herself over the edge. Looking down, she sees her body smashed on the rocks below and knows she is dead. When colonists settled in Australia, groups of men would chase a group of Aboriginals until, having nowhere to flee except over a cliff, they would throw themselves off and die. It was a kind of Sunday sport, an easy way of ridding the area of what they could only see as 'vermin'.

When asked if she had heard that story, Martha looked blank. She had no idea what I was talking about. I thought, 'Is she living out her mother's madness?' I do not think she is psychotic or stupid. She is repeating night after night the murdering of her soul. It is a nightmare in search of an audience who can help find meaning in the terror. Who inside her has written this 'dream'? Who is the director of this drama?

Counter-transference

I do not dream hopeful dreams for Martha, but I cannot get her out of my mind. She haunts me day and night. I had very little feeling while with her. I experienced a state of mind like a concreteness of affect, a lack of anything one could hold. Perhaps I had taken on her numbness. This is the incredible 'non-person' quality that comes from transgenerational trauma. Her hopelessness stays with me. I tell her story over and over to colleagues.

Three years later, I pick Martha up from the needle exchange bus. She is pregnant. She tells me she was really great now that she was having a baby. Her foster aunt later told me that having the baby saved her and she was doing just fine.

Processing the pain

With schizoid and autistic states, a new, different space is created, one that blocks any movement to and from the original space. The schizoid, autistic or narcissistic defence is a perversion of the real chaos. Only by release from this stasis can movement to the abyss occur and, from that, a new beginning. In therapy or deeply moving life experiences, there is a freeing from this block to allow an inward journey to the core nothingness, where something may begin.

I end with a story that fits so well with Frances Tustin's (1981, p.191) concept of at-one-ness and the overflowing of ecstasy as against the nightmare of its rupturing. Barinya is a rehabilitation centre for serious alcohol and drug users of Aboriginal descent. This village-like, live-in complex has a treatment centre that involves people moving from therapeutic group to group during the day (*Dadirri*), eating nourishing food, having lots of physical sport and activity, and thus developing a different lifestyle in a therapeutic community. A young man from this rehabilitation unit speaks in a session where I am present, but unknown.

> I have never been free of alcohol and drugs since I was 12 years of age. I have had a stormy past where I never worked and did all sorts of things to get drugs. I stole, I begged, I sold myself sexually. I have been clean for six weeks now. I can tell you it has not been easy. I am taking each day at a time. It is a nightmare and I did not think I could do it, but it is getting better now. This morning I went in the bus to Smokey Cape lighthouse. From the green hill I saw the sun rising over the ocean. I felt something peaceful inside me, a kind of beautiful feeling of belonging as part of what I was seeing. I knew this was what I had been trying to find through taking drugs. I have been looking for this space all the time but drugs and alcohol didn't give me this space. They gave me numbness, no life. I do not know how long it will last or if I will have it again, but I know I have had this feeling and I will always know I have had it.

Note

1 The author wishes to acknowledge her co-workers at Gunawirra, many years' mentoring by Mike Eigen and supervision by Jeff Eaton from Seattle. All have helped her develop and continue to challenge her own thoughts.

References

Bion, W.R. (1977). *Seven servants*. New York: Jason Aronson.
Cowan, J.G. (1994). *Myths of the Dreaming: interpreting Aboriginal legends*. Santa Rosa, CA: Atrium; Bridport: Prism.
Eaton, J.L. (2010). Personal communication.
Eigen, M. (2006). The annihilated self. *Psychoanalytic Review*, 93(1): 25–38.
Farrelly, E. (2003). *Dadirri: The spring within*. Darwin: Terry Knight and Associates.

Guntrip, H. (1968). *Schizoid phenomena, object-relations and the self*. London: Hogarth Press and the Institute of Psycho-Analysis.
Isaacs, J. (2005). *Australian Dreaming: 40,000 years of Aboriginal history*. Sydney and London: New Holland.
La Mothe, R. (2006). Constructing infants: anthropological realities and analytic horizons. *Psychoanalytic Review*, 93(3): 437–477.
Mitchell, S. (trans.) (1992). *Tao Te Ching*. New York: HarperCollins.
Tracey, N. (ed.) (2000). *Parents of premature infants: their emotional world*. London: Whurr.
—— (2009). Precreative space. *Psychoanalytic Review*, 96(6): 1025–1053.
Tustin, F. (1981). Psychological birth and psychological catastrophe. In J.S. Grotstein (ed.), *Do I dare disturb the universe*. London: Maresfield, pp.181–196.
Ungunmerr-Baumann, M.R. (1993). '*Dadirri*: listening to one another'. In J. Hendricks and G. Hefferan (eds), *A spirituality of Catholic Aborigines and the struggle for justice*. Brisbane: Aboriginal and Torres Strait Islander Apostolate, pp.34–37.

Chapter 11

A bicultural approach to working together

Conversing about cultural supervision

Trudy Ake and Sarah Calvert

'Cultural supervision' is a term used in the human sciences to refer to an engagement around the impact that 'culture' in varying forms (e.g., ethnic, queer) has on work where practitioners engage with others, usually from a framework representing their own cultural background.

We met when we both worked within New Zealand's state-funded health system in Tauranga Moana in the Bay of Plenty. Our relationship developed in a wider network of relationships, Māori and *pākehā* (see the Glossary at end of this chapter), professional and/or personal. For nearly thirty years, we have been developing our connection as *tāngata whenua* and *manuhiri* in respect to our work (mostly Sarah Calvert's) and ourselves. We began this journey as people, although culturally and professionally different, working with adults, children and families, in the same organizational space. We have come to regard the way the relationship – both professional (multi-layered) and personal (generational, networked) – has developed as a way of thinking about what occurs in cultural supervision. This chapter is part of our conversation about this process.

Introductions

Trudy: Ngā mihi nui ki a koutou.
Greetings to everyone
Tuatahi ki te Atua i runga rawa, tēnā koe.
Firstly to God above, greetings and acknowledgments.
Tuarua ki te Kingi, ki a Tūheitia, tēnā koe.
Secondly to the Māori King, Tūheitia, greetings and acknowledgments.
Tuatoru ki ō mātau mate, haere, haere, moe mai.
Thirdly to our loved ones who are no longer with us, farewell, go, and rest easily.
Ki a koutou Ngāti Whātua, te mana whenua o Tāmaki Makaurau, tēnei te mihi.
To Ngati Whatua, the tribal host of this region Tāmaki Makaurau I acknowledge you.
E ngā mana, e ngā reo, e ngā kāranga maha.
To the prestigious and powerful, to all languages and to the many esteemed guests.
Tēnā koutou, tēnā koutou, tēnā koutou katoa.
I respectfully greet and acknowledge you all.

Nō Aotearoa ahau.
I am from New Zealand.
He Māori ahau.
I am Māori.
Nō Tauranga Moana me Taupō-nui-a-Tia.
I come from the tribal regions of Tauranga Moana and Taupo-nui-a-Tia.
He uri ahau ō Ngāti Ranginui me Ngāti Tūwharetoa.
I'm descended from the tribal nations of Ngati Ranginui and Ngati Tuwharetoa.
Ko Trudy Ake tōku ingoa.
My name is Trudy Ake.
I am a social worker in private practice. I work in Māori development, research within Te Ao Māori, and professional and cultural supervision with individuals and groups.
Sarah: Born in England, I have lived most of my life in New Zealand. I am a clinical psychologist, mostly working in forensic settings, with a private psychotherapy practice.

Cultural supervision

Although practitioners (primarily using Western models) have long worked with those from other cultures, there has been limited attention to the impact cultural 'difference' has on the relationship and the work. Colonization of otherness has occurred as much in the human sciences as in the geo-political sphere. Much of the professional literature has focused on assessing competence to work with those who are other (Gloria, Hird and Tao, 2008; Ancis and Marshall, 2011). More recent literature examines the frame used in cultural supervision (Sommer, 2011) and on what attributes might make cultural supervision worthwhile or not (Hair and O'Donoghue, 2009; Quek, 2012). Although the literature is still sparse, there is significant evidence that the supervisory relationship is the most critical factor determining the value and usefulness of the process (Hernandez, Taylor and McDowell, 2009; Wong, 2012).

In Aotearoa (New Zealand) there has been a dialogue (with words, goods, money and, in the past, guns) for over 200 years about how we should engage with each other and each's otherness (Colquhoun, 2002). Māori often despair that non-Māori will 'never get them'. We grapple with the meaning of a Treaty (of Waitangi, 1840) partnership and how that is to be given real 'life' in everyday relationships and worlds. This process has been articulated professionally by social workers, social science researchers, psychologists and other professionals (e.g. Simpson and Ake, 2010). Linda Tuhiwai Smith (2007) coined the phrase 'tricky ground' to refer to discourses in these between spaces – complex, uncertain, shifting.

A respectful relationship between cultural supervisor and clinician becomes the foundation upon which to examine and reflect on the world presented in cultural supervision. Accepting the integrity and skills the 'other' has to offer in Māori clients' recovery process, the cultural supervisor supports clinicians to maintain their discomfort and curiosity as they navigate with the client and their world. Cultural supervision provides an opportunity to unpack Māori clients' reported experience of their lives, assisting clinicians to comprehend better the cultural world these clients inhabit that shapes their lives.

Using a group or one-on-one approach, cultural supervisor and clinicians examine traditional Māori values that would consciously or unconsciously influence the client and their *whānau*. We seek to understand the client's experience through a Māori cultural lens, considering how this may have influenced choices made and future opportunities. We look for Māori, client-specific anchors the clinician may use to unlock the client's situation and begin to plot a recovery path that will lead client and *whānau* to restored balance.

Working cross-culturally can be challenging, professionally and personally. It provides opportunities to reflect critically on practice and gain a larger window into another cultural landscape. Self-directed learning experiences to increase knowledge and appreciation of Te Ao Māori are encouraged.

Although many contemporary Māori may not have their personal cultural map well defined consciously, their ethnicity, *whakapapa* and life stories express their experience as Māori living and growing up in Aotearoa. This experience is shaped by personal and *whānau* experiences that have been influenced by Māori history pre- and post-Treaty of Waitangi.

Māori are wonderful weavers of *harakeke* (flax). This practical craft has spiritual, instructional, environmental and functional dimensions. Traditional and modern Māori often use weaving as a metaphor when articulating roles and relationships between people and with communities. Relational matrix or weave is central to cultural supervision because it places relationships and ways of knowing another above theory and rules/requirements. Our relationship has been, and continues to be, a weaving, sometimes a surprising weaving, of the threads and colours of our lives and those of others. We have sat with each other in sadness (at *tangi* and funerals). We have laughed, eaten, worked and argued. We know each other's *whānau* and their histories.

***

Trudy: So remind me, how did this start?

Sarah: I had been involved in social change movements, not just feminism, but also working with Māori women such as when Broadsheet published *Māori Sovereignty* (Awatere, 1984). Once I formally started working, especially at Greenhill in 1979, with a number of Māori staff and clients, I thought I needed to attend to how my clinical work was for clients. Although I had some exposure (unusually) to thinking about this during university training, especially with Jim Ritchie, really I had never been asked how who I was and what I did might be for Māori or, indeed, for others from differing backgrounds. I thought if I was going to do this, I needed it to be a real, challenging experience that would not allow me to avoid my privilege. I looked for someone who would challenge and extend my practice with *tāngata whenua*. You are a strong, passionate advocate for Māori and a very skilled social worker with enormous knowledge using Western models. We had friends and colleagues in common. I knew you would be challenging but that we had areas of common language and already something of a relationship.

Trudy: It has been a long time. My children were all little when we began. When you started your private practice, then went to Child, Youth and Family, you asked me not only to continue for you but to come to the whole team.

Sarah: I remember the shock for some of them when you asked about their memories of knowing Māori because you began so firmly with the relationship, just as you keep doing. How did you begin with your cultural supervision model?

Trudy: It began as a child with my father enquiring about my school day. He always asked, 'Who did you see?', meaning which Māori people did I see. He would say: 'Where were they from [location, family residence]? Who were they [names, sibling and parent names]? What did they do and say? How were they? Were they fast moving, bright, confident, good at catching a ball, quiet?' He would then tell me how I was connected to them and something about them [such as they were hard workers, kind, resourceful people, or where they came from]. Their identity and my connection to them was the emphasis.

Sarah: You translated that into my experience, requesting me and my team become mindful and present with the environment we live in – the space clinician, client and their *whānau* share – that we walk the land, learn to know the peoples, their names and history. I have wonderful memories of how that changed me, how I lived on Aotearoa's landscape. I remember driving around Tauranga Moana looking at the hills, thinking of the legends that speak to that landscape, slowly coming to feel familiar with the words. For example, the legend of Patupaiarehe told of sadness, despair, identity, resolution, boundaries and friendship. That legend personified the human condition. Both Māori and non-Māori could relate to it. We saw how the people we met with daily within our roles fit into that landscape. Names told me so much about how they fit into their world. Understanding that changed how I worked. That's when I understood *whakapapa* [pronounced *fakapapa*] or genealogy is a fundamental principle permeating Māori culture. It is a paradigm of cultural discourse, providing the basis for establishing, enhancing and challenging relationships between individuals, *whānau*, *hāpu* and *iwi*. It is a living thing, a way of conceptualizing and being with Māori. It includes the genealogical descent of all living things from the gods to present time. Since all living things, including rocks and mountains, possess *whakapapa*, it is a basis for organizing knowledge in respect of the creation and development of everything. *Whakapapa* implies deep connection to land and ancestral roots. To trace one's *whakapapa*, it is essential to identify the location where one's heritage began. *Whakapapa* links all people back to the land, sea, sky and outer universe. Consequently, the obligations of *whanaungatanga* extend to the physical world and all beings in it. Now I would never meet a Māori client without beginning in a formal way to acknowledge who they are, where they come from, offering the hospitality of relationship in that process. Can you think of a key moment that put it all together into a practice model?

Trudy: It happened in the late 1970s, at a multidisciplinary psychiatric inpatient team meeting. We were twenty professionals, led by a consultant psychiatrist. One older Māori woman held a leadership role. I was the youngest, a new practitioner, about 23 years old. The client, a 14-year-old, working-class *pākehā*, attempted suicide to get away from her father who was sexually abusing her. After a brief outline of the circumstances, the consultant said: 'We will refer this case you Trudy because, as Māori, you will understand the issues she is facing since Māori see incest as a normal part of their cultural life.' I was stunned. I waited for the older Māori woman to refute this crazy assertion. She was silent. I responded in higher-than-usual voice: 'Well it's not usual in my family.' Later, I was able to reflect on that experience, which included: a prejudiced psychiatrist; a *Kuia* rendered silent, therefore powerless, by a racial assumption; having to draw from my own experience to challenge colonist assumptions asserted by a dominant professional and take a public stand on matters of my culture – a role usually occupied by elders and leaders.

Sarah: How did you manage that challenging situation?

Trudy: I went home and talked to my father. I asked him about the racial assumption and the *Kuia*'s silence. His response made total sense. It was pragmatic, not moral or legal. He gave an example of why incest was prohibited within Māori culture. He started with our shared farm experience, breeding sheep and cattle. Weak, unhealthy animals would be produced if stock were inbred, father to daughter or granddaughter. Māori had to be strong to defend our land. We could not afford to have weak people or we would lose it. Without land, we are nothing. As to the silenced *Kuia*, he shook his head, looked down and said nothing. I then researched the topic. I found no evidence to support the doctor's assertion that Māori culture accepted incest as normal. I asked friends and colleagues for research supporting this assertion. The only reference I found was in *Penthouse* magazine.

Sarah: How did this experience inform your practice?

Trudy: It informed how I analysed and responded to assumptions about Māori from both Māori and non-Māori. I continued to be guided by my father and to have a voice that spoke of a Māori world I inhabited. I noted with sadness that many Māori directed themselves to non-Māori social workers, counsellors, therapists, because they believed incest was integral to their tribal customs, culture, their own *Tikanga*. Māori clients had been groomed by perpetrators and their corrupted worldview had been accepted by professionals. I was saddened and angered to find non-Māori colleagues accepting this assertion. Māori clients were being supported professionally to distance themselves from their abuse and their cultural identity. From this sadness and anger the following model emerged:

1. Seduction and coaching of children by family perpetrators to believe abuse is normal.
2. Naming the practice clinically, then developing culturally affirming metaphors and insights to enable Māori clients to become healed and whole. Supporting practitioners to comprehend the centrality of cultural identity to recovery. Māori clients can value *whakapapa*, identity and our place in Aotearoa and still abhor perpetrators' violence and exploitation.
3. Supporting and challenging colleagues to consider culturally affirming interventions to strengthen Māori clients' identity as Māori.
4. Examining the unconscious and conscious culture – gaining insight into the fact most Māori, professional and client, 'can't be what we are not'. We are always and forever Māori.

From those considerations, further developments included:

a. Donobedian (2002) began the study of quality in healthcare and medical outcomes. His research framework includes five steps: obtain data on performance; analyse patterns; generate hypotheses; take action based on the hypotheses; assess consequences of actions taken.
b. To Kadushin's (1992) 'tasks of supervision', I added the Māori cultural model and examples, including high (formal) culture and daily (informal) culture, and conflict and challenge.
c. *Pūrākau*/legends. When clients are disconnected from their *whakapapa*, they can be (re)connected to *Papatūānuku* and her children as a birthright of all Māori.
d. *Tāngata whenua* and *manuhiri*: roles, expectations, boundaries.

Sarah: Can you summarize key ideas informing your work?
Trudy: Cultural competence is built on clinical competence. First you must be competent in your craft, including being open to seeing the world from your client's point of reality.

In cultural supervision the relationship is asymmetrical. The cultural supervisor is the *tuakana*, leading and focusing. The *teina* is the practitioner seeking insight into the client's cultural world.

The cultural supervisor may need to examine cultural rules by reference to case studies in various settings and by consultation with cultural experts. It is unrealistic to ask a *Kaumātua* to be knowledgeable in clinical/ethical/moral matters beyond the scope of their domain. We do not expect non-Māori elders to be experts beyond their scope, yet there are multiple examples where respected Māori elders are expected to advise beyond their domain.

All culture is prior to us and shapes us in core matters like good/bad, ugly/beautiful, clean/dirty, fair/unfair, funny/cruel, right/wrong, truth/beauty, love/duty, polite/impolite, proper/improper.

Sarah: I thought of many examples of how I use this model and the work we have done and also of what you and Mary wrote (Simpson and Ake, 2010). I learned about the centrality of relationship. Taking time for relationships, for simply being with other. Knowing the other, and what that really means with Māori (history, location, etc.). Taking food when you meet with someone, even learning to bake *rewena* bread. You've taught me about walking the area I serve – now Tamaki Makaurau (Auckland) but then the Bay of Plenty – learning history, legends and knowing the people (*whakapapa*). For Māori, the past continues to live on and be part of the present. Careful exploration of the past often uncovers parts of a story about how something is now, at an individual and larger level. All this has become so central to my being with Māori that I am pulled up short when others don't do this in their work.

You encouraged thinking about how behaviour differs in different cultures and to be open to thinking about our responses to that difference, as well as having the knowledge to observe and engage those processes. The best example for me is your teaching about how Māori tend to work with conflict in a more circular, sometimes seemingly indirect fashion, allowing many dialogues to develop before someone, usually a *Kuia* or *Kaumātua*, cuts through the talking (often with a story, myth, example, proverb, prayer or some other accessing of other domains) and a solution is developed. I have seen this happen many times.

One of the most significant things I heard you say is: 'Culturally, safe practice is simply good practice.' Good work will be culturally safe because you cannot have good practice that is not. You taught about *mana* and the need to tolerate conflict and disagreement, to stand one's ground and meet the challenge. It has been very helpful clinically to see that the way someone is responding is a way of testing the safety of the space and the relationship, whether I am willing to be in the space with them. You also commented that culture is a point of separateness that can be used by a therapist who wants/needs distance.

You discussed the value of myth, story, prayer and ways of accessing what people think and feel is appropriate for them. Your expression 'From defeat to hope' underscores the need for inspiration, helping people find it through learnings from their culture. 'Words are lovely,' you said. 'Their rhythm and beat provide hope, like a heartbeat.'

Trudy: I wonder if you remember that young Ngā Puhi woman I assessed. Closed in by her life and experiences, she was unable to speak about herself or her background. Initially, I only found very minimal things about her. I consulted with you, seeking a way to connect with her. You encouraged me to think about the history of her *whānau*, *hāpu* and *iwi*. When I went back, she spoke about her dreams. They made no sense and frightened her, but she sensed they contained important meaning about her distress. She drew them. You helped me find out how her dreams related to losses her *whānau* and *hāpu* suffered prior to Europeans coming and afterwards. Your support helped me support her in exploring and understanding what she carried from the past and how that created such fear in her that she felt herself mentally unwell.

Trudy: For Māori, dreams can be the key. They are known as *moemoea*, when our forefathers or mothers come and guide us. For this lady, navigating around her mental health condition and general unease was challenging. We had to stay with the cultural map that she holds in her experience, recognizing how this map is generational, finding an incident that unlocked her, providing the opportunity to acknowledge and address the issue and furnish the cultural map to assist her in navigating the presenting mental health condition, creating a path toward restoration of balance.

Sarah: At the end of our work, she and I shared *rewena* bread she brought and cake I brought. We spoke of stories which make us who we are, her story and mine. For me, that shared relational space defines cultural supervision and good clinical practice.

Trudy: Cultural competence requires some historical, cultural and linguistic knowledge. In New Zealand, this includes knowledge of the Treaty of Waitangi, Māori values, pronunciation and knowledge of who is *tāngata whenua* in the areas you work in. Stories of bicultural relational journeys provide us ways of seeing ourselves. It is about looking past differences, yet being informed by them.

***

Our presentation ended with the New Zealand Chapter of IARPP singing a *waiata*. Such songs are usually offered after a significant speech or discussion to give *mana* to what has been said. The following was sung.

Ka waiata ki a Maria / Hine I whakaae / Whakameatia mai / Te whare tangata.
Hine pūrotu / Hine ngākau / Hine rangimārie
Ko te Whaea / Ko te whaea / O te ao.

***

Trudy: I think the late Bishop Max Mariu wrote this *waiata*; readers can hear versions of this *waiata* on YouTube (including one by an American choir).

***

Trudy and Sarah celebrated acceptance of this chapter (and their hard work) by attending an international rugby game between the Springboks (South Africa) and New Zealand (Aotearoa) with 60,000 other New Zealanders.

Glossary

Aotearoa	New Zealand
hāpu	descendants of a shared ancestor
iwi	groups of *hāpu* (descendants of a shared ancestor)
Kahui Ariki	first family of the Tainui people; descendant of the first Māori King, Pōtatau
Kaumātua	elder (respected) Māori male
Ka waiata	Māori Catholic hymn, venerating Mary, mother of Jesus, for accepting her role as mother of the future. The song is also sung at non-Catholic gatherings to praise the role of all mothers as '*whare tangata*', mothers of all people.
Kuia	elder (respected) Māori female
mana	authority (ascribed or achieved) to make decisions
manuhiri	respected and valued visitors
Māori	First Nation (indigenous) people of Aotearoa (New Zealand)
moemoea	dreams
Ngā Puhi	northland tribal people
pākehā	descendants of settler population, predominantly British
Papatūānuku	Mother Earth, from whom all are descended
patupaiarehe	mythical Māori fairy-like people who live in the bush, hills and misty mountain tops
rewena	Māori (sourdough) bread
Tainui	tribal people, Waikato region
Tāmaki Makaurau	Auckland city and surrounding sea, islands, hills, volcanos
tāngata whenua	indigenous people of New Zealand
tangi	traditional Māori funeral
Tauranga Moana	location including Tauranga city and surrounding sea, islands and hills
Te Ao Māori	Māori (socio-cultural) world
teina	younger sibling
tikanga	traditional Māori customs and appropriate behaviour
Treaty of Waitangi	treaty between Chiefs of Aotearoa and Queen Victoria of Britain; foundational document of the Nation
tuakana	elder sibling

waiata	song
whakapapa	genealogy
whānau	family, kin
whanaungatanga	a process wherein Māori identify themselves and confirm their relationships

References

Ancis, J.R. and Marshall, D.S. (2011). Using a multi-cultural framework to assess supervisees' perceptions of culturally competent supervision. *Journal of Counselling and Development*, 88: 277–284.

Awatere, D. (1984). *Māori sovereignty*. Auckland: Broadsheet.

Colquhoun, G. (2012). *Jumping ship and other essays*. Wellington: Four Winds Press.

Donobedian, A. (2002). *An introduction to quality assurance in health care*. Oxford: Oxford University Press.

Gloria, A.M., Hird, J.S. and Tao, K.W. (2008). Self-reported multicultural supervision competence of white predoctoral intern supervisors. *Training and Education in Professional Psychology*, 2: 129–136.

Hair, H.J. and O'Donoghue, K. (2009). Culturally relevant, socially just social work supervision: becoming visible through a social constructionist lens. *Journal of Ethnic and Cultural Diversity in Social Work*, 18: 70–88.

Hernàndez, P., Taylor, B.A. and McDowell, T. (2009). Listening to ethnic minority AAMFT approved supervisors: reflections on their experiences as supervisees. *Journal of Systemic Therapies*, 28: 88–100.

Kadushin, A. (1992). *Supervision in social work*, 3rd ed. New York: Columbia University Press.

Quek, K.M. and Storm, C. (2012). Chinese values in supervisory discourse: implications for culturally sensitive practice. *Contemporary Family Therapy*, 34: 44–56.

Simpson, M. and Ake, T. (2010). Whitiwhiti korero: exploring the researchers' relationship in cross-cultural research. *Journal of Intercultural Communication Research*, 39: 185–205.

Smith, L.T. (2007). On tricky ground. *The landscape of qualitative research*, 1: 85–113.

Sommer, C.A., Derrick, E.C., Bourgeois, M.B., Ingene, D.H., Yang, J.W. and Justice, C.A. (2011). Multicultural connections: using stories to transcend cultural boundaries in supervision. *Journal of Multicultural Counseling and Development*, 37(4): 206–218.

Wong, L.C.J., Wong, P.T.P. and Ishiyama, F.I. (2012). What helps and what hinders in cross cultural clinical supervision: a critical incident study. *The Counselling Psychologist*, 41: 66–85.

Chapter 12

Identity amongst differences
A personal account of a *pakeha* psychologist working in a New Zealand Māori Mental Health Service

Ingo Lambrecht

New Zealand's indigenous people name themselves *tangata whenua* (people of the land). In Māori *reo* (language), *pakeha* denotes whites. According to my cultural supervisor, Naida Glavich, cultural advisor for Auckland and Waitemata District Health Boards, *pakeha* comes from two words, *pa* and *keha*. *Keha* is a ghost-like white figure. When Māori sit and row in their *waka* (canoes), they face forward. When Captain Cook and his men arrived in 1769, they rowed from ship to land with their backs to the direction they were rowing. Seeing them rowing backwards, Māori concluded they were able to look through the back of their heads, like ghosts. *Pa* in Māori means 'to touch', so whites are 'ghosts you can touch'.

I have been 'touched' by my work at Manawanui Oranga Hinengaro Mental Health Services for Māori in Auckland. Usually, when I mention I work there, psychology colleagues politely say: 'Oh really? That's interesting.' The subtext is generally: 'Why as a white would you work there? It's a political minefield, the service is usually bad, and by the way, they will eat you alive. Why with your seniority and reputation are you taking this risk? This is a career dead end.' Of course, they don't say this, because most are politically correct.

Noticing this subtext, I asked myself, why am I working here? It is not that I was unaware of the at times unfair but understandable reputation of some Māori Mental Health Services. Some have been badly staffed. Many Māori staff, coming from disadvantaged classes and academic backgrounds, have been poorly trained and managed. Many have provided excellent treatment under very difficult circumstances. I was touched by remarkable work done, despite adversity and poor infrastructure. The subtext was sometimes accurate, but was equally true of some general mental health services.

My history plays a role in my curiosity. I obtained psychotherapeutic and psychological training at a South African anti-Apartheid university, where I worked in townships and private practice. I am acutely aware of the entanglement of personal and political factors.

It is impossible to understand Māori Mental Health Services without reference to New Zealand's political history. They came about in the mid-1980s in response to increased Māori referrals to mental health services where they did not receive adequate care, since many cultural factors were ignored or misdiagnosed as psychiatric phenomena. In the 1940s and 1950s, white psychologists noticed Māori were absent from psychiatric asylums. They assumed this was because of their healthy lifestyle, strong *whanau* (extended family) orientation and supportive communities. In the 1960s and 1970s, more Māori moved to cities and towns to find work (Kingi, 2007). Losing their rich rural connections, they encountered loneliness and alienation. Economic pressures, largely due to colonization, cultural genocide and debilitating poverty contributed to rapidly increasing referrals to mental health services (Durie, 2001).

Māori are now over-represented in psychiatric inpatient units (Oakley Browne, Wells and Scott, 2006). They more frequently receive diagnoses of schizophrenia or severe mood disorder. Entanglement of the personal and political remains active. The political past haunts the present mental health of Māori, like many colonized, indigenous peoples. Personal trauma is political trauma. Trauma fragments meaning, personally and politically. There are 'attacks on linking' (Bion, 1984a) personal and political processes.

Integrating clinical and cultural–political practices within mental health services is important across the world. Globalization widens the context in which clinicians perform healing duties. Research demonstrates that indigenous service users around the world prefer integrated cultural and clinical practices (Lambrecht and Taitimu, 2012). This is true whether they are minorities, like the Sámi people in Norway (Sexton and Sørlie, 2009) or Canadian Inuit (RN Health Society, 2010), or majorities, as in South Africa, where 70 to 80 per cent visit traditional healers before accessing mental health services (Robertson, 2006). Service users politically call for integrating clinical and complementary cultural mental health care. What is not clear is how integration is applied on the ground. Every cultural context requires its own form of integration based on a mental health service's clinical capacity and the needs of specific indigenous people.

Whenever I had Jewish clients in South Africa, I always at some point held the Holocaust in mind. A political holding was necessary to address the fact that I am German. The aim was to explore the shadow in the room, wonder about projections and shards of meaning, and about how each individual tries to survive and make sense of his or her life. In Soweto township, when black clients heard voices, I needed to appreciate that it might not be a sign of madness, but a call from ancestors. Once I met people on the road to a sacred cave. They had travelled many miles because of a dream. In South Africa, dreams are at times followed to the letter. Their 'manifest content' (Freud, 1981) determines actions. In this case, the dreamer felt called to visit a shamanic cave on the border of Lesotho. Similar integration of the clinical and cultural applies to my work in New Zealand.

New Zealand's 1840 Treaty of Waitangi, the central document addressing the complex, fraught relationship between Māori and Crown (state), is very relevant to the political entanglement with mental health. We need to consider its broken promises, land promises and cultural genocide. As Naida Glavich put it, *pakeha* needed the treaty, not the Māori. It is beyond this chapter's scope to address the many issues (e.g. translation errors, like questions of 'sovereignty' versus 'governance'), but I am bound by the Treaty to protect Māori health, rights and *tikanga* (culture).

The Treaty was first applied within the mental health system in 2000 in terms of three 'Ps', giving Māori the right to 'Participation' (access, service), 'Partnership' (power relations) and 'Protection' (health, culture) (Tapsell and Mellsop, 2007).

Māori Mental Health Services are the result of biculturalism. In the face of white cultural dominance, they are for Māori, by Māori. This approach has good clinical support in many other countries (Griner and Smith, 2006). Biculturalism, a political activity to protect Māori tradition, language and practices, will ultimately benefit everyone. At times the concept unfortunately functions like a monolith in political discourse. The splits and paranoia of political correctness function like a 'primitive superego' (Klein, 1975), freezing us into discursive forms suggesting early defences – black and white options without dialectical subtlety (Linehan, 1993). There is much silence and resentment around biculturalism which, at times, is used moralistically.

Māori are not trying to induce guilt. Like any of us, they just want what is due to them. I have no issue even with collective guilt, for as a German male, white South African, *pakeha* male, I trump anyone in that regard. I have benefitted from the dominance of European culture in New Zealand, although I only arrived in 2002. I am in a position to challenge myself and systems to consider the darker aspects of political and cultural dominance and to take personal responsibility for history.

Taking responsibility for history, just as in our own inner work, starts shaping a different future. It addresses and makes us conscious of historical repetition, the return of the repressed, and hopefully leads to healing and reparation. It is often harder for victims of history to consider their darker inner, personal parts in political processes. Considering racism, I could state that I am racist or have racist parts. That fact does not have to water down my awareness of the horrific experiences of racism experienced by indigenous people. As a white male, I cannot know what it is like to be Māori. I can, however, tell you why I enjoy working at Māori Mental Health Services, and what the edges are between us.

I enjoy the challenge of working in other cultures. All have rich histories, traditions and myths that allow for different healing opportunities. For example, at Manawanui I am currently working with one client, V, who has given me consent to write about this work. During frequent admissions to inpatient units, she has been diagnosed with schizophrenia, bipolar disorder, even psychosis NOS. In our work, V started to consider her childhood abandonment. A pivotal point in our understanding her rapid, painful, at times self-destructive responses in relationships related to her being raised by a young mother, overwhelmed by poverty, who sought solace in substances. To survive, mother became a sex worker, finally abandoning V to child protection services. In foster care, V was regularly sexually abused by a caring grandfather figure. As V worked with her anger, ambivalences, difficulty separating and need to cling to abusive relationships, she engaged her confusion about what is imagined versus real in relationships and the world.

We discussed how V's mother was part of a larger process of Māori urbanization. V's abandonment may be directly related to that process. Her mother migrated from her *whanau* and relations in Hawke's Bay to Wellington in the 1970s. If V had grown up in her *iwi* (rural tribe) and mother was unable to cope, other *whanau* members would have stepped in to care for her. V would not have lost contact with *whanau* and *tikanga* (culture). Her personal trauma is directly related to the political trauma of land loss and urbanization.

We could wonder with Lacan (1998) whether V's psychosis resulted from not having a clear path from the dyad to a working compromise. Failure of paternal function to introduce suitable limits, even cultural ones, may have left her in terrible limbo, unable to come to grips with limits. V finds satisfaction in the Imaginary, where she can find magical solutions. The Imaginary is sought to address developmental and traumatic challenges. Her madness manifests in racing thoughts and frantic joy of being in contact with God and solving problems for Māori.

As V began to integrate her personal development with her political history, she found it easier to acknowledge herself as Māori. In the past, this had been a source of shame, not pride. Shame triggered intense dissociative denial, leading to risky behaviours, such as substance abuse that, in turn, triggered uncontrollable racing thoughts and feelings, culminating in a crashing arrival at an inpatient unit. This cycle repeated as the personal was denied in the face of the political and cultural. In years of psychotherapy, V became more confidently Māori, providing a secure base for a new identity. She had suffered the shameful, deep hurt of being a second order citizen, a feeling that paralleled her feelings at home of being secondary to the sexual abuser's needs. As V worked through painful inner constellations, a new cultural and political intersubjectivity emerged. With healing came the capacity to express herself through political art and exhibitions. Meeting new people who acknowledged her, she was surprised at her success.

When considering Māori identity, Bion's (1984b) no desire and no memory is relevant. I can recite all the politically correct matters, but the person with me may not identify with Māori culture in a straightforward manner. Some identify strongly with Christianity. Some identify more with Western cultures and lifestyle. Some, although identifying with Māori culture, may not want to see a Māori professional. I am curious as a therapist to listen to where a person comes from, how identities and relationships are formed, what patterns occur in specific stories. These are always in some way intertwined with political and traumatic histories of the land. By listening to the gaps, the unknown, ruptures, impasses, underlying dilemmas, the political, cultural and personal, as well as the pain, it becomes possible to figure out what may be helpful.

The Manawanui Māori Mental Health Service adopted the holistic Māori Mental Health Model, *Te Whare Tapa Wha*, composed of four pillars of wellbeing (Durie, 2001): *whanau* (family health), *hinengaro* (mental health), *tinana* (physical health) and *wairua* (spiritual health). These pillars hold the protective space of health and wellbeing for Māori and, I would argue, for most people. Unfortunately, this model has become concretized as politically correct. Most clinical psychology students can provide a rote answer about *Te Whare Tapa Wha*. It has become part of mental health discourse, a colossus that begins to mean very little with overuse. Although people can ramble off the model, they often make only very superficial use of it, if at all.

Te Whare Tapa Wha can provide opportunities to access thinking that Western psychology struggles with (body–mind issues, political–systemic processes) and to work with 'anomalous' experiences belonging to the *wairua* (spirit) aspect of the model (Randal, Geekie, Lambrecht and Taitimu, 2008). This part can incorporate findings of parapsychological research. Māori practitioners and clients are often grateful when their worldview and 'anomalous' experiences are not seen as crazy, or just 'cultural', as they are often considered within academic Western psychological discourse. I often apologize to the *tohunga* (Māori shamans) that Western psychology has many unresolved taboos and resistances in this area despite scientific evidence (Radin, 2006), an embarrassing situation, given psychology's claim to be scientific.

Although deceptively simple, *Te Whare Tapa Wha* is in fact a sophisticated, inclusive model, giving therapeutic options, allowing psychoanalytic thinking to occur as much as many other perspectives. With far more space for innovation, I can experiment more freely and even risk applying ancient techniques.

Given the *whanau* (family) aspect of the model, 'good-enough holding' (Winnicott, 2005) needs to occur on personal, political, cultural and spiritual dimensions. At a Māori Mental Health Service, these dimensions are openly acknowledged, making it, for me, an enjoyable workplace. I have freedom to use long-term psychotherapy because the *hinegaro* (mind) is respected. I am grateful I don't have to fight for long-term psychological interventions, which some of my colleagues have to justify within the general mental health system's medical model. I can also wonder about integration of the cultural and clinical. This kind of dialogue shifts biculturalism away from the merely moralistic to the creative and curious. I find this deeply enriching.

There is a shadow side to Māori identity, as with all cultural and political identities. The Māori service often prides itself on cultural holding through the importance of *whanau* (family) – a process that is both light and shadow. We often mention in our service that we are a *whanau*. In many cases, this gives *tangata whai ite ora* (persons seeking wellbeing) a sense of belonging and connection within a wider web of relations. Sometimes it feels *whanau* gets evoked too often. *Whanau*s can be toxic. Clinical and managerial leaders have at times not protected members of this *whanau* from their own bad and questionable practices. At times, Māori staff have been made into mere taxi drivers and shoppers for *tangata whai ite ora*.

Sometimes people claim the cultural high ground, making even Māori staff feel non-Māori, prompting demoralization. Senior Māori psychologists have left because they felt undermined by other Māori staff's cultural bullying. I have sought to tackle this darker aspect by being very clear that regardless of who might be right or wrong about culture, abusive interactions remain abusive no matter who speaks. We can understand this as identification with the aggressor, and still question such behaviours. Acknowledging darkness helps. Zero tolerance for abusive interactions between team members or *whanau* diminishes it.

As a *pakeha* psychologist, being the other, even the unknown other, can, ironically, be helpful. Although rich connections within Māori culture can work for you, they can also work against you. Imagine going to a psychotherapist who is your cousin second degree. Imagine the therapist is related to your odd aunt, or knows of your tipsy uncle. A client told me yesterday she won't see Māori therapists because they don't keep confidentiality. She has had numerous experiences where information leaked to family and friends.

In this service, I hold the intersubjective space (Stolorow, Brandchaft and Atwood, 2000), focusing on the alliance, listening to relational eddies and knots, negotiating and mirroring 'mentalizing' (Bateman and Fonagy, 2004). I address personal and political histories, moving beyond empty articulations. These principles are equally valid with all New Zealand's inhabitants.

Finally, I would like to consider spiritual holding (*wairua*) – an important cultural, even political component of Māori life, as with many indigenous peoples. Although Māori Mental Health Services acknowledges *wairua* as one of the four pillars of *Te Whare Tapa Wha*, how to integrate this into psychotherapeutic practice is not always clear. Working outside the medical model, I can risk applying practices that lie outside Western psychology. I can talk to clients about a 'transcendent function' (Jung, 1957) within, and 'anomalous' experiences, much more than I could amongst many whites. When these issues are raised, some psychoanalysts and psychologists become very conservative, very 'white'. For example, projective identification is a weird, wonderful concept and process. It could be considered a special case of telepathy. When one mentions 'telepathy', an experience that has been successfully researched (Carter, 2012), many psychoanalysts balk, yet other tribes and cultures do not since they know it through experience (Lambrecht, 2016).

Spiritual holding requires us to make space to talk about 'anomalous' experiences. My experience from many parts of the world is that indigenous people are wary of white people's rejection of such phenomena as unreal, imagined or hallucinatory. Many whites merely provide politically correct postmodern lip service in discussing these events. It is important to explore and validate their reality. To do so requires respect for the reality of the Māori world.

When I met some *tohunga* (Māori shamans) from Wellington, it felt like coming home in terms of my experiences in South Africa sitting amongst *sangomas* (shamans). When I can talk about my shamanic training, it is understood in a way not possible with most psychoanalysts given their materialistic and often simplistic empirical framework. Many psychoanalytic thinkers have a poor understanding of many states of consciousness that other cultures have investigated and researched carefully (Lambrecht, 2014).

To find the centre and limit of a culture, entering the field of the healer is helpful. Healers, such as shamans and psychoanalysts, hold the history, stories, secrets and shadows of a culture. I enjoy being with *tohungas* rather than politicians because the experience is lived rather than made monolithic. Through them I hear the history of the deeper mind, the *hinengaro* (mind) and *wairua* (spirit).

Māori Mental Health Services have given me very special opportunities for which I am very grateful. Returning to the question I have often faced about why would I work here, my reply is, why would I not?

References

Bateman, A. and Fonagy, P. (2004). *Psychotherapy for borderline personality disorder: mentalization-based treatment*. Oxford: Oxford University Press.
Bion, W. (1984a). Attacks on linking. In Bion, W. *Second thoughts: selected papers on psychoanalysis*. London: Karnac, pp.93–109.
—— (1984b). *Attention and interpretation*. London: Karnac.
Carter, C.D. (2012). *Science and psychic phenomena: the fall of the house of skeptics*. Rochester, VT: Inner Traditions.
Durie, M. (2001). *Mauri ora: the dynamics of Māori health*. Auckland: Oxford University Press.
Freud, S. (1981). *The interpretation of dreams*. Harmondsworth: Penguin.
Griner, D. and Smith, T. (2006). Culturally adapted mental health intervention: a meta-analytic review. *Psychotherapy: Theory, Research, Practice, Training*, 43(4): 531–548.
Jung, C.G. [1916] (1957). The transcendent function. *The collected works of C.G. Jung*, vol. 8. Princeton, NJ: Princeton University Press.
Kingi, T. (2007). Māori mental health: past trends, current issues, and Māori responsiveness [monograph]. *Matariki*, 1(1): 51–80.
Klein, M. [1946] (1975). Notes on some schizoid mechanisms. In R.E. Money-Kyrle (ed.), *The writings of Melanie Klein*, vol. 3. London: Hogarth Press, pp.1–24.
Lacan, J. (1998). *The four fundamental concepts of psychoanalysis*. London: W.W. Norton.
Lambrecht, I. (2014). *Sangoma Trance States*. Auckland: AM Publishing.
—— (2016). Wairua: following shamanic contours in psychoanalytic therapy at a Māori Mental Health Service in New Zealand. *The Fenris Wolf*, 9, in press.
Lambrecht, I. and Taitimu, M. (2012). Exploring culture, subjectivity, and psychosis. In J. Geekie, P. Randal and D. Lampshire (eds.), *Experiencing psychosis: first-person and research perspectives*. London: Routledge, pp.44–54.
Linehan, M. (1993). *Cognitive behavioral therapy for borderline personality disorder*. New York: The Guilford Press.
Oakley Browne, M.A., Wells, J.E. and Scott, K.M. (eds). (2006). *Te Rau Hinengaro: The New Zealand mental health survey*. Wellington: Ministry of Health.
Radin, D. (2006). *Entangled minds: extrasensory experiences in a quantum field*. New York: Paraview.
Randal, P., Geekie, J., Lambrecht, I. and Taitimu, M. (2008). Dissociation, psychosis and spirituality: whose voices are we hearing? In A. Moskowitz, I. Schafer and J. Dorahy (eds), *Psychosis, trauma and dissociation: emerging perspectives on severe psychopathology*. Chichester: John Wiley & Sons, pp.333–345.
RN Health Society (2010). First nations' traditional models of wellness. Environmental scan in British Columbia. www.fnhc.ca/pdf/Traditional_Models_of_Wellness_Report_FIN-_2010.pdf (accessed 29 August 2013).

Roberston, B.H. (2006). Does the evidence support collaboration between psychiatry and traditional healers? Findings from three South African studies. *South African Psychiatry Review*, 9: 87–90.

Sexton, R. and Sørlie, T. (2009). Should traditional healing be integrated within the mental health services in Sámi areas of northern Norway? Patient views and related factors. *International Journal of Circumpolar Health*, 68(5): 488–497.

Stolorov, R.D., Brandchaft, B. and Atwood, G.E. (2000). *Psychoanalytic treatment: an inter-subjective approach*. London: Routledge.

Tapsell, R. and Mellsop, G. (2007). The contributions of culture and ethnicity to New Zealand mental health research findings. *International Journal of Social Psychiatry*, 53, July: 317–324.

Winnicott, D.W. (2005). *Playing and reality*. London: Routledge.

Chapter 13

The good son
Psychotherapy with a 65-year-old man with the diagnosis of Asperger syndrome

Susan Rose

> 'Holy shit, Bird,' I whispered through my teeth. 'At least try to be normal. You have to at least try.'
>
> (Krauss, 2006)

The message on my answering machine was to the point. 'My name is Lorne. I want to speak to you about therapy.' The voice sounded like a mature man. The words were spoken in a monotone, somewhat robotic fashion. Later, he told me he was ending treatment with Dr M, 60 miles from his home. This psychologist had evaluated Lorne several years earlier, giving him the diagnosis of Asperger syndrome. Closing his practice and suggesting Lorne find a therapist closer to where he lived, Dr M referred him to me, since I work with individuals on the autism spectrum. Lorne and I began meeting once a week. He wanted help navigating his relationship with his parents, with his 'meltdowns' and developing the capacity to meet and marry a woman.

Before describing our work, I will briefly discuss key concepts associated with autistic spectrum disorders. In recent years, there has been a surge in interest and research in this area, with much change in our understanding. Currently, autistic spectrum disorders are understood as a complex set of neurobiologically based developmental conditions first identified, independently, by Leo Kanner, an American psychiatrist, and Hans Asperger, a Viennese paediatrician. Kanner (1943) described 11 patients with 'Early Infantile Autism'. He suggested these children are born lacking the usual motivation for social interaction. He felt they lacked the biological preconditions to take in the social world and make it part of themselves. They also displayed difficulties with symbolization, abstraction, understanding meanings and major disturbances of communication. Three were mute. The others' language was marked by echolalia, literalness and pronoun reversals. Kanner used the word 'autism' to convey their self-contained quality. He also felt, erroneously, there were major maternal personality deficits.

Asperger (1944) wrote of four boys between the ages of 6 and 11 with 'autistic psychopathy'. Despite seemingly intact cognitive and verbal abilities, they had significant difficulties in social integration. They displayed unusual speech patterns, often talking in a robotic fashion. They frequently had very strong interests in esoteric subjects that they talked at length about with what often seemed to be complete disregard for the listener's interest. Asperger described them as 'Little Professors'.

Because of World War II, Asperger and Kanner were unaware of each other's work. Their patients shared many attributes, such as problems with social interaction, affect and communication, and unusual interests. Despite the overlap, there were some major differences. Kanner's descriptions have been associated with classical autism, while Asperger syndrome's higher-functioning, more verbal, intellectually intact people were diagnosed with the syndrome that now bears his name.

Autism was not in the *Diagnostic and Statistical Manual of Mental Disorders* (*DSM*) until the third edition (American Psychiatric Association, 1980), where it appeared along with several other childhood disorders in a new category, Pervasive Developmental Disorder. PDD conveys suffering from severe impairments in multiple areas. DSM–IV (1994) expanded this category, including Aspergers for the first time, along with Autistic Disorder, Childhood Disintegrative Disorder, Rett Syndrome and PDD Not Otherwise Specified (NOS).

Researchers found these diagnoses were not reliably and consistently applied across settings. There was diagnostic confusion and considerable overlap, particularly of PDD-NOS and Aspergers. Confusion was compounded by the fact that three categories (Rett syndrome, Aspergers, PDD-NOS) shared the same diagnostic code, 299.80. To address these concerns, in the fifth edition of *DSM* (2013), PDD has been replaced with 'Autism Spectrum Disorder', a continuum bounded by severe autism at one end and by less significant but nonetheless life-long social impairments at the other. Individuals on the spectrum display difficulties in two core domains: social communication and interaction, and fixed interests and repetitive behaviour or activity. Symptoms must be present in early childhood, limiting and impairing daily functioning.

Uta Frith (1989) and Simon Baron-Cohen (1995) postulated that autistic individuals have a central processing deficit: weak high-level cohesive thought processes. Frith utilized the metaphor of a strong-flowing river that pulls together large amounts of information. With a strong need for central coherence, non-autistic individuals typically give priority to understanding/remembering the gist of a message, not the message verbatim. Without this high-level cohesion, pieces of information remain just that, of limited use in long-term adaption, leaving individuals in a fragmented, incoherent world with wide repercussions for multiple domains of life including communication and social interactions (Frith, 1989).

Perhaps because they lack a strong need for coherence, individuals on the spectrum have difficulty with mentalizing activities in which one attempts to pull together information to 'read' the minds of others and theorize about what they are thinking and feeling. As Fonagy and Target (1998) wrote: 'Mentalization or reflective function is the developmental acquisition that permits children to respond not only to another person's behavior, but to the child's conception of others' attitudes, intentions or plans' (p.92). Children begin demonstrating mentalizing at about 3 to 4 years of age (Wellman, 1990). Before then, they have difficulty understanding that their thoughts, feelings and beliefs might differ from those of another person. Once they begin mentalizing, children respond to others according to their theories of how others, as well as themselves, think and feel. 'Theory of mind' refers to this emerging understanding that they, as well as other people, have thoughts, knowledge, beliefs and desires that influence their behaviour (Baron-Cohen, Leslie and Frith, 1986; Leslie, 1987; Attwood, 1998). Ability to infer what others believe allows the individual to predict how he or she will behave (Baron-Cohen, Leslie and Frith, 1985) – a crucial component of social interactions and interpersonal relationships. For individuals with autism, the world can be a confusing, mysterious and at times frightening place due to their impaired capacity to fathom others' thoughts and feelings.

Most research and writing on autistic spectrum disorders has focused on children. They do not vanish when they reach adulthood. Autism impacts all phases of life. These individuals face all of life's challenges with increased difficulty as they frequently misread social cues that underlie and govern relationships. They often feel like foreigners in a strange land – observing, not quite part of the culture. Temple Grandin, a well-known professor with autism, is known for writing and activism on autism. She described herself as an 'anthropologist on Mars' (Sacks, 1996). Some wish to simply 'blend in' and be accepted by 'neurotypicals', but lack the tools and understanding necessary to accomplish this.

Functional limitations do not mean an absence of needs, psychodynamics or emotional development (Topel and Lachmann, 2008). With this mind, I will discuss my work with Lorne as he confronts the challenges of aging, caring for elderly parents, siblings, dating and mortality, all through the veil of autism.

I met Lorne when he was 62. His sister, Natalie, six years younger, was a lively, well-co-ordinated child who may have displayed signs of mild autism. When she was four, a severe concussion left her with major brain damage. Functioning at a four-year-old level, Natalie lived at home until it became increasingly difficult for the family to care for her. At age 16, she was sent to a boarding school for children with developmental disabilities. At 21, she became a ward of the state, and resides in a facility two hours away. The family maintains regular contact. Since traveling is difficult for them, usually, Natalie's caretakers bring her to them.

Lorne was raised in a middle-class family. His mother understood he was facing significant challenges, despite strong intellectual endowment. She attempted to obtain treatment for him, but in the early 1950s autism was just beginning to be recognized. Help was not readily available. A diagnosis of anything along the spectrum was never entertained. Lorne arrived for our first session with three psychological evaluations in hand. The earliest dated back to 1953, when he was six. Two early evaluations described him as being of high average intelligence, with strong verbal abilities. The earliest observed that he seemed socially confident, speaking in a loud voice and frequently standing up during the testing. He made bids for reassurance, often asking 'Is this right?' after responding to a question, suggesting insecurity. His evaluation nine years later (age 15) noted: 'He is not making a wholly satisfactory personal, social and emotional adjustment. He is a rather shy person who appears to lack confidence in himself and in his abilities.'

Lorne graduated from a small private school, then attended a high-pressured college. Living at home, unable to keep up with academic demands, he quit after a year and a half. Eventually, he finished at another college, then obtained work in sync with his need for precision.

When he was 25, mother insisted he live on his own. Although this was challenging, in retrospect he realizes it was a gift. Mother helped him find an apartment nearby, move, learn to cook and budget. While providing considerable support, she taught him independent living skills.

After holding his job for 35 years, Lorne retired at age 60, then entered treatment with Dr M. Without the structure and predictability work provided, loneliness and depression arose. When I met Lorne, he had structured his retired life. Having taught himself bridge, he attended a senior centre several times a week to play with the 'old ladies'. He played monthly Dungeons and Dragons with two former colleagues and visited with mother and father (ages 91 and 94).

I will focus on the third (final) phase of our work and on pervasive issues. Initially, Lorne articulated his wish to meet a woman and marry. He had never really dated or been intimate with a woman. It soon became clear that it was hard for Lorne to distinguish between his wants and needs and those of his parents. He worried about who would be there for him when they were gone. His wish to please and obtain their approval became painfully clear. We called this aspect of him – attempting to become the son they wanted, introjecting their wishes without critical evaluation – 'The Chameleon'. For example, he informed me he might take a month or two off during the winter to vacation in a warmer climate. A few months later, he told me his parents thought it wasn't safe for him to travel alone. He should only go with a girlfriend. When I explored his feelings about this (he had travelled alone to Florida, Hawaii, Israel, Europe), he stated he needed to be a good son. Stridently gesturing, he repeated that good sons obey parents. Attempts to untangle his opinion from theirs met resistance. Gradually, a shift occurred. Lorne took on what he thought was my opinion: 'I am going to go away. I've done it in the past. I need a vacation. If I wait till I have a girlfriend, I may never go away.' The next session, we were always back to square one, with no acknowledgement or recognition of previous discussions.

Initially, these interactions frustrated me. We always seemed to be back to what his parents wanted. I needed to accept that change would only slowly be achieved. When I discussed what transpired between us, Lorne could reflect, calling himself a 'people pleaser'. Since he has difficulty understanding others' internal states, attempts to please were doomed as he tried to please based upon mechanistic understanding of what others desired, rather than addressing more subtle emotional issues.

Eight months into our work, his mother was diagnosed with cancer. She would not survive. Mostly, Lorne was able to go about his normal routine, missing only a handful of our sessions. He visited and drove her to appointments. She still tried to care for him, fixing him up on a blind date with her radiology technician, perhaps feeling this immigrant would be less likely to pick up on Lorne's idiosyncratic personality and mannerisms.

Lorne felt sad and worried about who would care for him and father when mother was gone. (Since he has no 'clothing sense', she picked out his wardrobe.) As Lorne saw it, she was the glue holding the family together. Lorne seemed more worried about losing a caretaker than a loved one. He would have to care for father. Quoting from a movie, he repeatedly said: 'I'm the last one in the boat.' His emotional state resembled Sacks' (1996) description of Temple Grandin. Feelings for others were present, but greatly attenuated, lacking the emotional resonance many experience.

Lorne's mother died five months after diagnosis. He 'stepped up to the plate', making all funeral arrangements. A year later, he arranged for the tombstone unveiling and conducted the service. He radically altered his life to devote himself to father's care. Dividing his time between New York and tending to father in a different state, Lorne shops, helps pay bills, takes father to the doctor and assists when Natalie visits.

Lorne's treatment focused on helping him adapt to his new life, father's demands, mother's death and new feelings that have emerged, including anxiety about who will be there for him when he is older, and perhaps frail and infirm.

Following mother's death, Lorne spoke of missing her. He carries her driver's license in his wallet. I explored how he always apologizes for feeling sad. He acknowledged this was a new feeling, not something he was accustomed to sharing, emphasizing he must be strong since he's in charge now and must take care of father and Natalie.

Often he brought up father's anger at his spouse for dying. If this 'stupid woman' had gone to the doctor regularly, cancer would have been caught earlier, and she could have lived. Lorne appropriated these beliefs without evaluating them. Away from father's influence, he could achieve some objectivity and independence of thought, enabling him to better accept mother's death. His anger and sadness dissipated as he came to understand that he and father could have different views and that it was not his duty to accept all that father believed. This achievement was tenuous.

As Lorne settled into caring for father, wanting to please and taking on others' opinions (particularly father's) reappeared in full force. Simultaneously, this has been a time of significant growth.

'My father says I'm not his son.' So began a session six months after mother's death. 'He says she had an affair with my uncle while he was in the army. Even a few years ago, she would disappear for several hours!' Father thought she 'fooled around' with this uncle while father drove them in his car. As we discussed this matter, Lorne began wondering if father's age (95) had something to do with bringing this up. It was difficult to hold on to the idea that father could be incorrect as this would require relinquishing his belief in father's strength and status as family 'leader'. Lorne repeatedly stated it was filial obligation to believe everything father stated. He struggled to understand they could have different opinions and beliefs. Due to his literal thinking, he felt it was dishonest to simply placate father when the latter made accusations. Challenging father was futile. Additionally, Lorne worried about father's ultimate demise, fearing it would leave him alone in a frightening world. However, one thing that Lorne began articulating was the impact of father's statements. He reported a broader range of affects. Father's statements made him sad, angry and fearful. Experiencing different feelings simultaneously was new.

At times Lorne wished father would move to assisted living in New York, then Lorne could see him daily. They visited facilities. None met Dad's approval. He claimed they were too expensive, although he had significant resources. One day Lorne stated he felt father should stay where he is because 'that is what he wants'. It was a significant step that he could understand father's wishes and subordinate his feelings. He was not blindly wishing to be the 'good son'. This felt more mature and nuanced, with Lorne thinking through what father wished and required and committing himself to supplying it as best he could.

Five months after mother's death, Lorne stated with pride that father says he is doing a good job. To Lorne's surprise, he enjoyed caretaking, feeling a new closeness with father. Lorne finds it comforting to sleep in the same bed, cuddling, intertwining legs and playing 'footsie' with father.

While enjoying companionship with father, Lorne began experiencing loneliness and worried about who would be there for him when father was gone. After discussing these issues, he took matters into his own hands, contacting Natalie's facility to see if he could ultimately live there. They responded positively. Drawing up a will, he wanted father to be executor. It was painful to imagine life without all-powerful father taking care of and protecting him. Ultimately, he asked younger cousins to be executors.

Loneliness was harder to resolve. Fuelled by paternal pressure, Lorne wanted to meet a woman. I encouraged him to examine what he desired. He wanted to please father. He felt his lack of a spouse had disappointed both parents, making him feel like a failure. He also feared being alone, wanting a woman to take care of him. In time, Lorne stated that since he enjoyed taking care of his father, he would like to take care of a woman, too. He wants a companion with whom he can do things. Desire for love and intimacy has not entered his equation. Lorne noted he doesn't know what love is, but does know the joys of companionship.

When Lorne placed an ad on a Jewish dating website, one woman seemed interested. They went out to dinner with father. He told Lorne not to date her because she was deformed and Lorne would end up taking care of her, rather than vice versa. Lorne didn't contact her again, feeling he needed to comply with paternal wishes. Lorne had not observed any deformities, but felt maybe he simply hadn't noticed them. He was unable to see that he and father could have different takes on how he should lead his life. They both approached choice of spouse in a concrete, objective, need-based fashion. The woman's feelings and the concepts of attraction and desire did not enter their formulations.

Reaching out to other women, Lorne was rebuffed. His profile read in part: 'I need a person to guide me in the relationship – that is tweak me out of my comfort zone and share my interests. I need someone who will establish a leadership role while not being too domineering – teach me.' After we discussed how others might interpret his profile, he rewrote it using the mantra 'less is more'. Entering unchartered waters, Lorne's capacity to understand the unspoken language of dating and flirtation is limited. He feels alone and handicapped, like an observer, unable to break a mysterious code. He realizes his dating skills are decades behind those of others. Sometimes our interactions about these matters are somewhat humorous. For example, we discussed a woman with whom he made tentative plans to play bridge at his senior centre. Lorne did not follow up with her. When I asked him how he thought she felt, he replied: 'I don't know. Remember, I'm autistic and don't have empathy.' When I looked quizzically, he responded, 'I know. She probably thought I wasn't interested.'

Lorne's evolving relationship with me has been crucial to his gains. Initially, I was Dr M's replacement. He looked to me as someone who could clarify issues and reassure him. Our relationship deepened after his mother's death. Loss likely intensified maternal transference, making him more available to the therapeutic process. The death evoked stronger feelings and exposed him to a greater range of affect with father. An example of our deepened connection occurred when I cancelled a session due to weather. The next week, Lorne told me he had been worried about me in the snow. He was glad I hadn't come in. He thought of me as the younger sister he never had since Natalie had always remained a little girl. Having lost mother and sister, he did not want to lose any more females. He now flirts with me, saying things like, 'I could kiss you for that, but of course I won't.' He also offers to teach me and my family bridge 'off the clock'. In these examples, he plays with, but maintains, the therapeutic frame.

Lorne's connection to me was tested when it became clear he would have to pay for sessions. Although I charge him a low fee, it was hard for him to accept paying when he could see someone else who takes his insurance. Proud of his ability to stick to a budget and care for himself, spending makes him anxious. Such expenditures would not have paternal approval. He asked me to refer him to 'another provider'. I said I could, but that he seemed to feel people are interchangeable, and this belief was probably associated with Aspergers. He was surprised, but able to discuss how difficult it is for him to pay and the anxiety it evokes. He said it would take a while to get used to it. He has – a truly significant, independent act.

Lorne shows increasing capacity to reflect upon his thoughts and inner world. For example, he told me what he had done one week with father, ending with 'Isn't that something?' He frequently ends sentences with this phrase. I find it stifling. There isn't much to say other than 'Yes.' This day, Lorne paused and said, 'I wonder why I always say this,' leading to a discussion of how these clichés modulate anxiety. I believe this ability to reflect upon experience in the safety of a containing relationship is central to the work with such patients. We help them cultivate curiosity about the workings of their minds – their thoughts, feelings and underlying motives – and help them extend this curiosity to others' minds. While we may take this ability for granted, for Lorne it is what will help him navigate the wide divide that separates him from much of the richness life has to offer.

References

American Psychiatric Association (1980). *Diagnostic and Statistical Manual of Mental Disorders*, 3rd ed. Washington: APA.
—— (1994). *Diagnostic and statistical manual of mental disorders*, 4th edition. Washington: APA.
—— (2013). *Diagnostic and statistical manual of mental disorders*, 5th edition. Washington: APA.
Asperger, H. (1944). Autistic psychopathy in childhood. In U. Frith (ed.) (1991), *Autism and Asperger syndrome*. New York: Cambridge University Press.
Attwood, T. (1998) *Asperger's syndrome: a guide for parents and professionals*. London and Philadelphia: Jessica Kingsley.
Baron-Cohen, S. (1995). Mindblindness: an essay on autism and theory of mind. Cambridge, MA: MIT Press.
Baron-Cohen, S., Leslie, A.M. and Frith, U. (1985). Does the autistic child have a 'theory of mind'? *Cognition*, 4: 37–46.
Fonagy, P. and Target, M. (1998). Mentalization and the changing aims of child psychoanalysis. *Psychoanalytic Dialogues*, 8: 87–114.
Frith, U. (1989). *Autism: explaining the enigma*. Oxford: Blackwell.
Kanner, L. (1943). Autistic disturbances of affective contact. *Nervous Child*, 2: 217–250.
Krauss, N. (2006). *The history of love*. New York: W.W. Norton.
Leslie, A.M. (1987). Pretense and representation: the origins of 'theory of mind'. *Psychological Review* 94(4): 412–426.
Sacks, O. (1996). *An anthropologist on Mars*. New York: Vintage.
Topel, E. and Lachmann, F. (2008). Life begins on an ant farm for two patients with Asperger's syndrome. *Psychoanalytic Psychology*, 25(4): 602–617.
Wellman, H. (1990). *The child's theory of mind*. Cambridge, MA: MIT Press.

Chapter 14

Creativity, identity and social exclusion
Working with traumatized individuals

Marilyn Charles

We are social beings, and discover ourselves in interaction with others. People who are 'different' are at a disadvantage, particularly in the early years, when the challenge of becoming part of the social structure is at stake. In childhood, difference tends to be marked as a problem, often leading to bullying and social exclusion. Difference becomes further problematized in adolescence, during those uneasy years in which adult identity is being consolidated. The very qualities that mark us as unique and special can feel dangerous if they also mark us as too distant from our peers. Evidence mounts regarding the damaging effects of social exclusion, experiences that deauthorize and dehumanize the developing sense of self, at times catapulting the victim into a terrible void of deprecated otherness (Charles, 2012, 2013). Tensions between internal and external demands can result in psychotic symptoms, signs of strain that are often transitory and can be moderated in psychoanalytic therapy if we can recognize the healthy developmental desires that may be obscured by the symptoms.

The dilemma of facing alikeness and difference is particularly challenging when working with individuals struggling with psychotic experience. Although psychosis is often thought of as a physiological disorder, most often people are driven mad by experiences that push them outside the social order. In this way, the symptoms associated with psychosis mark a struggle to make sense of self and other in a world in which the comfortable signs and guideposts we normally rely on are skewed or missing. Even though difference can mark exceptional qualities, how one learns to read one's own difference has implications for all subsequent development. That fact makes it important for the clinician to recognize that personal characteristics that are found in gifted individuals are also found in those at risk for severe psychopathology. Most people who experience psychotic symptoms do not develop chronic or severe disorder. The crucial factor seems to be how those experiences – those markers of difference – are read. Drawing on the attachment literature and psychoanalytic theory, and then using a case for illustration, I will explore ways in which idiosyncrasy that is punished in childhood can obstruct the potential for creativity and leave the young adult isolated and alienated from him/herself and others.

The importance of early relationships in self-development

We come into the world already to some extent configured in our parents' minds. We receive the world as it is offered to us, and our ideas about ourselves develop in the context of early relationships with caregivers. One crucial developmental challenge involves being able to identify and disidentify with important others so that we can find ourselves in relation to others who are both like and unlike ourselves. The attachment literature has shown ways in which early relationships with caregivers can provide a secure foundation that builds a strong identity and, with it, resistance to trauma and stress. Empathic attunement from a secure object recognizes the child as a separate, sentient being. This developmental process is confounded when caregivers are not able to have the child's needs or feelings in mind, a lack that provides insufficient grounding for the developing self. Self-development is further obstructed when traumatic experiences disrupt the internalization of affective self-regulation so crucial to all later wellbeing. Often, the most insidious trauma is not overt. Unresolved trauma is passed along the generations, such that the intergenerational transmission of unresolved trauma and loss has been implicated in the type of disorganized attachment associated with social, emotional and physical problems in childhood and later life (O'Connor, Bureau, McCartney and Lyons-Ruth, 2011).

Attuned parenting builds resilience as the caretaker moderates the child's distress through soothing tone, gesture or touch, providing an experience-near sense of recognition and understanding. As the child actively practises these soothing functions, they become internalized as part of the implicit memory system, coming forward in times of stress. The internalization of affective attunement has profound implications for all later psychical and emotional wellbeing, including the development of cognitive capacities (Krystal, 1988). Harsh and inconsistent parenting, in contrast, interferes with the internalization of effective soothing functions, thereby impeding development. Such parenting has been linked to what Main and Hesse (1990) term a *disorganized attachment* style, characterized by disorientation and stereotyped, inconsistent or contradictory behavioural patterns. Parents who are not able to mirror the child's experience and provide a consistent frame of reference impede the development of consistent and organized strategies for self-regulation. Such deficits leave the child at the mercy of heightened, overwhelming affect under stress. Overwhelming affect itself can disrupt cognitive capacities, thereby further impeding the child's ability to manage life's challenges.

Although psychosis is often thought of as a biological disorder, genetically driven, evidence increasingly points to relational deprivation and disruption, traumatically driven. Evidence suggests that relational trauma can lead to psychosis by disrupting self-development and, at the extreme, leaving the self in pieces, fragmented, with insufficient connecting links. These types of dissociative processes have been associated with profound difficulties in affect regulation that result in a breakdown in self-development (Liotti, 1999). If we look through the lens of disorganized attachment as described by Main and Hesse (1990), we can see two relational pathways to psychosis. The first path is associated with abuse or neglect and is characterized by a lack of a consistent and organized strategy of affective self-regulation that precludes the development of a coherent, integrated self. The second path is linked to families who are struggling with unresolved trauma or loss and is characterized by a breakdown in a more generally organized and consistent strategy of affective regulation, manifesting as a self that coheres sufficiently to function relatively effectively under normal conditions but not sufficiently integrated to hold together under strain (Van Ijzendoorn et al., 1999).

Peer relationships and social exclusion

Complicating this picture, children who have not been able to build and sustain a secure base in relation to caregivers are more likely to experience difficulties in building and sustaining relationships with peers (Jacobvitz and Hazen, 1999). The failure to develop the foundation afforded by a coherent self and effective coping mechanisms makes the child particularly susceptible to peer victimization. Temperamental factors also come into play. The sensitive child who is anxious and submissive is more likely to be bullied than his or her more aggressive counterparts (Olweus, 1994). In addition, ineffective coping strategies leave the child more reactive to stress, thereby further exacerbating difficulties in peer relationships (Myin-Germeys and van Os, 2007).

Children are highly sensitive to difference in others and quickly learn whether to be curious and engaged, or fearful and distancing. Unrepaired, social exclusion not only results in impoverished relations with others, but also with oneself. This lack of repair points to caretakers' failures to recognize and contain the distress of the developing child. Such containment is particularly important for the child for whom social engagement does not come easily but who might, with assistance, learn to bring her own talents to bear in interactions with others. Studies that trace the effects of social exclusion in childhood point to individual difference factors and personality characteristics, such as shyness and sensitivity, that are implicated in both creativity and severe psychopathology. Recognizing characteristics that *might* result in adaptive creative engagement but, under conditions of adversity might also lead to psychosis, helps us better understand the plight of the gifted individual who also experiences psychotic symptoms.

Shame

Evidence mounts regarding the damaging effects of bullying and social exclusion, and the dire consequences of peer victimization (Charles, 2013). During the school years, the child is developing a sense of self in relation to others. Experiences of competency and efficacy build a sense of mastery and confidence in one's ability to manage life challenges, whereas difficulties in coping and failures in social adaptation can lead to feelings of inefficacy and hopelessness, a cycle that can become self-perpetuating. Research affirms that situations that are uncontrollable and also involve social-evaluative judgements are most stressful and most difficult to recover from (Dickerson and Kemeny, 2004). Experiences of social exclusion and marginalization, in particular, lead to social humiliation and to shame, a virulent and self-perpetuating emotion that amplifies feelings of inferiority and low self-esteem (Birchwood, Meaden, Trower, Gilbert and Plaistow, 2000). Recurrent experiences of shame can result in scripts that hold expectations of humiliation, defeat and victimization that are self-validating and therefore resist moderation or repair (Tomkins, 1962, 1979, 1982). These expectations are, in part, self-validating because they inhibit reengagement with others in ways that might ease the distress or alter the expectation.

Peer relationships inform one's sense of self in relation to others. Positive relationships help to develop a sense of belonging in the social world, whereas bullying and social exclusion mark one as different and inferior, leading to the types of negative assumptions about oneself and one's interpersonal world that enhance the vulnerability to shame (Platt and Freyd, 2011). Shame itself designates the person as inferior and alienated from the larger social surround, making it a particularly toxic affect. Shame and loneliness have been found to be the most problematic sequelae reported by adults who had been victims of bullying in childhood (Carlisle and Rofes, 2007). Unlike guilt, shame does not easily lend itself to repair because it is the self, not one's actions, that are implicated. Shame breaks the interpersonal bonds, inviting withdrawal and avoidance of the very interpersonal engagement that might prove reparative. Vulnerability to shame has been linked not only to interpersonal difficulties but also to the types of cognitive and affective difficulties associated with psychopathology more generally (Tangney, Wagner and Gramzow, 1992), likely in part because of the tendency for shame to amplify affect, thereby inhibiting reflective function (Tomkins, 1982).

Tomkins describes shame explicitly as a 'specific inhibitor of continuing interest and enjoyment' that is evoked by a 'perceived barrier to positive affect with the other' (1982, pp.377–378). It is, therefore, a decidedly interpersonal affective state. Because of its inhibiting effects, shame not only impedes social interactions but also makes it more difficult for the individual to sustain curiosity in the face of novelty and to take the types of risks required for new learning and the mastery of important developmental tasks. This is the critical moment Bion (1977) refers to in terms of the constant choice between seeking knowledge or turning a blind eye. Turning away from the challenge precludes the very experiences of mastery that invite further exploration and help to build positive self-regard. These experiences of mastery are also implicated in the development of mentalization and metacognitive capacities (Fonagy, Gergely, Jurist and Target, 2002; Lysaker, Erickson et al., 2010). Metacognition involves the ability to obtain sufficient perspective to distance oneself from one's immediate experience and thereby to reflect on one's own thoughts and feelings in relation to the thoughts and feelings of others. Shame inhibits our ability to look outward and thereby closes down perspective.

Metacognition and mastery

Notably, Lysaker and his colleagues include mastery under the overarching rubric of metacognitive capacities. They define mastery in terms of the ability to make use of one's knowledge about the mental states of oneself and others in pragmatic ways that facilitate adaptive coping with life challenges (Lysaker, Erickson et al., 2010). Psychosis is associated with deficits in metacognitive capacities (Lysaker, Olesek et al., 2011). These deficits have been linked to difficulties with executive function, such as mental flexibility and inhibition (Lysaker, Warman et al., 2008), and also to difficulties in coping (Lysaker, Erickson et al., 2011). Gumley (2011) suggests that unsuccessful coping may be the key mediator between trauma and impaired metacognition, noting that whereas avoidant coping styles (in which shame is implicated prominently) can serve as a protection against painful thoughts, memories and experiences, a high price is exacted in terms of decrements in affect regulation and cognitive capacities.

Difficulties in coping also interfere with the development of strong and positive peer relationships. Children who have not developed secure attachments with parents and learned adaptive coping are more likely to be excluded and bullied. This fact is of concern because of the links between bullying and peer victimization and severe psychopathology, most particularly psychotic spectrum disorders (Schreier et al, 2009). Data from developmental studies and attachment research shows not only the importance of early relationships in building resilience in young people but also that *early deficits can be moderated* with sufficient attention to the quality of later relationships (Mayes, Fonagy and Target, 2007; Schwandt et al., 2010). This data is good news for those who work with individuals struggling with psychosis and also affirms the importance of early intervention to attenuate the difficulties and thereby inhibit further traumatic events from occurring. Notably, studies show that early intervention can reduce the likelihood of chronic psychotic disorder (Seikkula, Aaltonen, Alakare, Haarakangas and Keränen, 2006). Even when intervention does not occur until adulthood, attention to the developmental milestones that have not yet been met, and to the metacognitive capacities needing to be built and supported, can help the individual to move beyond the impasse, as we will see in the case to follow. Such interventions take a stand, insisting that the problem relates to the person's experience, which can be changed, rather than to the person him or herself in some way that cannot.

This stand is particularly important in light of data that shows a strong link between trauma, social exclusion and psychosis. This link highlights the importance of building and reinforcing social links for vulnerable individuals (Charles, 2009; Seikkula, Aaltonen, Alakare, Haarakangas and Keränen, 2006), rather than following the current cultural trend towards management of symptoms. The idea of not being able to rely on one's own mind is a frightening one, making it all too easy for the clinician to try to ease his or her own discomfort with thoughts of finding 'the right medication' or other ways to 'solve' the 'problem'. The problem of psychosis, however, is more complex (Charles and O'Loughlin, 2013). If we take seriously what our patients tell us about the etiology of their distress, we see that psychosis emerges over time in relation to problems in living that cannot be worked through sufficiently to regain equilibrium. The failure to achieve mastery is experienced as further proof of deficiency, thus compounding the alienation and pushing the individual further into autistic means of relieving distress. Increasingly, research confirms how even somewhat 'normal' trauma, such as bullying and social exclusion, can intrude itself and disrupt normal development in ways that lead to psychosis (Charles, 2013). This recognition of the traumatic origins of psychosis breaks into our reassuring fantasy that psychosis could not happen to *us*; it could only happen to *them*.

We live in a manic society, with the idea that if we just did more, moved faster, tried harder, everything would be fine. Problems in living tend to be seen not as something to face and understand but rather as a sign of failure. If we were really doing it right, we wouldn't be depressed, or anxious, and certainly not psychotic. And yet, it is precisely that type of alienation from self and experience that leaves us at greater risk of developing psychotic disorders. Learning to recognize one's own thoughts and feelings in relation to the thoughts and feelings of others, then, can be a crucial part of any recovery process. That type of learning is integral to the psychoanalytic process, in which the process itself models the type of curiosity in the face of perplexity that is a fundamental factor in moving towards hopefulness from despair.

Increasingly, we can recognize that psychosis marks, in part, a failure in adaptation. Those struggling with psychosis often show deficits in the types of metacognitive abilities – or 'reflective function' – so crucial to the development of resilience. Lysaker and his colleagues (2011) have noted the importance, in this regard, of being able to recognize one's thoughts and feelings, such that one can track those thoughts and feelings as distinct from and in relation to the thoughts and feelings of others. As Winnicott (1971) shows, one can only truly find one's self in relation to another who is present with, but separate from, oneself. Only then can we do the further work of being able to locate oneself in relation to one's desires, and in relation to one's world, which then affords the kind of traction we need in order to be able to struggle with the inevitable adversities that life brings. Psychoanalytic psychotherapy, at its best, helps an individual to begin to recognize what is at stake and to begin to make a claim for his or her own desires in ways that others can support or at least give feedback about. Such work requires, in part, finding sufficient hope to be able to begin to build the kind of frustration tolerance we need in order to create a life for ourselves (Charles, 2012).

Working with psychosis

Bion (1977) saw the crucial juncture of development as the constant choice between seeking knowledge and turning a blind eye. When knowledge has meant pain without the possibility of mastery or repair, facing a challenge can feel impossible, terrible and even foolish. And yet, what we can't see inevitably entraps us. The therapist, then, is charged with trying to keep his or her eyes open so that the story that has resisted telling might be told. This process is complicated by shame and is further impeded by whatever cannot be known within the family, factors that were crucial in the case to follow.

I find that working with psychosis requires an utter honesty that can be difficult to sustain. There is at times a terrible fluidity of boundaries that can make me both utterly transparent and oddly opaque such that I am always in danger of being both read and misread. With 'Greg', for example, dangerous signs and signals intruded into our work together, signs that were not visible to me except insofar as our process provided clues, or when he would tell me after the fact of some difficulty he had encountered. Being in my presence at all was complicated, as he was never certain to what extent he was being 'bugged' or otherwise at terrible risk. Even when he felt relatively safe during the session, as he left, without my presence to reassure him, he would become certain of the dangers that had, indeed, existed in the consulting room and which he had just escaped. This lack of object constancy made contact even more dangerous.

Accepting what Greg told me regarding his sense of himself as fundamentally different from all other human beings, I took seriously whatever information he was able to give me, so that I could have a better sense of his universe and how it was configured. Being able to register the signals being read, to consider the meanings attributed, and then find my way to my own reading is useful in being able to navigate the divide between self and other, particularly with one whose interpersonal world is configured so differently from my own. This challenge is both difficult and tenuous, particularly given my *own* desire to misread my failures of attention, interest or understanding. In such moments, we may long for some Authority to defer to, to avoid the discomfort of having to stand on our own *inner* authority. In this difficult work, we continually face the challenge of finding sufficient integrity to remain present in the moment and find our way through it together. Although theory can help us in meeting that challenge, we also need to be vigilant not to impose the theory between ourselves and our patients as a way of managing our anxiety and titrating our distress.

This issue of mastering the challenge rather than looking to a Master seems to be at the heart of a shift Lacan makes in his later seminars, describing a triadic interdependent structure he refers to as a Borromean 'knot' (Lacan, 1972–1973, 1974–1975; Vanheule, 2011). This model opposes his previous hierarchy in which a conventional or normative solution was equated with health, and focuses instead on how meanings are linked together for that particular individual. We can see this as a shift away from his emphasis on the *Name of the Father*, a Law that constrains and determines Meaning in a more general sense. In this way, the later model de-pathologizes psychosis and invites us to consider more directly what is at stake for the individual in this position, who is trying to work through meanings as they have been presented to him or her – meanings that may not make sense from one perspective and yet are experienced as fundamentally and absolutely important *and* in which may be lodged crucial facts that have not yet been made conscious.

Lacan (1974–1975, 1975–1976) uses the term *sinthome* to designate an idiosyncratic solution to the problems of existence that then also becomes the *key* to the meanings displayed and implied by that solution, as we note the ways in which the meanings are knotted together. The three rings of the knot represent the levels of the Real, the Imaginary and the Symbolic order. So, then, the symptom *itself* marks the particularity of the individual in terms of how meanings are configured. It holds and displays, and in that way begins to tell the story. This term holds respect for the meanings being carried. Rather than merely a symptom of pathology, the sinthome is an important puzzle waiting to be explored, a key to the individual's mystery. This move on Lacan's part recognizes that there *is* a logic, a structuring at work, that may be too idiosyncratic to be comprehensible outside that realm. From this perspective, there is no substitute for the clinician's willingness to intuit and inhabit, as best we might, the universe of the other.

This stand also insists that one cannot presume authority when questions of individual existence are at stake. This is an inherently ethical stance, a statement of a value system that demands that we recognize the inherent narcissism at the base of our presumptions regarding the 'illness of the other', a narcissism that threatens to deauthorize the very subject we are trying to support. Like Bion, therefore, in Lacan we find a determined slipping away from definite meanings and prescriptions that would pre-define the course of treatment. To the contrary, if we are to face the challenge head on, our task is to *learn the language* of the other sufficiently to be able to recognize the gaps and elisions, the condensations, the ways in which meanings are organized and formulated by that individual.

Particularly when working with someone who struggles with psychosis, I notice that it is easy to find myself in the position of 'correcting' or challenging the system of meanings I encounter, as though if the person just saw things my way, everything would be so much easier. And yet, it is only when we can avoid correcting or challenging that idiosyncratic system of meanings that we can perhaps recognize the logic sufficiently to be able to invite a conversation that is *in relation to* that system. From that position, we can obtain a better sense of the meanings *as they exist*, the ways in which they function for the person and how those meanings tell a story that cannot otherwise be deciphered. It is important to stay close, to be both attentive and attuned, in order to track the meanings as they are displayed by the individual. It is only at that point of meeting that we might be able to consider together ways in which that system *fails* him or her in relation to his or her *own* desires. From that position, we are best able to speak in relation to the person's productions without overriding, intruding or trespassing (Apollon, Bergeron and Cantin, 2002).

Part of our dilemma is the very concreteness of meaning for the individual who struggles with psychosis, a concreteness that leaves little room for perspective or reflection. And so, paradoxically, in a culture in which madness is read as a physiological process, *there is a move towards the concrete that threatens to meet the psychotic in that very place in which words are no longer layered and meanings cannot be investigated*. In contrast, if we take seriously what is at stake in the negotiation between self and other, we can see that our understanding, itself, can be fundamentally crippling as, for example, in the case of diagnoses, which offer our patients a language that *may* be clarifying and organizing but can also be *dis*organizing, *writing over* the individual and further obscuring him from view.

Psychosis, creativity and resilience

Working at the Austen Riggs Center, a private psychoanalytic psychiatric hospital in Western Massachusetts, has offered opportunities to try to make sense of the often unclear line between creativity and psychosis. The foundation of Austen Riggs is its open setting that leaves patients free to choose to participate – or not – in any of the programme offerings, including entering treatment or ending it. Reliance on 'examined living' helps us talk with patients about how they are making use of their treatment without mandating any particular path. This stance helps us to locate the subject who has become lost in relation to his own desires, and to invite him to think seriously about his feelings and desires in relation to those of others around him, who may be similar and different in various ways. In that way, we attempt to provide opportunities to help build his metacognitive capacities and, with these, his ability to withstand and more effectively cope with the inevitable life challenges that arise.

In addition to providing four-times-a-week intensive psychoanalytic psychotherapy, the therapeutic community programme allows patients to explore what it means to be a citizen within a community. Formal and informal interactions in this environment of examined living afford opportunities to talk about the problems one encounters in interactions with others rather than merely suffering through them. We find that it is often the individual who has been designated 'psychotic' who stands to the side sufficiently to be able to report back to us some of what has been excluded from the conversation. As one patient remarked in a process group (in reference to an encounter that had no real engagement or vitality), 'It's like the popcorn without the butter.' Such novelty of perspective can be illuminating, and yet, though such remarks can be seen to hit the mark quite pointedly, they can also be pushed to the side as irrelevant, depending on our willingness to engage deeply in the moment and allow ourselves to associate relatively freely.

The psychotic individual him or herself, however, may not have sufficient resilience to be able to sustain faith in the products of his or her own mind in the face of the incomprehension of others. Increasingly, I think of resilience as a marker for the type of reflective functions so crucial to finding one's way in the world, the types of functions built and strengthened in psychoanalytic psychotherapies. The ability to reflect on one's thoughts and feelings in relation to the thoughts and feelings of others involves capacities that are built over time through interactions in the social environment. For those who have been wounded by and have receded from such interactions, trying to move beyond the point of impasse can feel increasingly impossible.

I have a particular interest in creativity and in people who may stand at the margins because of the idiosyncrasy of their perspective. How such an individual finds his or her way in the world while retaining individuality is always foremost in my mind. My interests in creativity and in psychosis have led me to investigate ways in which psychosis may mark underlying capacities that have been thwarted and find their creative expression in the symptom. If we can set in abeyance our own concreteness and shift towards a psychoanalytic perspective, symptoms that at the manifest level might seem bizarre or nonsensical can be read as communications from the unconscious that cannot be spoken more directly. Learning to 'read' one's self and to be able to track one's thoughts is the work of psychoanalysis, as the patient struggles against internal constraints and inhibitions towards a more creative engagement.

Projective testing at times affords a glimpse into these layered meanings and, with them, into the individual's creative capacities. For example, in a study examining the Rorschach responses of creative individuals who struggle with psychosis, we found that one group was characterized by a tendency to massively constrict, whereas individuals in a second group allowed themselves free rein, offering wildly idiosyncratic responses that were difficult for the interviewer to locate (Charles, Clemence and Biel, 2011). A third group, however, were able to ground their imaginations sufficiently to offer unique and idiosyncratic responses that were well grounded in the blots themselves. Tracking individuals over time, within the context of ongoing psychoanalytic treatment, we could see that some were able to move from the overly constricted or overly disinhibited response set towards a more genuinely creative expression, a freer free association. Notably, patients with the poorest outcomes tended to be in the constricted group. As such, both their psychotic liabilities and their creative potential might be overlooked by the inattentive observer.

In part, I have found working with individuals struggling with psychosis so rewarding because there is so much at stake. The suffering of not being able to find one's way into the social surround can be profound and utterly debilitating. If we recognize ways in which psychosis marks a developmental failure, then we are invited to look beyond the particularities of the symptoms displayed and attempt to recognize where the failures lie. In this way, we take a stand with the patient regarding our belief, not that something is *wrong with them* but rather that something has *happened to them* that needs to be better understood in order to be able to move beyond the impasse. This happening-to-them marks not the experience of victim but rather a recognition of the difficulty, at times, of facing life's challenges and yet the importance and possibility of so doing.

To explore and explicate this dilemma, I will present a case of paranoid psychosis that could also be conceptualized in terms of severely delayed psychosocial development. With traumatized adults, we find ourselves working with the child and adolescent, as well, making it important for the clinician to have a good understanding of psychosocial development so that she can recognize the milestones that have not been met. Such was the case with Greg, who, in spite of his fine intellect and dogged work ethic, had been unable to attain most of life's challenges, aside from his ability to obtain an 'A' when one was offered. Life beyond the parameters of a formal school setting had left him utterly unmoored and floundering. Thinking about his early life in relation to the milestones he had not achieved afforded Greg a way of thinking about himself as a real human being embedded in a social context, rather than the grandiose, autistic robot he initially presented to me. Together, we began to build a narrative in which his current problems made sense, and through which we could imagine that they might possibly be relieved.

Case illustration

Greg sought treatment at the insistence of his mother because of severe psychotic episodes initially linked with stimulant abuse. He, himself, did not believe he needed treatment but did appreciate the respite from his mother's 'care' and concern, which he experienced as terribly intrusive and overriding of his needs, feelings and experience. In spite of his initial report of having no symptoms or concerns, he was eventually able to allow me to see the virulent paranoia that he was desperately trying to contain and yet still surfaced in moments of extreme strain.

Severely constrained and inhibited, Greg had found it difficult to make use of his talents in his life. Rather, much of his intellect and creative potential had gone into the elaborate fantasies he contrived to make sense of his feelings of intense anxiety, shame and impending doom. Greg's story was notable in terms of a history of bullying combined with parents who were not able to help their son find his way in the social surround and manage the bullying that had left him profoundly isolated and alone. Instead, socially isolated themselves, they encouraged him to turn towards academic achievement for the satisfactions he could not find in human interactions. Perhaps most notably, in light of our understanding gleaned from the attachment literature, neither parent had been able to mourn effectively the child they had lost before Greg was born.

Greg's solution to the shame and humiliation of social exclusion had been to withdraw, not only from social interactions, but also from the life of feelings. His primary source of pride was his arrogance and his investment in an accomplishment so stellar that it inevitably eluded him. This stance also afforded him little tolerance for the types of failures that are inevitable by-products of learning. When I met him, the presumption that he had no feelings and no interest in people or social interactions was utterly convincing, and yet he was also able to recall a brief time in high school when he had enjoyed being part of a community.

Although my clinical practice is largely informed by object relations theory, some of my fundamental values are Lacanian. Primary is the idea of the Subject Caught by the Desire of the Other. If we take seriously the dilemma at the core of this conceptualization, it becomes critically important to try to locate each patient in relation to his or her desires rather than losing him or her behind his or her (or our) ideas of what is or should be wanted. With Greg, who was initially adamant in wanting – and feeling – nothing, locating him in relation to his desire was the salient challenge. When he first presented, he could tell me that he had no feelings or social interest, that he had been bullied as a child and had spent most of his younger years in front of a television screen. He had, however, had that one brief time in his teens at a farm in another state where he had felt like part of a community. This memory was the only bit of data that belied his utterly asocial presentation.

Over time, we could begin to see cracks in this armour but Greg remained convinced that therapy was useless and that change was impossible. As he became embroiled in a series of conflictual relationships with women he experienced as intrusive and controlling, I developed the idea that there were two kinds of people in his world, modelled roughly after himself and his mother. Greg corrected me, however, saying that there was only one type of person. Until then, I had not realized that he saw in himself the terrible narcissism and lack of care he encountered in his mother. Given this model, in which people are driven only by self-interest, what could he make of a therapist who pretends to be interested in *him*? What nefarious purpose might I be serving? He seemed caught between the hope that I *might* be helpful to him in some way, a fear that I might be stupid or deluded (and thereby possibly delude him and leave him ashamed at having been taken in), and the terrible paranoia about bugs and tapes and conspiracies that would envelop him as he left our sessions. Telling me about these fears became a mark of his attempt to not believe in them.

As Greg told me about his early life, I was struck by how alone he had been. His parents were each more solidly married to their work than to one another and he could not recall spending any time together with both parents as a family. His greatest source of comfort had been his nanny, who was let go when Greg reached age five. The following year, when his parents called him in to tell him of their impending divorce, he was frightened because they seemed so much more sombre than when the nanny had been let go. According to his report, however, this change did not really affect him because it merely continued the pattern to which he was accustomed, of spending time with each parent separately.

Considering his early life in relation to milestones never achieved afforded Greg a way of thinking about himself as a real human being embedded in a social context, rather than an automaton with no feelings or interest in other people, or even in learning anything about himself. Such learning, he said, could only bring shame by telling him that there was something others might know that he did not. Over time, I was to learn that his shame was so intense and so easily evoked that any evidence of another perspective was almost intolerable. The shame made it difficult for him to learn anything aside from the myriad facts he acquired alone in his room. His social inhibition had become so severe that it was difficult for Greg to even earn a living. He found himself caught between his shame and impotence at being unable to earn a living and the utter impossibility of facing others enough to be able to seek employment. Even acknowledging a desire as yet unmet seemed too shameful to contemplate such that, in our work together, our conversations tended to circle around in crazy ways, as I became the voice of possibility in relation to his stance of utter hopelessness. Where, then, might be a place where we could stand together?

From a Lacanian perspective, we can all become lost in relation to the Desire of the Other, which holds the possibility of an unlimited jouissance. The challenge is to accept the inevitability of lack – of limit – so that we might be able to recognize and articulate our own particular desire. From this perspective, I try to avoid being caricatured as the One who Knows, so that I might invite the patient to become the Subject of the inquiry. And so, with Greg, I took the position that I had no way of working with him unless there was something on which he wanted to work. For some time, there seemed to be nothing he wanted, and no place where he could locate a desire. We seemed to be at an impasse until one day he spoke about his desire to leave treatment, and I recognized in this a desire that was truly his own.

'Great,' I said. 'That's something we can work on together.' And we did. I helped him find a way out of inpatient treatment, one in which he would have support but also greater autonomy. But then, just as the door was about to close behind him, Greg felt less constrained and was better able to think about what he might want, aside from just leaving. He spoke about his recognition that there were aspects of his treatment that he had not been able to make use of, and wondered whether he might be leaving prematurely. That moment was a crucial one. It marked the beginning of Greg being in charge of his treatment in a way that he could feel and make use of. Subsequently, we learned a great deal about the narrow margins within which he was able to have any hope or pleasure. As he began to work on his own projects, and I learned to stay out of the way, we were able to recognize together patterns that were useful to him in beginning to plan his activities and, eventually, his life.

For Greg, it was extremely useful when I tracked for him his experiences and tried to make sense of them in a developmental context, in part because it invited him to be more curious about his own ideas and feelings. This tracking helped to provide conceptual anchors within which Greg was able to better recognize and understand some of his own difficulties. Much of our early work involved conjectures about what it must have been like for him at various stages of his early life, given the context and characters he described. As we began to build a narrative in which we could locate a child with needs that were not being recognized, and developmental milestones that were not achieved, Greg began to have a sense of himself, not as impossibly flawed but rather as in need of maturation and further development. Learning, then, became less a narcissistic injury and more something that carried the potential for growth, and perhaps even pride, although we could also recognize that real learning for Greg occurred only when he could take in some bit of information and make use of it himself.

Particularly important was the moment when I tracked for him the experience of shame, as a cut breaking into a moment of pleasure or interest. This conceptualization related directly to his own experience such that he began to be intensely curious about shame *as an experience-near phenomena*, an interest he was able to bring into his conversations with peers. He became so preoccupied with the concept that he was able to break through his inhibitions about speaking openly or honestly, and began to engage quite directly in conversations about the experience of shame and its various effects. These conversations attenuated the shame while also inviting greater connection and understanding, helping to repair and strengthen the interpersonal bonds between himself and others.

The capacity to recognize a problem in context has been crucial to breaking into Greg's concrete and universal presumptions of meaning. Much as Apollon, Bergeron and Cantin (2002) describe, a dream can be a pivotal point in working with psychotic patients because the dream can be recognized as one's own production in ways that the symptom cannot, particularly for those who are profoundly paranoid. Greg's dreams helped us to locate him in relation to his fears *and* to his desires. His initial dreams were cloaked and hidden: first, an elaborate desk that belonged to his father with important papers in it; then a dream of a girl who was 'not my Mom' and people in costumes. Then, in the ninth month of treatment, he reports a dream that vivifies his paranoid anxieties.

> I dreamed there was a small nuclear reactor behind the community centre. Everybody said it was safe but I didn't believe them. I did my own calculations and concluded that we needed an additional half inch of steel plating in order to make it safe. Dr E had designed it and I knew she wouldn't admit she had made an error. So I didn't tell anyone but I ordered the steel plates online and I was going to install them. But, in the end, I didn't want to have to explain so I just lay down in my room waiting to die. She was the foremost expert so I knew no one would believe me. I think the idea of no one believing me is related to K [a female patient] not believing me. In the dream, I never see another human being. In the dream, I just walk through the double doors of the Community Centre. I examined the reactor but I didn't touch it; I wouldn't want to get contaminated. It was in a separate outbuilding. Then I went through this dark corridor – the connector – it was very long and no one else was around. I was doing calculations – setting up equations in a notebook – the answers became apparent.

In his associations, he said:

> I felt both afraid but also kind of lethargic and unmotivated. So, even though I had the necessary equipment, it was too much effort to explain and I wanted to avoid a showdown. K said Thursday that she doesn't believe me. I can't blame her because I wouldn't believe me either. I have no credibility. It's frustrating. A lot of effort would be required to convince Dr E that she had made a mistake. The feelings were about a lack of trust. I didn't trust them. I didn't think they would trust me.

Then, a week later, a major turning point came when Greg reported his first dream about me:

> I had a dream about you [he said, with excitement]! We were in your office; it wasn't this office but it was your office. You wanted me to go to this charity dinner for the National Drowning and Maritime Victims Association – NDVMA – and the whole time I felt so guilty because I felt that I failed you. It was in San Diego – it was a long way to go but I wanted to try because I felt so guilty for failing you. You made this PowerPoint presentation – I only looked at the first slide – there was something wrong with it – it didn't work.
>
> The dream was really emotional. I felt bad – it wasn't just guilt. I felt bad because I had the sense that you had no ulterior motives – you really believed that this would be good for me. I really believed your intentions were pure. That made me feel even worse for failing you – failing to learn anything here. It mirrors how I feel in the waking day – It's like I'm not getting it. The presentation was shaped like a hexagon – like that bankrupt solar panel maker – those were in the shape of a hexagon.
>
> I had a false memory Saturday. M told me the title of a movie. I didn't remember the name but I remembered clearly the form of it – it was a noun, a comma and then a descriptive phrase. But when I went back, it wasn't that. It was very troubling. I have such a clear memory but it didn't really happen. I've had a handful of other false memories. I don't like it. I find it very unsettling. I don't like being wrong but these are not opinions, they're factual memories. I might have to rely on other people – I want to at least be intellectually self-sufficient.

In Greg's associations to the dream, we see his difficulty in even considering relying on me, and we also see him grappling with his awareness that he cannot necessarily rely on the products of his own mind. Bion (1977) talks about the importance of bi-nocular perspective. For Greg, this vantage point can only be found by allowing himself to think about my perspective as not only different than his own but also as potentially useful or reliable. He had hoped that by not letting people in he could keep himself safe but now he can see that his isolation feeds his persecution. And yet, how to live in a world with other people remains a dilemma, particularly in relation to his mother, on whom he has a terrible dependence.

For Greg, closeness with another person has involved the threat of being utterly submerged and destroyed: annihilated. His mother – and individuals who reminded him of his mother – were experienced as dangerous objects to avoid or pacify. During the time we worked together, he first avoided his mother entirely but then learned to manage her by literally keeping the telephone at arm's distance when he could not tolerate her speech. There is something about this metaphor, of both needing the connection with the other but also needing to be able to attenuate the contact and control what is taken in and when, that began to figure prominently in our work. There were times when even my acknowledgement of his success could take away the vitality he had managed to build. The ease and speed with which pleasure could be banished was remarkable. Notably, this process is similar in form to the prosody of his experience of shame, the ways in which shame results from disrupted curiosity or pleasure. We learned to recognize that this pattern of disrupted pleasure leading to shame was so pervasive that even positive recognition imposed the Other upon him in ways that could destroy his fragile connection with his own inner pride or pleasure. From that perspective, I had to be able to recognize myself as the well-intentioned but dangerous other of his dream in order to have any idea at all about the terrain in which he needed to learn to navigate.

Greg continued to struggle to discover himself in relation to others without getting lost. Over time, the danger he experienced in relation to maternal figures became less dire and more manageable. He was even able to spend time with his mother without a resurgence of his psychotic symptoms. At one point, he brought in his laptop to play for me a news story that showed how dangerous it can be to trust others. We were able to recognize together how dangerous trust can be and yet how fundamental to living life as a human being. Eventually, Greg was able to secure employment with someone he had known from his college years, someone who had known him when he was functioning well. Finding someone who could have him in mind as the competent, creative highly intelligent young man he was, while also knowing enough about his current challenges to be able to afford him some sense of safety, enabled Greg to finally obtain his wish to leave treatment and, with that, his utter and regressive dependence on his mother.

Our patients invite us into realms of experience that may be similar in some ways to our own but inevitably also differ profoundly. Psychoanalysis affords us a perspective from which to meet in the middle and entertain possibilities in ways that carry the potential for their realization. At best, we are blind companions on a journey and depend on our patients to show us the way. With Greg, being able to be with him and to be like him in some ways but also respectful of the very real differences that separate us helped him to develop conceptual anchors through which to confront his humanity as a social being with feelings and needs, while also recognizing the differences that define his particularity. From this perspective, he was better able to recognize his experience as his own, and to be able to give words to it and thereby to detoxify the terrible fears that initially would entirely envelop him when he would leave my office. Over time, our developing intimacy no longer had to be eradicated by paranoid ideas about what I might be plotting against him. Rather, I could be the misguided but well-intentioned person of his dream, who may not have all the answers but also, just possibly, may not take him over or destroy him. This nascent safety enabled him to build his sense of his own ideas, his own feelings and his own mind, in relation to others that may be similar or different in important ways.

As we ended our work together, Greg's retreats to safety were no longer quite so devastating because they were not so absolutely private. They could be talked about and even joked about within the safety of a relationship that was becoming good enough to negotiate some of the developmental passages that had been foreclosed and abandoned. For Greg, trust was not only elusive – it was highly dangerous. Relying on another person brought him dangerously close to the scenes encoded in memory of utter shame when his interest and affiliative moves had been met by absence or ridicule. The work he had done in treatment, however, helped him to recognize the potency of those old scripts, which afforded him the possibility, at times, of being able to reflect on and work through a difficult moment rather than being utterly immobilized by the fear of encountering it.

At the end of our work together, Greg was no longer the robot who had no interest in feelings and no need of other people but rather a sensitive individual who often found machines more compatible companions. He could acknowledge that he does, indeed, have feelings, and could use those feelings as signals that relay information about his internal states rather than as signs that mark the intrusion of alien external forces. Being able to recognize, albeit in some ways uncomfortably, those qualities he does share with other human beings helped Greg to broaden his sense of himself, his desires and also future possibilities. His increasing ability to tolerate being amongst people who may not be entirely like him but with whom he shares common needs for esteem and affiliation enabled Greg to achieve *his* goal – to be able to go back to work and thus to achieve the independence he had longed for but which, when we met, had been utterly out of reach.

References

Apollon, W., Bergeron, D., Cantin, L., Hughes, R. and Malone, K.R. (2002). *After Lacan: clinical practice and the subject of the unconscious*. Albany: SUNY Press.
Bion, W.R. (1977). *Seven servants*. New York: Jason Aronson.
Birchwood, M., Meaden, A., Trower, P., Gilbert, P. and Plaistow, J. (2000). The power and omnipotence of voices: subordination and entrapment by voices and significant others. *Psychological Medicine*, 30: 337–344.
Carlisle, N. and Rofes, E. (2007). School bullying: do adult survivors perceive long-term effects? *Traumatology*, 13: 16–26.
Charles, M. (2009). Psychosis and the social link: fighting chronicity through human connections. *Bulletin of the Michigan Psychoanalytic Council*, 5: 33–44.
—— (2012). *Working with trauma: lessons from Bion and Lacan*. New York: Jason Aronson.
—— (2013). Bullying and social exclusion: links to severe psychopathology. In M. O'Loughlin (ed.), *Working with children's emotional lives: psychodynamic perspectives on children and schools*. New York: Jason Aronson, pp. 207–226.
—— Clemence, J. and Biel, S. (2011). Psychosis and creativity: managing cognitive complexity on unstructured tasks. In L. DellaPietra (ed.), *Perspectives on creativity*, vol. 2. Newcastle upon Tyne: Cambridge Scholars, pp. 107–122.
—— and O'Loughlin, M. (2013). The complex subject of psychosis. Special issue: Psychosis, M. Charles (ed.). *Psychoanalysis, Culture and Society*, 17(4): 410–421.
Dickerson, S.S. and Kemeny, M.E. (2004). Acute stressors and cortisol responses: a theoretical integration and synthesis of laboratory research. *Psychological Bulletin*, 130: 355–391.
Fonagy, P., Gergely, G., Jurist, E.L. and Target, M. (2002). *Affect regulation, mentalization, and the development of the self*. New York: Other Press.

Gumley, A. (2011). Metacognition, affect regulation and symptom expression: a transdiagnostic perspective. *Psychiatry Research*, 190: 72–78.

Jacobvitz, D. and Hazen, N. (1999). Developmental pathways from infant disorganization to childhood peer relationships. In J. Solomon and C. George (eds), *Attachment Disorganization*. New York. Guilford Press, pp. 127–159.

Krystal, H. (1988). *Integration and self-healing: affect, trauma, alexithymia*. Hillsdale, NJ: The Analytic Press.

Lacan, J. (1972–1973). *The seminar of Jacques Lacan, Book XX*, J.-A. Miller (ed.), B. Fink (trans.). New York: W.W. Norton, 1998.

—— (1974–1975). *Seminar XII: RSI*, C. Gallagher (trans.). Online at www.lacaninireland.com/web/published-works/seminars (accessed 3 July 2016).

—— (1975–1976). *Seminar XII: Joyce and the Sinthome*. C. Gallagher (trans.). Online at www.lacaninireland.com/web/published-works/seminars (accessed 3 July 2016).

Liotti, G. (1999). Disorganization of attachment as a model for understanding dissociative psychopathology. In J. Solomon and C. George (eds), *Attachment disorganization*. New York and London: Guilford Press.

Lysaker, P.H., Erickson, M., Buck, K.D., Procacci, M., Nicolò, G. and Dimaggio, G. (2010). Metacognition in schizophrenia spectrum disorders: methods of assessment and associations with neurocognition and function. *European Journal of Psychiatry*, 24: 220–226.

——, Erickson, M., Ringer, J., Buck, K.D., Semerari, A., Carcione, A. and Dimaggio, G. (2011). Metacognition in schizophrenia: the relationship of mastery to coping, insight, self-esteem, social anxiety, and various facets of neurocognition. *British Journal of Clinical Psychology*, 50: 412–424.

——, Olesek, K.L., Warman, D.M., Martin, J.M., Salzman, A.K., Nicolò, G., Salvatore, G. and Dimaggio, G. (2011). Metacognition in schizophrenia: correlates and stability of deficits in theory of mind and self-reflectivity. *Psychiatry Research*, 190: 18–22.

——, Warman, D.M., Dimaggio, G., Procacci, M., LaRocco, V.A., Clark, L.K., Dike, C.A. and Nicolò, G. (2008). Metacognition in schizophrenia: associations with multiple assessments of executive function. *Journal of Nervous and Mental Disease*, 196: 384–389.

Main, M. and Hesse, E. (1990). Parents' unresolved traumatic experiences are related to infant disorganized/disoriented attachment status: is frightened and/or frightening parental behaviour the linking mechanism? In M. Greenberg, D. Cicchetti and E.M. Cummings (eds), *Attachment in the preschool years: theory, research, and intervention*. Chicago: University of Chicago Press, pp.161–182.

Mayes, L., Fonagy, P. and Target, M. (2007). *Developmental science and psychoanalysis: integration and innovation: developments in psychoanalysis.* London: Karnac.

Myin-Germeys, I. and van Os, J. (2007). Stress-reactivity in psychosis: evidence for an affective pathway to psychosis. *Clinical Psychology Review*, 27: 409–424.

O'Connor, E., Bureau, J.-F., McCartney, K. and Lyons-Ruth, K. (2011). Risks and outcomes associated with disorganized/controlling patterns of attachment at age three years in the National Institute of Health and Human Development Study of Early Child Care and Youth Development. *Infant Mental Health Journal*, 32: 450–472.

Olweus, D. (1994). Annotation: bullying at school – basic facts and effects of a school-based intervention program. *Journal of Child Psychology and Psychiatry*, 35: 1171–1190.

Platt, M. and Freyd, J. (2011). Trauma and negative underlying assumptions in feelings of shame: an exploratory study. *Psychological trauma: theory, research, practice, and policy*. Advance online publication. doi: 10.1037/a0024253.

Schreier, A., Wolke, D., Thomas, K., Horwood, J., Hollis, C., Gunnell, D., Lewis, G., Thomson, A., Zàmmit, S., Duffy, L., Salvi, G. and Harrison, G. (2009). Prospective study of peer victimization in childhood and psychotic symptoms in a nonclinical population at age 12 years. *Archives of General Psychiatry*, 66: 527–536.

Schwandt, M.L., Lindell, S.G., Sjöberg, R.L., Chisholm, K.L., Higley, J.D., Suomi, S.J., Heilig, M. and Barr, C.S. (2010). Gene–environment interactions and response to social intrusion in male and female rhesus macaques. *Biological Psychiatry*, 67: 323–330.

Seikkula, J., Aaltonen, J., Alakare, B., Haarakangas, K. and Keränen, J. (2006). Five-year experience of first-episode nonaffective psychosis in open-dialogue approach: treatment principles, follow-up outcomes, and two case studies. *Psychotherapy Research*, 16: 214–228.

Tangney, J.P., Wagner, P. and Gramzow, R. (1992). Proneness to shame, proneness to guilt, and psychopathology. *Journal of Abnormal Psychology*, 101: 460–478.

Tomkins, S.S. (1962). *Affect. Imagery. Consciousness*, vol. 1. New York: Springer.

—— (1979). Script theory: differential magnification of affects. In H.E. Howe, Jr. and R.A. Dienstbier (eds.), *Nebraska symposium on motivation*, vol. 26. Lincoln: University of Nebraska Press, pp.201–236.

—— (1982). Affect theory. In P. Ekman, W.V. Friesen and P. Ellsworth (eds). *Emotion in the human face*, 2nd ed. Cambridge: Cambridge University Press, pp.353–395.

Van Ijzendoorn, M.H., Schuengel, C. and Bakermans-Kranenburg, M.J. (1999), Disorganized attachment in early childhood: meta-analysis of precursors, concomitants, and sequelae. *Development and Psychopathology*, 11: 225–249.

Vanheule, S. (2011). *The subject of psychosis: a Lacanian perspective*. London: Palgrave.

Winnicott, D.W. (1971). *Playing and reality*. London and New York: Routledge.

Part IV

Internal experience of likeness and difference in the therapist

Chapter 15

An autobiographical account of the analysis of an analyst who endured complex childhood trauma

Johanna Tiemann

As analysands and analysts, we stand at the interface between theory and experience. We are in a unique position to contribute to the articulation of what is effective in analysis by sharing our experiences of being patients in our personal analyses. From the 1950s through the 1970s, a small body of literature was amassed describing such experience (Jung, 1973; Guntrip, 1975; Little, 1981). This practice seemed to have fallen by the wayside until recent years, when there has been an efflorescence of analysts' candid descriptions of their analyses (Stolorow, 2007; Bornstein, 2011; Deutsch, 2011; Dimen, 2011; Levin, 2011; Wixom, 2011). I deeply appreciate the uniqueness of these authors' contributions. They open highly personal discussions of phenomenology that stand in contrast to usual attempts to describe patients' experiences secondhand.

I intend to expand upon this dialogue by placing my analysis within the context of my history of developmental trauma. Presuming that many of us have brought traumatic experiences into our analyses, I am surprised at the lacunae in this literature of descriptions of the impact of trauma and how its aftermath compels its analyst–survivors to find help. Part of the reason we stop short of sharing these highly personal struggles may be that we believe we must present ourselves as masters of our individual psychologies, and trauma is notoriously indomitable. The irony of this pretense is heightened by the fact that one person's analyst is often another analyst's patient. When we write, however, it is easy to fall into the trap of presenting patients' experience of their pathology as categorically different from ours.

I am comforted by Davies' (1999) statement: "The old notion that the analyst, by dint of training analysis, now holds some privileged access to superior mental health seems a form of rather arrogant self-protection and denial." (p.187) Fortified by her statement and Stolorow's (2007) description of his experience of trauma and its crippling effect on his life, I feel motivated to 'come out' as a trauma survivor and contribute to the discussion of the first-hand experience of trauma and its aftermath. I will share some of my history and comment on Stolorow's phenomenological descriptions as they pertain to my own experience.

I was the fourth and last child born into my family. Three of us were born with visible birth defects that promised lifetimes of social, psychological and physical challenges. I shared with my brother the fate of being born with a cleft lip and palate. The most likely cause is that my mother drank too much during her pregnancies.

I believe my particular journey into the realm of enduring trauma began at two months with my first neonatal surgery, which, at that time, was typically performed without anesthesia.[1] I am certain that the assault of surgery on my lip, palate and nose, with its implications for feeding and self-soothing, had considerable detrimental effects. These were compounded by my mother's depressed state following the birth of yet another child with a defect. Early mirroring was compromised by the fact that I wore my defect on my face.

Psychological and neurological sequelae of trauma are mediated by interpersonal matrices. That I was born with a 'flaw' is true. That I came to see myself as inherently flawed and became a profoundly fearful, mistrustful person is the product of the traumatogenic emotional landscape created in my early attachments.

My family environment presented conflicting messages regarding just how different I was from others. My parents' stated philosophy was to raise us as if we were "just normal kids", yet my father told me I would never look normal, the scar on my lip would never go away, and unless I was vigilant about clearly articulating my words, what he termed my "cleft lip and palate speech" would be detectable and repellent. Although I desperately wanted to be normal, my only chance at approaching normality was more surgery, which loomed as a horrifying eventuality. Until I was well into adulthood, my father urged me to have more operations, contemptuously stating that I shouldn't "walk around looking like that." Because there was little room for my feelings about my defect, I came to feel my parents viewed it as their tragedy much more than it was a shared tragedy with me.

My parents' inability to put themselves in my shoes is further illustrated by the following story. The day before surgery, when I was 11, my father drove me to a hospital in New York City. I was shocked and frightened by the atmosphere of the inner-city hospital. I had to share a small room with two other girls; one appeared near death. My father left, and I began to cry. I comforted myself with the knowledge that my mother would be by my side when I awakened after surgery the next morning, but when I awoke no one was there. A nurse told me my mother had been, but departed. She left me a turkey wishbone as a present. It would be three days before I received my sole visit from my family during my five-day hospitalization. They telephoned once or twice. I dialed their number over and over but could not reach them because I did not know about area codes.

I agree with Stolorow's (2007) view of developmental trauma in which he describes it as emerging from an intersubjective context in which there is a breakdown of the child-caregiver system of mutual regulation, especially in relation to painful affect. "From recurring experiences of malattunement, the child acquires the unconscious conviction that unmet developmental yearnings and reactive painful feeling states are manifestations of a loathsome defect or an inherent inner badness." (p.4) Early medical interventions set the stage for my pathology, but the actual catalyst was the depressive, threatening, intersubjective field in which I grew up. Perceiving my parents as condemning my inner and outer flaws led to my conviction that I was wholly repugnant.

Nevertheless, as a young child, leaving my mother induced in me an engulfing sadness. I would desperately cling to her because her presence sustained my very being. As I grew older, my parents' continuous scorn for my persistent difficulties separating led me to condemn myself for my not-yet-understood need for a sustaining attachment. I was very proud when I taught myself to feign indifference in the face of my mother's comings and goings. Underlying my outward show of apathy regarding her absence was profound panic and pain. I hoped I would outgrow these feelings, but, when I still felt devastated when leaving my mother as a teenager, I began to fear that I would always feel thus.

My profound sense of defectiveness was reinforced at school where I endured gazes that felt like they were filled with repulsion, questions about what happened to my lip, and constant teasing and physical threats from the meaner kids. As I grew older, I could not accept the idea that people did not focus on my scar and misshapen upper lip. This self-perception would never alter. To this day, my misshapen lip is always the dominant feature I see in my reflection.

When I left my parents' home to go to college, I felt the full force of my inability to sustain a sense of internal coherence on my own. I experienced being thrust into a dangerous world with no means of survival. I reacted with a full mind–body protest – a continuous state of panic. I had a terrifying feeling of being entirely untethered, as if doomed to float endlessly in absolute isolation. Unable to contain my fear and pain, I wept uncontrollably. Feeling utterly alone, I regarded the other students as hostile strangers contemptuous of my struggle. Similarly to Stolorow (p.14), I was certain they were incapable of understanding my emotional state; after all, they were 'normal.' In spite of clear indications to the contrary, I continued to believe my mother would rescue me if only I could make her understand that I felt as if my line to vital oxygen had been cut, and that I was certain I could not breathe on my own.

With enormous effort, I was able to achieve some semblance of normalcy and fulfil academic obligations. My hope that I just had a bad case of homesickness soon proved ill-founded. During my second year, I entered a hypomanic state culminating in a defining moment of my life. While attending a concert, my mind wandered to the fact that it was the birthday of my childhood friend Ginny, who had recently committed suicide. I noticed a woman across the hall that resembled Ginny. She seemed to be looking at me. Convincing myself she was Ginny's ghost, I became terrified. My panic surged out of control when I realized that if I actually were seeing a ghost, there was no one to tell, no one would believe me. Suddenly, I had the horrifying sensation of my will being taken over, or hijacked, by another mind that urged me to scream, or jump off the balcony. I feared I might be possessed. I since have learned that this psychological event is called a "passive influence/interference experience" (Kluft, 1987; Putnam, 1997), now considered a dissociative phenomenon.

For decades I struggled with this other mind that seemed to live side by side with the mind I recognized as my own, goading me towards self-destruction, generally by violent or humiliating means. When triggered, the other mind scanned the environment for the information needed to generate a worst-case scenario, then compelled me to act. The list of ideas that would come to me was very long, including screaming obscenities, jumping out of windows, and various forms of self-mutilation and self-humiliation. Each time the other mind was activated, it was as if it were the first time, fresh in its horror. I felt helpless against its power. Although I never enacted the ideas of the 'other mind', I withdrew from numerous activities that triggered such assaults.

I sought therapy several times during this long span of time, but after many disappointments I came to feel that there was no hope for me. After moving to New York City, I was referred by a friend to my seventh therapist, whom I would come to call "my analyst". Upon meeting her, I knew she was different. I perceived that my revelation to her of my inner world neither frightened her nor made her distance herself from me. Her relativistic orientation, coupled with an empathic listening stance, created an interpersonal ambience that came to be safe enough. Her approach was in stark contrast to other therapists who attempted, early in treatment, to challenge my 'illogical', contradictory, trauma-generated perspectives, forcing me to embrace the 'truth' embedded in their alleged objective reality. For example, regarding my humiliation about the scar on my lip, therapists have said something like: "I never would have guessed that you had a cleft lip. I don't see anything." This kind of intervention left me feeling further humiliated, misunderstood and abandoned. This new therapist's responses to me, emphasizing mirroring, validation, holding and, eventually, mutuality (Long, 2007), indicated she knew how desperately I needed to have my suffering taken seriously.

After years, I believe I have found what Stolorow calls a "relational home" with my analyst. Let me share with you my experience of this home and its function for me. In my solitary experience of the full affective burden of trauma, which I have come to equate with my dissociative moments, I feel absolutely isolated. I do not believe I can be joined in the horror that dominates my affectivity. I am as alone as I imagine I will be in death. I discovered in my analyst an accepting other who listens, takes me seriously and genuinely attempts to understand me. I feel I am present in her mind, and that an aspect of my relationship with her has taken up residence within her. When I am overtaken by unbearable feelings, if I can find my way home, I experience her as sharing the burden. When I cannot feel my connection with her, I move into the painful dissociated state that I described, alternating with an experience of being completely shut down and robotic. I feel like my very life has been drained from me. Reanimation occurs once again when I feel deeply understood and accepted by her, and my affectivity becomes reintegrated into my sense of existence. I feel accompanied through life and develop a sense of belonging, safety and calm.

While on internship, before my analysis had revealed my own traumatic past, I was assigned an intake with a homeless man. Shortly after beginning the session, he indicated our meeting was a waste of time. "Unless you have picked food out of a garbage can, you will never understand me." Taken off guard, I said nothing, but thought, "Of course I can understand you. You just have to help me to." I was concerned about completing the intake, but felt that the whole undertaking was at best pointless and, at worst, experienced as dehumanizing by him. I finished the meeting as soon as I could, but ruminated on his statement and my inability to come up with a response. I thought of clever ways I might have engaged him. For example, I could have asked, "Does that mean that *anyone* who picked food out of the garbage can understand you?" or "If I went down to the street right now and ate from a garbage can, would I be able to understand you?" As I thought about this vignette recently, I realized my reaction was self-protective on many levels. When face to face with someone who had lived on the streets, I actually brought very little to the table in terms of life experience to aid in vicarious introspection. Relative to this man, I was a privileged person. I felt guilty and helpless, and like a bad therapist. My attempt to pull myself out of these bad feelings involved outsmarting the man – picking apart his logic, showing him he was wrong. In my self-absorption, I missed his primary communication: 'You cannot understand me.' Might I have come to understand him? I think that at the time it would have been very difficult for me because I still had not understood the full weight of my own traumatic past. I now know that it is not by dint of being traumatized that an analyst can understand another's trauma. Rather, it is only after the trauma has been worked through that the analyst's knowledge and experience can come into positive play in the treatment of a traumatized patient.

In his critique of Stolorow, Philip Ringstrom (2010) voices concern that Stolorow ennobles trauma by suggesting it guides the traumatized individual to a morally superior existence. I believe ennobling trauma only occurs when the victim does not fully grasp the implications of his or her victimization. Before my analysis, I believed my capacity to endure suffering made me stronger and wiser than other young women.[2] While they were busy worrying about hair and makeup, I pondered the meaning of life, art and music. This grandiose vision of myself allowed me to hold on to a primordial tie to what I regarded as my parents' tough stock and bolstered my denial of actual victimization by them. This survival strategy provided a refuge from the pain of my actual experience. Until I could tolerate the knowledge of my victimization and traumatic past, I was disempowered. I remained in isolation, living out the limited view of myself that evolved from my early attachments. I came to see that my suffering did not entitle me to more respect. I learned that the facts of my life story were actually quite humbling. They are a cause for mourning of time lost in suffering and loneliness. Coming to terms with these truths has made me more generous, more compassionate towards the suffering of others, and keenly aware that we are all more similar than different. Life can be joyous, but it surely is difficult for everyone, whether apparently normal, or not.

Notes

1 To protect the child, neonatal surgery was often performed without anaesthesia (Anand and Hickey, 1987). The prevailing theory, now strongly refuted, was that the newborn's brain is not yet wired to sense pain.

2 Alfred Adler's formulation of organ inferiority and the inferiority complex contribute to the understanding of my state of mind at this time. These words in particular describe my situation: 'The material of life has been constantly bent on reaching a plus from a minus situation' (Adler, 1964, p.97).

References

Adler, A. (1964). *Social interest: a challenge to mankind*. New York: Putnam.
Anand, K.J.S. and Hickey, P.R. (1987). Pain and its effects in the human neonate and fetus. *The New England Journal of Medicine*, 317(21): 1321–1329.
Atkinson, J. (2002). *Trauma trails, recreating songlines: the transgenerational effects of trauma on Indigenous Australians*. North Melbourne: Spinifex Press.
Bornstein, M.B. (2011). A psychoanalyst's story: a simple discovery after years of searching. *Psychoanalytic Inquiry*, 31(6): 554–565.
Davies, J. (1999). Getting cold feet, defining 'safe-enough' borders: disintegration in the analyst's experience. *The Psychoanalytic Quarterly*, 68: 184–208.
Deutsch, R.A. (2011). A voice lost, a voice found: after the death of the analyst. *Psychoanalytic Inquiry*, 31(6): 536–542.
Dimen, M. (2011). Lapsus linguae, or a slip of the tongue? A sexual violation in an analytic treatment and its personal and theoretical aftermath. *Contemporary Psychoanalysis*, 47: 35–79.
Guntrip, H. (1975). My experience of analysis with Fairbairn and Winnicott. *International Review of Psycho-Analysis*, 2: 145–156.
Jung, C. (1973). *Memories, dreams, reflections*, rev. ed., A. Jaffé (ed.). New York: Pantheon.
Kluft, R.P. (1987). First rank symptoms as a diagnostic clue of multiple personality disorder. *American Journal of Psychiatry*, 144: 293–298.
Levin, C.B. (2011). Soft assembly: expanding the field of therapeutic actions in (my training) analysis. *Psychoanalytic Inquiry*, 31(6): 570–583.
Little, M. (1981). *Transference neurosis and transference psychosis*. Northvale, NJ: Jason Aronson.
Long, S.W. (2007). A relational perspective on working with dying patients in a nursing home setting. In B. Willock, L.C. Bohn and R.C. Curtis (eds), *On Deaths and Endings*. New York: Routledge, pp.237–246.
Putnam, F.W. (1997). *Dissociation in children and adolescents*. New York: Guilford Press.
Ringstrom, P.A. (2010). Trauma and human existence: autobiographical, psychoanalytic, and philosophical reflections by Robert Stolorow. *Psychoanalytic Psychology*, 27: 241–249.
Stolorow, R.D. (2007). *Trauma and human existence*. New York: The Analytic Press.
Wixom, J. (2011). Just do it. *Psychoanalytic Inquiry*, 31(6): 543–549.

Chapter 16

Same old story?
Consistency and change in the analyst's work over time

Michael Stern

Being an analyst has never been easy. Intensive training, scrutinizing supervision, personal analysis, institute politics, long, lonely hours and the responsibility inherent in the endeavour – these have been some of the challenges facing analytic practitioners. Historically, the analyst's role was defined to a considerable degree by restrictions and limitations: 'We are obliged to sharply curtail the instinctual gratifications permissible in our interactions with patients ... and to sustain a genuine neutrality toward whatever each analysand brings forth, regardless of our personal preferences, ethics, and values' (Abend, 1986, p.564). But once one was declared a psychoanalyst, one was bestowed a reassuring authority. Fully analysed, properly supervised and faithful to theoretical purity, the analyst's personal life could comfortably move to a fairly anonymous background. This is no longer the case. As conceptualization of the therapeutic process changed in the direction of recognizing interpersonal, relational and intersubjective influences, the analyst's space became more relevant, creating a need for ongoing self-observation.

When experienced therapists write about their work, they almost invariably state that as time went on they became more comfortable and self-confident. It's a reassuring self-assessment. We settle on a way of being and working that allows us to feel balanced and productive. We learn a skill and, as we apply it over years of practice, we stamp it with our identity that in itself keeps evolving. The following are some factors that, based on my experience, affect one's work over time.

Personal and professional identity

That people change over time is one of the basic premises of psychoanalysis and psychotherapy. Through psychosexual, developmental and relational stages, analysts have seen their patients as ever evolving, developing and maturing. Recognition of the analyst as a living, breathing person has certainly grown, but analysts still struggle with the question as to how their personal lives affect their work and, therefore, how much they should, or can, leave outside the consulting room.

Analysts do not arrive at their careers as blank screens. We come to analytic training with fairly well-developed beliefs about what matters in life, a kind of moral and ethical map that guides us as individuals and gradually as analysts

(Hagman, 2000, p.69). This map developed in relationships with caretakers, was affected by family dynamics, and fine tuned in social interactions. It defines the meaning of caring, the understanding of personal responsibility, the boundaries of right and wrong. It offers a personal and professional anchor, yet may continue to shift as the practitioner goes through life, moulded by personal, interpersonal and social influences. Life events, maturation, aging and social changes inevitably impact practitioners' views of life and of what makes it work, both for themselves and for their patients. Though analysts may wish to adhere consistently to particular theoretical and practical guidelines, their use of them is bound to be affected by the state of their lives.

There is tension between this individuality and the historical emphasis on psychoanalytic rules and technique. In my case, psychoanalytic training was originally provided by well-informed, classically trained analysts, many arriving as refugees from Nazi Germany. They offered a rich, textured, but singular frame of reference that I found difficult to apply to all the people I was working with, especially in a cultural milieu that was quite different from the theory's European origins. Issues that I considered critical to meaningful living, to personal responsibility and commitment to the common good, which were woven early on into my familial and social fabric, had no easy access to the kind of interventions I was taught to provide.

Even as alternative theoretical and practical approaches became available, the internalized attentiveness to what a good analyst should *not* do made going out on a limb, following my own intuition, taking a chance, a guilt ridden, often secretive occurrence. This is, of course, not to say that being guided by theory impedes good, creative practice. Faced with the ambiguities of our work, clear, workable standards offer affirmation and reassurance. But theoretical protection comes at a price – a greater concern and worry about 'doing it wrong'. Psychoanalysis as a discipline has never looked kindly on deviations from prescribed rules and practices. Regardless of ongoing changes in theory, the field has a propensity to view currently held positions as requiring strict adherence. But in a field in which facts are few, theory is always in danger of being wrong, even disastrously so. I still flinch at the way I dealt, thankfully many years ago, with devastated families of schizophrenic teenagers. Armed with the then accepted theory of the schizophrenogenic mother, I listened for and naturally found the many flaws, mistakes and errors committed by caretakers.

In what applies to all theories, Levenson (2008) wrote: 'Psychoanalytic positions usually begin as clinical innovation. Analysts see a new way of working that enlivens therapy ... but what begins as clinical innovation often ends in dogma' (p.91). Commitment to a particular approach may be so strong that, as Cooper (2010) noted, 'Some patients complain that the analyst loves his technique more than he loves his patient' (p.372). Poland (2006) pointed to defensive misuses of theory in efforts to ward off anxieties associated with living life immersed in the lives of others.

The field has certainly changed. 'This is no longer your mother's psychoanalysis' (Lionells, 2005). Adjustments to the times have been made. But the tendency to imagine a virtual supervisor looking over one's shoulders continues long after one has completed formal training. Is a given intervention legitimate? Is this too much self-disclosure? Am I imposing my own values? What eventually replaces such strict oversight is more complex self-evaluation, affected by one's ability to move the patient closer to an authentic life and by the therapist's own proximity to personal integration and fulfilment. The seasoned analyst can then exercise greater freedom in moving away from the script. A senior Freudian analyst related an incident in which a young male patient obligingly spoke, session after session, of his relationship with his mother. Recognizing the obsessionally compliant nature of the reporting, the analyst finally erupted 'Mother, mother, mother. That's all I hear about!' – not the kind of intervention beginning analysts would bring to supervision.

The analyst's personal life

Over the years, analysts inevitably go through changes that profoundly affect their lives. Among the more dramatic, cited in the literature, are their personal analyses (Levine, 2009), pregnancy, relocation (Sherby, 2005), serious illness (Colson, 1995; Buechler, 2009; Pizer, 2009), divorce (Basescu, 2009), immigration and aging. All require an emotional rebalancing while maintaining a steady hand in addressing patients' needs. Therapists have struggled with related issues of self-disclosure and its unintentional consequences. What often emerges, even in recently published papers, is a tension between the classical expectation of non-disclosure and a realization that many of the therapist's life events become quite obvious pretty quickly. Therapist and patient may informally conspire to ignore their recognition, but only the most self-absorbed or impaired individuals will fail to recognize pregnancy or significant illness for long.

There are developments in a therapist's life whose impact is less dramatic yet more lasting. Little has been written about the impact of family and, particularly, of guiding one's own children through struggles often similar to those of patients. (This is one area in which the perceived danger of self-disclosure may create somewhat of a taboo, e.g., not wearing wedding bands, no family pictures in the office, etc.) And yet, years of parenting leave their mark. At the very least, one learns humility and caution in one's predictive ability, in one's accuracy in assessing another person's potential and psychological resourcefulness.

I found that being a clinician and parent informed both experiences. Clinical training made me a more patient listener, not so quick to jump in with solutions or to rescue either patient or child. Being a parent taught added respect for the creative resilience of people, a reminder that father/therapist does not always know best. I have learned that though some opportunities for intervention are better than others, one rarely gets only one chance to make a point, and that even if acknowledgement is slow in coming, good, caring input within an ongoing trusting relationship is usually internalized and integrated.

With successive children we become more flexible, less alarmed by minor crises, less fearful of expressions of anger and aggression, more reliant on what we have seen and done before, and more humble as we allow ourselves to be inspired by each child's uniqueness. I believe the same thing happens in regard to patients as we see more and more of them. We offer them the balanced perspective they lack as they enter therapy. We are less impressed with tantrums, more immune to manipulation, but also more hopeful and optimistic than they can be at the moment.

Though personal crises may temporarily constrict the analyst's participation in the analytic space and reduce flexibility and resilience, life experience may provide tools to better withstand such impact. We become better transferrential objects in that we can tolerate being seen as bad and ugly while containing our defensiveness. We can be better than we are elsewhere. A colleague recounted an exchange with an adoring female patient. The woman repeatedly indicated her admiration for his smarts, skills, personality and looks, to which he finally responded: 'Yes, my wife says the same thing ... about her analyst.'

In the theoretical shifts of recent years the concept of enactment has been at centre stage. Sometimes defined as the more sophisticated cousin of acting out, the concept shines the light on the inner machinations of the analyst, and specifically on ways in which his or her efforts to maintain the frame are challenged by his or her needs and wants. This has not made the analyst's life easier. Chused and Raphling (1992) suggest that attention to the analyst's unconscious motivation resulted in today's analysts no longer having the same confidence in the correctness of their interpretations or their theoretical assumptions as did their predecessors (p.90). Mitchell (2000) addressed this problem in writing about love: 'Part of the analyst's responsibility is to participate in and enjoy that love while it seems facilitative of the analytic process, but not to enjoy that love so much that it becomes a vehicle for the analyst's own pleasure in a way that occludes his focus on the patient's well being' (p.139). Early in my work I saw a young woman, only slightly younger than me, an aspiring actress, whose transferrential contempt and disdain were relentless. She saw me as a dull, unfashionable bore who had probably never in his life been to the theatre. I soldiered on bravely, withstanding assault after fierce assault. I flew to England for a weekend, then, during my first Monday session, as my patient announced her next audition, I could not resist dropping, in a most nonchalant manner, 'Oh yes, I saw it in London last night.' How sweet it was! Looking back, I suspect that with more experience I could have resisted this blatant attempt to be seen as cool and sophisticated. I may be more secure and comfortable with where I am and better poised to see through my patient's pretences.

Aging

Experience comes with age, and the analyst's age is bound to be a factor in the course of treatment. How can it not, considering that the therapeutic instrument, at least in contemporary psychoanalysis, is always the person of the analyst? Hirsch (1993) addressed age as it may affect countertransference enactments, pointing to changes in perceptions, needs and notions of helpfulness. As a young analyst, it was impossible for him to put aside his romantic interest in young female patients, or to not be disappointed when such interest was not coming from them. While awareness of sexual attraction thankfully remains part of one's experience over time, it is increasingly accompanied by parental protectiveness and a richer appreciation of life's possibilities at any given age. I am currently working with two middle-aged women who are engaged in illicit extramarital affairs. While in the past I would have been more distressed by their 'breaking the frame', and possibly more concerned with saving their marriages, I can now see the fuller picture of unfulfilled needs, fear of unhappy aging and creative individual choices. I can better see their courage in admitting failure and taking responsibility for it, and am more optimistic that whatever direction their significant relationships take they will be all right. I can create a more confident distance between my own life and theirs, thus allowing for a genuinely accepting attitude.

At the same time, as one ages, working with younger patients may create a set of challenges. Ruderman (2002), writing about analysts reaching middle-age, pointed to 'envy in the countertransference, an envy associated, in part, with the therapist's mourning for lost or absent opportunities for gratification in her past life' (p.498). Longevity in practice has its dark side. 'Experience can improve the way in which people work, but ... one of the dangers that lies in wait for older analysts is that of believing, given their long experience, that in their professional life they know all there is to know' (Quinodoz, 2010, p.177). 'Analyst and patient alike can retreat from the daunting uncertainty of new and spontaneous interpersonal relatedness by viewing each other, over extended periods of time, in the familiar safety of mutually agreed-upon transference–countertransference understandings' (Cooper, 2010, p.377). Paradoxically, adds Cooper, an experienced analyst is more vulnerable to that danger as he has become acculturated and committed to the method.

Balancing who one is with how one works

No one can operate without theory. Cooper (1986) recommended 'that we know what our theory is, how it suits our character, and how each theory limits us in some direction' (p.584). A universal theory applicable to all treatment events (and all analysts) is not yet at hand, he noted. Analysts may experience conflicting desires of meaningful connectedness versus remaining safely hidden. In the end, choice of theoretical orientation may be affected by the ways these needs are balanced.

Another aspect of the problem rests on what Abend (1986) described as 'the residual propensity we seem to have for unconscious narcissistic fantasies of perfection, with which we invest others and toward which we continue to aspire, since derivatives of them contribute to the formation of our personal analytic ideals and idealizations' (p.565) and 'the secret, irrational, but persistent conviction that each of us alone feels these burdens far more than is proper, and far more than do our colleagues, although we regularly reassure one another that, on the contrary, these feelings are shared by all of us' (pp.564–565). (See also Morrison, 2008, on the analyst's shame.) 'We endure a strain in our work that takes its toll. We demand a self-discipline that few other professions can match. The analytic role at times is experienced as a straightjacket from which we long to escape' (p.257). 'Constant feeding leads to constant depletion' (Tallmer, 1992, p.393). Escape is not easy.

Efforts to find relief from these constraints have all too often led to professional and ethical violations. Experience does not always offer a good resolution. As we grow older, 'Not only do we become wiser, but probably our regressive tendencies also increase' (Laine, 2007, p.1180).

A common thread in writings of analysts who address changes over the years is a shift 'from analyst-technician to analyst-person' (Kremer, 1981) and from externally provided theory to greater reliance on informed personal engagement. Eagle (2001) highlighted 'effective presence' and 'therapeutic interaction' (p.47) as increasingly more central to his work than making the unconscious conscious. 'Insight is not necessarily the result of interpretation but may just as likely follow on empathic listening and understanding or a corrective emotional experience' (p.49). Writing about her work following illness, Buechler (2009) described it as 'a journey toward less reliance on intellect and insight and greater trust in an emotionally meaningful exchange' (p.67). Pine (2006) wrote about starting with the trio of neutrality, abstinence and relative anonymity, which sets a baseline from which he varies and to which he may or may not return. 'It depends on my judgment, a judgment made cautiously and backed by considerable experience and thought about what will be most useful in this particular treatment' (p.2). Others describe lowering unrealistic expectations.

Analysing responses of older analysts to a questionnaire, Tallmer (1992) found that 75 per cent indicated fewer ambitions of structural change, shifting instead to helping people live with greater comfort. With some unease, several respondents admitted being more discriminating in the kind of pathology they accept into their practices. Others indicated a degree of burnout, which Farber and Heifetz (1982) saw as a consequence of the non-reciprocated attentiveness, giving and responsibility demanded by the therapeutic relationship, as well as overwork, isolation and discouragement as a function of the slow pace of work. Cooper (1986) noted a threat of shifting from early excessive curative zeal to later excessive therapeutic nihilism. Among the tools for avoiding burnout, prescriptions of vacations, peer reviews, shorter days etc. were commonly suggested. More creatively, Pizer (2005) advocated bringing into sessions something outside one's particular analytic school or identity, such as a passionate interest that 'brings air, texture, and dimensionality into the enclosed space in which two people are engaged' (p.60). O'Leary (2008) wrote about the need to go beyond purely analytic technique, employing alternative resources such as spirituality and exercise to benefit both patient and analyst. Going a step further, Schachter and Kachele (2007) proposed nuanced use of explicit support, consolation, suggestion, persuasion and advice – techniques used in healing across many ages and societies – be added to traditional psychoanalytic treatment even though they are inconsistent with neutrality.

In the end, it's not the same old story. We may or may not get better over the years (see Clement, 1994) but in many significant ways we change. We are likely to develop a way of working that fits our personality, loosen theoretical guidelines and be more tolerant of failed therapies. At some point, we may reach a more or less stable plateau, a 'good enough' professional identity. In the process, if we allow it, we open to new possibilities just as much as we encourage our patients to do, and get to utilize personal resources that make our work uniquely individual.

References

Abend, S.M. (1986). Countertransference, empathy, and the analytic ideal: the impact of life stresses on analytic capability. *Psychoanalysis Quarterly*, 55: 563–575.
Basescu, C. (2009). Shifting ground: the therapist's divorce and its impact on her life and work. *Contemporary Psychoanalysis*, 45: 44–64.
Buechler, S. (2009). Love will do the thing that's right. *Psychoanalytic Dialogues*, 68: 63–68.
Chused, J.F. and Raphling, D.L. (1992). The analyst's mistakes. *Journal of the American Psychoanalytic Association*, 40: 89–116.
Clement, P.W. (1994). Quantitative evaluation of 26 years of private practice. *Professional Psychology: Research and Practice*, 25(2): 173–176.
Colson, D.B. (1995). An analyst's multiple losses: countertransference and other reactions. *Contemporary Psychoanalysis*, 31: 459–478.
Cooper, A.M. (1986). Some limitations on therapeutic effectiveness: the 'burnout syndrome' in psychoanalysis. *Psychoanalysis Quarterly*, 55: 576–598.
Cooper, S.H. (2010). An elusive aspect of the analyst's relationship to the transference. *Psychoanalysis Quarterly*, 79: 349–380.
Eagle, M.N. (2001). Reflections of a psychoanalytic therapist. In M.R. Goldfried (ed.), *How therapists change: personal and professional reflections*. Washington: American Psychological Association, pp.55–66.
Farber, B.A. and Heifetz, L.J. (1982). The process and dimensions of burnout in psychotherapists. *Professional Psychology*, 13(2): 293–301.
Hagman, G. (2000). The analyst's relation to the good. *Journal of the American Academy of Psychoanalysis*, 28: 63–82.
Hirsch, I. (1993). Countertransference enactments and some issues related to external factors in the analyst's life. *Psychoanalytic Dialogues*, 3: 343–366.
Kremer, M.W. (1981). The human dimension in psychoanalytic practice. *Journal of the American Academy of Psychoanalysis*, 9: 324–327.
Laine, A. (2007). On the edge: the psychoanalyst's transference. *International Journal of Psychoanalysis*, 88: 1171–1183.
Levenson, E. (2008). In search of the person in the patient: an interpersonal perspective on roles in the psychoanalytic relationship. *Psychoanalytic Dialogues*, 18: 89–94.
Levine, L. (2009). Transformative aspects of our own analyses and their resonance in our work with our patients. *Psychoanalytic Dialogues*, 19: 454–462.
Lionells, M. (2005). The person of the analyst: past and present (a plea for self-perception). *American Journal of Psychoanalysis*, 65: 327–332.
Mitchell, S.A. (2000). *Relationality: from attachment to intersubjectivity*. Hillsdale, NJ: The Analytic Press.
Morrison, A.P. (2008). The analyst's shame. *Contemporary Psychoanalysis*, 44: 65–82.

O'Leary, J. (2008). Putting it together while falling apart: a personal view on depression. *Contemporary Psychoanalysis*, 44: 531–550.
Pine, F. (2006). If I knew then what I know now: theme and variations. *Psychoanalytic Psychology*, 23: 1–7.
Pizer, B. (2005). Passion, responsibility, and 'wild geese': creating a context for the absence of conscious intentions. *Psychoanalytic Dialogues*, 15: 57–84.
Pizer, S.A. (2009). Love and existential exposure. *Psychoanalytic Dialogues*, 19: 80–86.
Poland, W.S. (2006). The analyst's fears. *American Imago*, 63: 201–217.
Quinodoz, D. (2010). *Growing old: a journey of self-discovery*. New York: Routledge.
Ruderman, E.G. (2002). As time goes by: life experiences and their effects on analytic technique. *Psychoanalytic Inquiry*, 22: 495–509.
Schachter, J. and Kachele, H. (2007). The analyst's role in healing. *Psychoanalytical Psychology*, 24: 429–444.
Sherby, L.B. (2005). Self-disclosure: seeking connection and protection. *Contemporary Psychoanalysis*, 41: 499–517.
Tallmer, M. (1992). The aging analyst. *Psychoanalytic Review*, 79: 381–404.

Chapter 17

The analyst as patient
Working from both sides of the divide

Emily Fucheck

We therapists do not often publicly discuss our experiences as patients. Notable exceptions include Margaret Little (1990), Harry Guntrip (1975), Sue Elkind (1996) and, most recently, Muriel Dimen (2011). These experiences affect more than our day-to-day lives; they also deeply affect our work. Our choice of therapist may have more of an influence in our consulting rooms than any other training element, including supervision, courses and fieldwork. The intimacy of the therapeutic dyad is so close to our relationships with our most primitive objects that it cannot help but be fundamental in forming our professional identities. At the same time, we don't often speak with other professionals, with the exception of our closest friends and colleagues, about our therapeutic experiences – particularly difficult ones – and we don't have a great deal of amassed literature about the effect that our experience as patients has on our understanding of ourselves and our theory of how our work is done.

I recently presented a spoken version of this chapter to a group of colleagues at a professional conference. I was overwhelmed with the response. Clinician after clinician came up to me to describe his or her own experience as patient, many of them traumatic, and thanked me for providing an opening for public discussion. I wished for a tape recorder to record as many stories as possible to begin sifting through the narratives that were being offered.

Many clinicians commented on how brave they felt I was to be presenting this paper. 'Were you afraid to be presenting this to a group of professional colleagues?' 'Perhaps it helps that this conference is occurring so far from home?' The conference was literally on the other side of the world from my own analyst and training institute, although there were colleagues from home in attendance. Those questions intrigued me as much as their narratives. What is the risk for us when discussing an experience as ubiquitous as our own personal therapies? Why is such discussion so frequently seen as 'outing' our analysts? The following is the presentation, followed by thoughts about why it received these responses, and what all this might suggest for future exploration.

Presentation

'You're not listening to me!! Why do you keep interrupting me with your thoughts when I keep telling you it's not what I want?!! You won't let me stay in my own experience, my own thought!' I listened to my patient, Annie, angrily express these feelings with horror and a clenching of my stomach. This was exactly what I had accused my analyst of less than a year before, marking an impasse that we never overcame. As this was not the first time Annie had struggled with this experience of me, I was scared and very confused by the parallel. I had felt so sure my analyst had failed me – was I failing Annie? I didn't think so ... But she, *clearly*, disagreed. Well, I thought, I must dig deeply to try to remain open to what was happening between the two of us. And so we continued what would remain an intensely difficult four months that left both of us with a sense of how fragile our connection can be. It also upended my concept of how my experience as a patient had shaped my analytic identity.

I arrived at this place with Annie after ending my own five-year treatment, four of which were while completing my Certification in Psychoanalysis. Things seemed to be going so well. I had been 'on the couch', using that space for reverie and deep reflection. I felt my analyst was a guide, collaborator and truly empathic listener. I trusted his opinion and allowed my own perspective to be swayed. At times, I took on his view of my life. It felt very relieving to me as I did not entirely trust my experience and found myself again and again looking for the wise parent to guide me into safer waters. He seemed more than willing to accommodate this need, with minimal questioning. Simultaneously, he encouraged me to develop my own voice, but, at times, stridently expressed his own. Certain people in my life were couched in unforgiving terms. I was so relieved to hear him call these people out, label them for their bad behaviours and numerous injuries to me and suggest that I was free to leave these relationships. I had never allowed myself this freedom, to just call someone a 'bad apple' and consider leaving him or her. This freedom allowed me to move deeply into my personal pain, sadness, abandonment, with him as facilitator and empathizer. My hurts seemed to resonate with him and this, too, was comforting.

I felt very close to him and believed I could say anything I needed to. I was confident in the treatment and in his investment in and, especially, protection of me. As I understood later, the need to believe in the other's investment in and protection of me is related to core areas of conflict that had not yet been consciously experienced in my work with him. My fantasy about his investment and protection of me was seriously challenged at one point when I decided to take a class he was teaching at our Institute.

Training analysts often teach classes. Should one's training analyst be teaching, it is Institute policy to give the candidate the choice to take the class with his/her analyst or do the work as independent study. I chose to take my analyst's class. We had been working together for some time and I felt secure in my ability to tell him whatever I needed to, and our ability to openly discuss what might come up. We didn't process this decision much in our work. We didn't discuss the class itself (its content and the way it would unfold).

I found myself completely unprepared for the fact that my analyst started the course discussing case material – not mine, but that of another patient. Suddenly,

I was confronted with the possibility, through his description of his counter transference, that he might not feel as invested in or protective of me as my fantasy had encouraged. It felt as though he had not taken care of me well, which may have had some validity, as he had not encouraged exploration of this upcoming classroom experience. Perhaps I was also surprised by my strong reaction to hearing him discuss another patient, as I had felt so secure in my ability to be his student. I felt painfully vulnerable and became preoccupied with his description of his patient. He was very candid about his reactions and thoughts, some of them negative, in a way that he was never candid in our sessions. This was, of course, understandable, but was still an emotionally overwhelming experience as it left me wondering what he 'really' thought of me. I think I was suddenly very, very aware of how little we had discussed the course. For some reason, the fact that *he* didn't prepare me for his counter-transference discussion left me feeling neglected and unprotected. I imagined that he had not thought much about me in the role of his patient taking his class, but was instead thinking of me only as a student. I noticed *I* had not thought to explore the class more deeply in our sessions. I was disappointed and confused by the fact that he had not made sure that I was aware of what he would be discussing, how the class was to be structured, and to leave sufficient space and time to really think ahead and process this information so that I could decide if I wanted to take the class. In hindsight, I was cavalier, unaware of my transference and some core themes that would be triggered, such as competition with my analytic 'siblings', desire to be exempt from any but the most positive countertransference, to be cared for/protected when I myself might not even know that I needed care and protection. Rationally or irrationally, I was hurt that my analyst had not seemed aware of these core themes and my cavalier attitude and, instead, accepted at face value my insistence that I felt completely secure taking his class. I had only a shadowy awareness of these thoughts and feelings. My ability to articulate my experience of that class came later.

The next day I called to tell him I had been very upset by the class. I expected he was going to respond with curiosity and a collaborative approach – here we were, faced with a particular challenge in navigating the complicated roles of student and teacher, patient and analyst, but we would discuss it and figure out what it meant and how to proceed. I was angry and anxious but also excited by the idea that something had happened between us that I didn't fully understand and I thought could deepen our work. I felt aware that some of my core issues had been touched on but was not clear yet as to what they were. I needed to voice my feeling that he had not prepared me for the fact that he would be discussing his own clinical material in our first class. I fully expected that he would be curious about why I was so upset. I also longed for some understanding about the situation that was eluding me. I wished he could recognize the hurt that was beneath the surface of my anger.

I was shocked by his response: 'Gird your loins.' Whoa, I thought. What is this?!! I was, for some reason, completely unprepared for his response, perhaps because of my own fantasy about the man I believed him to be, not an entirely false fantasy, but maybe one that left out crucial information about his limitations. He went on to say that I would have to have a thick skin if I was going to take the class. Why was he saying I needed to prepare myself for the worst, protect my most vulnerable self, not allow the class to bother me? I couldn't answer these questions. I felt shocked, with a sense of immediate, profound betrayal, perhaps because this felt like the opposite of the protection for which I longed. I told him I had to get off the phone. I don't remember exactly what happened immediately afterward but he must have realized something about my intense reaction because I recall he tried to backpedal and undo his comments a bit, either in that first conversation or by leaving a message for me afterward. The trust I felt in our profession had been deeply affected, as my analyst, considered 'senior', had after many years of work made a mistake that I felt was so basic. I feared I, too, identifying with him, could go through all of the training and decades of work, only to react as defensively to a patient.

I called a friend, also an analytic candidate, and spoke to her extensively about what had happened. I told her I was considering leaving the program. I expressed that it shook me to the core to have my analyst take such a defensive stance. 'Hasn't he read "the manual"?' I asked. 'Isn't "Psychoanalysis 101" to be curious and open to your patient's experiences and not tell her to "gird her loins"?!'

Sue Elkind (1996) wrote about the painful ending of two of her personal analyses. She conceptualized that a recurrence of her personal trauma was the result of the way her therapists created the following situation:

> This [her analysts'] countertransference resulted in the abandonment of an analytic stance and inability to preserve a sustaining therapeutic connection. The result was a *reenactment without understanding* of the trauma of abandonment that I had sought therapy to understand. The destruction of hope that this reenactment brought about was catastrophic to live through initially and then difficult to live with for some time.
>
> (p.168)

I, too, experienced traumatic 'reenactment without understanding'. I was aware something deep had been triggered by the classroom experience. I was hopeful that we would be able to mine my reaction for material that would add substance and weight to my understanding of my most basic interpersonal dynamics. As a practicing therapist and analytic candidate, I was cognizant that something potentially very rich had happened. My role also led me to very quickly understand the inverse, exactly what did *not* happen between my analyst and myself when I experienced his defensive response. This, in a brief yet intense moment, opened the door to deep disappointment and disillusionment.

Slowly, that evening I began to feel that my disappointment did not need to extend to my training and profession, but could remain in my analyst and my treatment. Although I was aware that there was a deeper transferential element in the intensity of my response, I was most able to identify a feeling of profound bait and switch. I was unprepared for his defensiveness and saw it as a rejection of my experience and a warning that I would not always be safe when criticizing him. It surprised me that there did not seem to be room for analysis. 'Gird your loins' felt like a period at the end of a sentence. This was not what I had experienced before. Instead, I had felt strongly encouraged to explore my feelings toward him, with his assurance that this exploration would be met with curiosity, analysis and non-defensiveness.

I returned to our next session with trepidation, but also interest in what we would uncover. He presented me with an apology when I entered the room. Initially, he found it difficult to fully explore this event. He asked me why I hadn't been prepared to hear clinical material. 'What did you think we would be talking about in our class?' he asked me. Fair question, I answered. I said I knew we would be discussing our own clinical material but had been utterly unprepared to start my first class and have *him*, my analyst, discussing his own. I asked why he didn't tell me ahead of time. As the session went on, he paused thoughtfully and replied, 'Maybe I was anxious about having you in the class.' Ah, I thought. Thank you. Now we can really talk about this.

My analyst and I did continue to discuss the event. During the year that followed we dipped into this episode in a fluid way. I began to think of it with pride, as something we had survived together and grown to understand. However, while I do believe we did survive something together and there is true value in that, I think my initial relief and satisfaction were based on the fact that we had both experienced a profound rupture in our connection that we were able to repair through mutual caring and respect. But it did not go deep enough. Much later I realized we only touched the surface and never really delved into the multi-layered transference that was uncovered.

Two and a half years went by. My analysis regained much of the richness and expression it had before the above experience. I began to feel a profound shift in my ability to stay more connected to what Winnicott (1956) calls one's 'true self'. However, there were moments in which I didn't completely trust that our relationship could absorb my challenges to his authority or his need to see me in a particular way. The exact way that my analyst saw me is difficult for me to define. Gill (quoted in Hoffman, 1983) describes an analytic stance in which 'Analysts have largely followed Freud in taking it for granted that the analyst's behavior is such that the patient's appropriate reaction to it will be cooperation in the joint work' (p.406). This statement feels appropriate to my treatment. I experienced my analyst as being open to exploration of his influence, but primarily as a tool to facilitate my cooperative involvement in our shared work. I experienced his vision of me as being a patient who would consistently cooperate. During this phase, I became more consciously aware of what could go wrong in my work with him when I diverged from cooperative involvement and, instead, openly reacted to his defensiveness.

About four and a half years into my analysis, we experienced another profound rupture. This was one from which we were not able to recover. I was in the throes of a serious, albeit manageable, extended illness that required me to rest as much as possible while I maintained my life commitments and practice. I chose to take a leave of absence from my analysis during this period that ended up lasting about four weeks. It was a messy leave of absence. I was unclear about how much time away I would need. I gave mixed signals about when I would be able to return. Because my illness was quite stressful, I only knew I needed to focus on my priorities, and hoped my analyst would support my decision to care for myself by allowing flexibility in cancelling my sessions.

In this time of profound shift in my life, I used my most intimate relationships in very different ways. Prior to this, my analyst had been my closest confidant. I had used the analytic space as a container for my most intense experiences, often at the exclusion of other relationships. At the time of my illness, I was working through the difficult yet growth-producing transition of having my other relationships become my most immediate emotional supports. I turned toward others in a way I had previously turned toward my analyst. I was asking him to step to the side and he was reacting in a way that I found intrusive, related to his own needs and anxieties.

I contacted my analyst to let him know about my illness and to tell him that I would need to cancel sessions for the week. I told him I would be in touch soon, giving him updates. He began calling daily, sometimes on my cell phone and my house line on the same day, leaving messages that said he was calling to see how I was. I recall feeling surprised and angry, as I had specifically asked that he wait to hear from me for updates. We also had a few e-mail exchanges, in which I attempted to give him a clear picture of how I was doing. His e-mails began to take on a more anxious, demanding tone, as he questioned my ability to function in my day-to-day life and asked to speak when I was recovering from a particularly tiring diagnostic test, which he knew about. I told him that he was overwhelming me with his communication and asked that he hold on to his comments and questions until I could return to analysis. I had to find a way to hold the frame when he appeared unable to do so. I was disappointed he had not understood my need for space and contained communication during those weeks.

Things did not go well when I returned to treatment. He described the experience as being similar to driving along at 60 mph and suddenly hitting a wall. I agree completely. We were not able to find a shared reality of what had transpired between us during the four weeks that I was away. The confusion, anxiety and resentment that had been communicated between us via calls and e-mails during my illness became intractably rooted as we tried and failed to find common ground.

I felt caught in a haze of trying to hold on to many different experiences simultaneously, including his past decency along with more immediate attacking and blaming behaviour. He sometimes made cutting remarks, while I was feeling deep pain and confusion over what was happening between us. 'You're being so cold,' he said on several occasions when I was sitting on the couch, unable to speak because I was overcome with sadness and emotion. I often left our sessions feeling like the enemy, having been criticized for being unable to let go of the previous months' events. He asked: 'Why can't you move on? What else do you want from me?' Had I read Sue Elkind's paper, I might have been able to articulate what I wanted:

> [There are] dual levels of trauma for patients when there is a rupture. The first level resides in the therapist's original upsetting action, and the second level in the therapist's subsequent failure to communicate a psychological understanding of why the action was upsetting, what primary vulnerability was activated in the patient, and that a primary vulnerability of the therapist might have been involved.
>
> (p.175)

One irony is that I *had* grown in my treatment so that I felt much stronger in asserting myself. I had gained significant confidence in my own voice as a direct result of our work. Therefore, I did not easily back down when my version of events or experience was questioned. I think it was a shock to my analyst. We spent many sessions fighting instead of exploring. Sometimes he asked what was wrong with our fighting and I would answer, 'I grew up knowing how to fight. Now I need something different. We don't seem able to get there.' Clearly, this was a clue to the transference lying beneath all that occurred, but we just were not able to move into that transference space in a deep, consistent, meaningful way.

I experienced my analyst's defensiveness as the primary factor in the way my treatment ended. My interpretation is that we tripped hard over something very deep for him that allowed him to apologize to me for certain behaviours that occurred and words that were spoken, but created such an overwhelming sense of vulnerability and anxiety in him that either he could not deeply explore the reasons he was reacting to me in the way that he was or he could not use this exploration in a manner that allowed him to consistently maintain a curious, non-defensive stance within our sessions. For example, in a session, he might be open to discussing the e-mails from my leave of absence. He would acknowledge what he said and express curiosity about my reactions. In a later session, when I might reference his e-mail, including the words that he used, he would once again deny having spoken them, and we would have to start the process all over again. When I expressed anger and anxiety over this, he responded inconsistently, sometimes with curiosity, other times with angry defensiveness.

I experienced much of his behavior as dissociated aspects of himself. It is possible that these were not truly dissociated; I cannot know his internal experience during this time, but only my understanding and analysis of his behavior. Here I think I am crossing another boundary, another taboo, by interpreting my analyst's behavior. Our analytic community has a rich history of conflicting theories, even confusion, over our understanding of the analyst's influence in the room and patient's interpretation of the analyst's behavior. Irwin Hoffman (1983) provides an excellent analysis of the differing ways clinicians have historically viewed these issues. As a community, we continue to use differing theoretical frameworks to understand the types of influence analysts have. Concurrently, we hold different views of the validity of patients' interpretation of their analysts' behavior. The following quote from Gill and Hoffman (1982) is 30 years old. I believe we are still struggling to fully validate the patient's experience of the analyst:

> Central to our understanding of transference is the notion that the analyst's behavior is invariably amenable to a variety of interpretations ... [We] may agree that the therapist has behaved in a particular way, one which could be construed as seductive, or disapproving, or whatever, only after some subtle aspect of his behavior is called to ... attention by another observer. This observer might, of course, be none other than the patient. He may notice something about the therapist's behavior or suggest a possible interpretation of it that most ... would overlook.
>
> (p.140)

In the spirit of Gill and Hoffman's observation, I will allow myself to briefly interpret my analyst's behavior. The defensiveness and, at times, real confusion with which he responded caused me to experience his behavior as quite split off from the prior norm of our interactions. He seemed to have trouble tolerating the reality of his actions, leading him to 'forget' things that he had done, such as sending certain e-mails. I was conscious of aspects of him that he appeared unable to consistently access, or even access at all, causing me to feel caught in a constant, uphill struggle as I attempted to express my experience of those disavowed aspects of him through my own self-protective and outwardly calm lens. There was little room for my own self-exploration.

In my view, my analyst and I were experiencing his anxiously disowned or dissociated behavior when he phoned and e-mailed me. I became suspicious that this was the case as we attempted to process the experience and could not find a mutually agreed upon, consistently experienced reality. Hypothesizing that this was a far more anxiety-ridden experience for him than that moment several years earlier when he had responded 'Gird your loins,' I wonder if it was more disavowed.

I know that I badly needed him to be able to own his behavior and take a different stance, one that was open to understanding me, in spite of my anger, and committed to curiosity about what was happening within both of us that was being acted out in the treatment. His defensiveness, aggression and avoidance of the disavowed experience that was with us in the room mirrored my history far too closely. What I needed was for him to rise above his limitations, to appreciate what was happening between us and find a way to integrate the behaviors that he could not own or even fully acknowledge, in spite of the anxiety involved.

This brings me back to Annie. In some ways our work together has been reminiscent of my work in my own analysis. We've been quite close and there's been something in our work which has always left me feeling as though I could identify with her pain, although we come from very different backgrounds and experiences. She's in a four-times-a-week treatment, as I was with my analyst.

She's trusted me deeply and has been easily influenced, particularly in the early years of her analysis. She's also struggled to find her own voice, often angrily.

Annie and I have also experienced moments of real rupture. While this has been intensely uncomfortable, it has created necessary space for Annie to express herself as separate from me and my desires. Her need for space, as well as my own within my own analysis, may be well characterized by Bion (1970): 'A certain class of patient feels "possessed" by or imprisoned "in" the mind of the analyst if he considers the analyst desires something relative to him – his presence, or his cure, or his welfare' (p.41). These moments of rupture have allowed Annie to explore territory that is hers alone.

These moments of rupture and subsequent awareness of difference have, at times, been our saving grace, allowing Annie room for a new expression of self. Through our shared tolerance of these often painful moments, we've slowly begun to build a new understanding of her that's allowed for far more open exploration of transference and countertransference. My attempts to take in her experience of me, mainly at times when what she describes feels most alien, have appeared to be instrumental in loosening the knot of an enactment as it has occurred. She has needed me to remain open to her experience of me, non-defensively, and particularly when her experience does not match up with my experience of myself. For her, it has been an issue of trust – in her own emerging voice, in my ability to listen without defensiveness, attack, or insistence that I know myself, including my motivations and intents, better than what her experience of me suggests.

My faith in my profession was shaken, again, when I left my own analysis and I've been thinking a great deal about the ways that we, as analysts, are effective and what happens to a treatment when we have limitations that just can't be overcome, particularly when we are confronted with our own dissociated or disavowed experiences as our patients bring them to us. The fear that surfaced years ago when my analyst said 'Gird your loins' surfaced again. I wonder about the ways that our limitations negatively affect patients, even after years or even decades of clinical work. Our experiences may be dissociated/disavowed precisely because they highlight moments that we might perceive ourselves, with or without our patients' agreement, as failures in our work and as vulnerable human beings. It's frightening as a patient to have such a difficult experience of one's analyst. It is also frightening to be the analyst coming up against one's own limitations, perceived failures and anxiety-provoking behaviors.

My need to distance myself from my analyst and his limitations, to be different from him at moments when I wondered, with panic, if I was actually the same, made me wish to avoid what Annie was saying in her treatment with me even more strongly than my usual defensiveness. It was incredibly hard to allow myself to realize that Annie may be aware of aspects of me that I was *not* and that she had a right to be angry about them. I recall a particular moment in one session in which she was telling me I was not listening and was instead competing with another therapist with whom she had had a family session. 'You're jealous,' Annie said. 'You're just trying to talk about what you're doing for me so that you don't have to feel like she could have given me something that you aren't or can't. But you're not *listening* to me.' In the moment, I could not connect to what she was saying at all. It did not resonate. I thought of my analyst and his similar reaction to me. I thought about how I was so sure I was on to something that he couldn't see, his dissociated or disavowed experience, and saw Annie across the room feeling equally convinced that she knew something about me that I couldn't own. I felt compassion for my analyst as I believe he tried his best to be with me at similarly difficult times, as he struggled and was confronted with the pain of the 'failure' of a previously successful treatment. I decided to behave differently. I took a deep breath and said, 'OK. I can't connect to this in the way you're describing but I want to try.' I sat quietly and listened. Things seemed to get better between us. I asked why she seemed less angry and appeared to have moved much further into her own experience as the session progressed. 'I knew you'd catch on eventually,' she said. 'You always do.'

I'm not sure that I always do. I found those months with her to be extremely difficult. It would feel that we had found our connection again, then it would be gone in an instant. The work up until that point had been very different. I realized part of that difference was that Annie had previously protected me from her rage. This was a great deal of what had made *her* an easily influenced patient. It was similar to 'driving along at 60 mph and hitting a wall'. It was disorienting, but I felt very hopeful during that crash. The fact that Annie was allowing herself to be angry felt like a turning point. I tried to hold on to the tiger's tail through those sessions, hoping I was creating enough space to allow her own voice and the need, particularly for separation, beneath the rage to come through. Some days it worked; some days it didn't.

One of the major disruptions in my own analysis that I have tried to work through in my treatment of Annie has to do with the ways that we, as analysts, work with our dissociated or disavowed aspects of self. It can be painfully difficult to be reminded that we are people first and analysts after that. At times, Annie has attacked me for being false, for saying one thing and doing another. At these moments, I've wanted very much to believe that I could rest in my 'knowledge' that I have more self-awareness than she; therefore, my experience is correct and Annie's is irrational. During those moments, it has occurred to me that this is false security. I know that outside my consulting room I don't always have that kind of self-awareness. I rely on the people closest to me to reflect aspects of self about which I find it impossible to be conscious. Could I really possess a consistent clarity of mind and experience in work that I don't have in the rest of my life? I realized the answer is no. This has made me more open to listening. I also wonder why this openness is so difficult. Perhaps it is because it is already such a difficult process to try to integrate disavowed experience. Having one's *patient* be the one to notice and tell you about it, can feel exponentially more vulnerable. Is there a myth and mutually shared fantasy that we, as analysts, are always completely open to self-examination and ownership of potentially disruptive, disavowed aspects of self so that nothing harmful can get played out with our patients? What purpose might this fantasy play in the consulting room? How do we navigate the often painful and intensely disruptive experience of having our dissociated or disavowed aspects of self enter the space? How do our experiences as patients, destructive and otherwise, profoundly influence our work and identity as analysts?

The things that occurred in my own analysis have clearly made me a better analyst to my patients. I used the word 'failure' earlier to describe what my analyst might have thought when working with me toward the end and how I, at times, perceived him. As the years have gone by and I have continued to process my experience as a whole, I've realized that I actually don't believe that my treatment with him should be called a failure. There were certainly failed moments. Time has, however, allowed me to recognize and appreciate the growth that took place. His continued influence, as my analyst, and humanness, both in his failures and in real moments of caring and connection remind me again and again of what we are all capable of being, particularly within the consulting room.

During the question and answer period after I presented my paper, I noticed the audience focused almost exclusively on the dyad of myself and my analyst. I don't think I received a single response to the parts of my paper relating to my work with Annie or my thoughts about the use of dissociative or disavowed experience. For some reason, I had not been prepared for this, and found it quite interesting. The audience members who spoke, and others who approached me afterwards, again and again wanted to share their own experiences as patients and comment on mine. There was a sense of pressure and relief to the tone of their stories, as though these were experiences that had been saved up for a long time, just waiting to be told.

These were in no way unwelcome responses. I had just not been prepared for them to be in such exclusion to the other parts of my paper. It made me wonder what my colleagues and I seem to need to share and why, at least some of us, have such a hunger to share it.

The discussion following the presentation also revealed another current, labelled as my 'bravery', related to a fear that I might be misunderstood or criticized by colleagues. One participant recommended I make sure I was in treatment before continuing to present this work to protect me from such criticism. Another feared I would be pathologized, a fate to be avoided at all costs. I found this current just as interesting as the first. I felt that instead of simply labelling him as 'bad' and myself as 'good', I had tried hard to express extremely painful moments in my analysis that might have allowed for rich mining of deep transferential material, but, instead, eventually ended my treatment, and that I then went on to try to learn from those painful moments so I *might* not repeat the defensiveness and subsequent traumatic 'reenactment without understanding' (Elkind, 1996) that I had experienced in my analysis. This chapter is not an attempt to pathologize my analyst. Instead, I have tried to highlight the particular, human limitations that occurred at particular points in my personal analysis. I have tried to use these examples to connect to the idea that we are people first and clinicians second and that this humanness means we will all experience our own vulnerabilities when we are confronted with certain experiences, including the possibility of failure, whether in a moment or an entire treatment. I was very angry and very hurt by the limitations I experienced in my analyst and within my treatment and, at times, was left with the feeling that he was not doing good work with me. Of course, this occurred in the context of transference, and, of course, my reactions could not have always been completely rational. It was my analysis, after all.

My intent in presenting this work is to discuss my experience as patient and analyst and think about the ways I have been influenced by this duality – the ways we are like our analysts but strive to learn from both the painful and exhilarating moments to become different, our own selves in our work and life. We can't help but identify with our analysts, as we are alike and hope to be doing the work we see them doing. This is probably even more strikingly felt by the candidate who hopes to have the same perceived success as the senior analyst. Additionally, we carry our analytic experiences within us. I found my parallel experience with Annie to be painful, but ultimately rewarding, as I allowed myself to face, head on, the ways that I was similar to my analyst in my capacity for personal limitation but also quite different, as well as how I had internalized him, the good and the bad, and the ways I had used my internalized experience of him to try to move beyond him in my work with Annie.

The ability to explore our defensiveness when we are asked to see our vulnerabilities and potential failures appears crucial. Because we have been patients and analysts, we are in an interesting position to explore defensiveness, particularly around dissociated or disavowed experience, from many different frames of reference that can provide for increased richness in our understanding of ourselves in and outside of our consulting rooms.

Returning to one question raised earlier, why is there a risk that public discussion of our treatments, particularly painful or traumatizing experiences, might be viewed as 'outing' our analysts? Is there a feeling of 'there but for the grace of God, go I', causing us to be protective of the other as a way of ultimately being protective of self? Outing our analysts can be an important outing of ourselves, as we are inherently alike. It is a way that we can examine the limitations we all bring to our work and provide a forum for better understanding of what can go wrong in a treatment. Sometimes therapeutic work is re-traumatizing, or even newly traumatizing, for a patient and we, as clinicians, may need the support of our community to discuss our experiences when things go wrong in our personal analyses.

Do we have a tendency to blame the victim in these situations, again in order to provide some measure of self-protection? Exploration of what goes right or wrong in therapy is a terribly complex endeavor. Two people are interacting on a deep level of intimacy for the purpose of bringing limitations, i.e., pathologies, to the surface so that healing can occur. I would argue that it is necessary to continue to discuss these limitations in ourselves and our analysts, as well as the ways we grow and heal as clinicians and patients in this process, in order to understand the nature of our clinical work more fully.

References

Bion W. (1970). *Attention and interpretation: a scientific approach to insight in psychoanalysis and groups*. London: Tavistock.

Dimen, M. (2011). Lapsus linguae, or a slip of the tongue? A sexual violation in an analytic treatment and its personal and theoretical aftermath. *Contemporary Psychoanalysis*, 47: 35–79.

Elkind, S. (1996). The impact of negative experiences as a patient on my work as a therapist. In B. Gerson (ed.), *The therapist as a person: life crisis, life choices, life experiences, and their effects on treatment*. Hillsdale, NJ: Analytic Press, pp. 159–174.

Gill, M.M. and Hoffman, I.Z. (1982). A method for studying the analysis of aspects of the patient's experience of the relationship in psychoanalysis and psychotherapy. *Journal of the American Psychoanalytic Association*, 30: 137–167.

Guntrip, H. (1975). My experience of analysis with Fairbairn and Winnicott (how complete a result does psycho-analytic therapy achieve?). *International Review of Psychoanalysis*, 2: 145–156.

Hoffman, I.Z. (1983). The patient as interpreter of the analyst's experience. *Contemporary Psychoanalysis*, 19: 389–422.

Little, M.I. (1990). *Psychotic anxieties and containment: a personal record of an analysis with Winnicott*. Northvale, NJ: Jason Aronson.

Winnicott, D.W. (1956). On transference. *The International Journal of Psychoanalysis*, 37: 386–388.

Chapter 18

The contrapuntal play of paradox
Likeness and difference in the theories of Otto Rank

Claude Barbre

The Palestinian theorist Edward Said wrote that

> most people are principally aware of one culture, one setting, one home; exiles are aware of at least two, and this plurality of vision gives rise to an awareness of simultaneous dimensions, an awareness that, to borrow a phrase from music, is *contrapuntal*, meaning counterpoised. For an exile, habits of life, expression, activity in the new environment inevitably occur against the memory of these things in another environment.
>
> (Said, 2001, p.186)

Commenting on Said's two-home characteristic of exiles, psychoanalyst Christopher Bollas points out that maybe we are all exiles in that we must leave original attachments and move to new environments where meaning arises from both memory and new creative initiatives (Bollas, 2003, p.8). Further, Bollas suggests that we can transfer Said's notion of exiles to psychoanalytic theory, proposing a 'psychic contrapuntal' (p.8) that recognizes the benefit of movement from one's primary place to a new location from which the self and others are seen in a different light. This idea contains foundations for therapeutic, empathic resonances – two or more independent life forces harmonizing and dissenting, interacting separately and together in contrapuntal play.

Keeping in mind Bollas's view of how the psyche may counterpoise experiences in regard to a psychic contrapuntal, and how in this respect we may all be exiles as we move from the vicissitudes of infancy to the worlds of growth and development, the writings of Otto Rank on likeness and difference emerge as a correspondent voice. For although Otto Rank began as a disciple of Sigmund Freud's early psychoanalytic writings, he was at heart a philosophical process thinker, seeing a progressive, creative process inherent in all phenomenon, including self-building. Sometimes he has been called a 'philosophical psychologist for his theories did not grow initially or primarily out of a concern with therapy, but rather out of a preoccupation with the meaning of life' (Menaker, 1982, p.5). In his view, both individuals and collectives evolve in an inevitable duality: individuation and a need to remain part of a larger whole – a conflict that can be resolved through creative will.

To understand Rank's thinking about the paradoxical domain of the creative potential brought on by the life force of the will – a striving that existentially abides in tension with human separation, anxiety, and guilt – let us review Rank's perspectives, such as the likeness and difference of creative will and counter-will, the artist and the *artiste manqué*, life and death fear, mortality and immortality struggles, and the therapeutic consequences of his theory.

Otto Rank's life evinces striving toward self-becoming – a creative will toward making an art of his life from enormous childhood challenges. From an early age, he wrote a diary, his daybooks (*Tagebücher*). Like Rousseau's *Confessions* (1782), these daybooks provided an instrument for discerning and structuring a self. They conclude with 'triumphant self-discovery of a genuine self-identity as an artist' (Homans, 1989, p.164).

Born Otto Rosenfeld in 1884, Rank was the second of two sons in a low-income Viennese family. Brother Paul was guided toward law. Otto worked at a machine shop as a locksmith's apprentice in late adolescence and earned a technical school diploma. In his first daybook (26 October 1903), he wrote: 'My father bothered himself little about me, and my mother found her satisfaction in the fact that we at least "lived" – that is, ate and went "decently" clothed. So I grew up left to myself, without education, without friends, without books' (Taft, 1958, p.10). Rank notes that his father, 'a quiet drinker', was prone to outbursts: 'I was alone with him in the house ... He bellowed hoarsely and struck his hands against the table until they bled, while I sat motionless in a corner, as if not alive but turned to stone ... Every one of us had a deep rage inside' (Taft, 1958, p.16).

Rank's daybooks reveal Nietzsche's and the humanities' large influence. At Rank's most desperate time at the machine shop, 'I had serious thoughts of suicide which, as Nietzsche says, helped me get past many a night and many a day. Then in reaction came a tremendous love of life and creative joy, which swept me into activity' (Taft, 1958, p.13). Lamenting 'the terrible emptiness and aimlessness of my present life ... I bought a weapon to kill myself. Afterwards the highest lust for life and the greatest courage toward death grew up in me' (ibid., p.29). This confrontation with life and death, self-creation and destruction, anticipates Rank's life-long empathy toward helping others discover creative will and lived meaning.

As he began his daybooks in 1903, Rank discovered Freud's writing. In August 1905, with the help of Alfred Adler, his physician, Rank presented Freud with a monograph about the artist and creativity from a psychoanalytic perspective. Inspired by Nietzsche's focus on self-creation, *The artist* (*Der Künstler*) attests to Rank's early preoccupation with the psychology of creative activity and the artist's personality. Rejecting 'explanations' of art and the artist in terms of causal psychology, for Rank, the artist symbolized human striving for self-expression, growth and change.

In this 21 year old, Freud recognized a creative will prevailing over his background's cultural and emotional poverty. In turn, Rank found a mentoring, paternal presence, a kindred spirit in Freud. In the new science of psychoanalysis, Rank discovered new material and theoretic nuance. *The artist* brought psychoanalysis into his language, employing the word 'artist' much as Freud did 'sexuality' (Barbre, 1997, p.250). The burgeoning emphasis on the spontaneous growth of the self and the undetermined potentialities of the psyche became for Rank the expression of will in theory and in life.

Reading the monograph, Freud was so impressed that he encouraged Rank to complete his university education, ensuring his ability to do so by making him the Psychoanalytic Society's secretary (the movement's first paid position). In October 1906, Rank moved out of his family home into an apartment near Freud's. At Freud's urging, Rank attended the gymnasium, and graduated in 1908. From his relationship to Freud, as in effect a foster son, Rank began to work with him in many ways. *Der Künstler* (1907), the first psychoanalytic work not written by Freud, was followed by *The myth of the birth of the hero* (1909), which included a section on family romance written by Freud. Rank completed a doctorate at the University of Vienna in 1911 – the first doctorate on the application of psychoanalysis to the humanities (*The Lohengrin Saga*). As Robert Kramer notes, 'For every edition of *The interpretation of dreams* since 1911, Rank helped Freud revise, word by word, every line of his case celebre of self-analysis' (Kramer, 1996, p.10). In 1914, Freud asked him to contribute two chapters on literature and myth to *The interpretation of dreams*, resulting in Rank's name appearing just below Freud's on the title page. That same year, Rank published *The double*, a work on identity, guilt, narcissism, fear of death, soul and desire for immortality. He became editor of *Imago* and *Internationale Zeitschrift* and director of *Verlag*, the new psychoanalytic publishing house. In 1919, he began private practice. Kramer (1996) captures well the close emotional relationship with Freud when he notes:

> He dined Wednesdays with the Professor and his family at Berggasse 19 before meetings of the Vienna Psychoanalytic Society, over which Rank, now vice-president, was president in Freud's frequent absences. The youngest and freshest of the Committee members, he held a unique position in the nucleus of the secret ring: Freud cosigned Rank's circular letters to the Committee, giving them an imprimatur the others did not enjoy ... Summing up Rank's vital role during these years, Hanns Sachs described him, simply as Freud's *Doppelganger*, his shadow: 'Lord Everything Else.'
>
> (p.12)

As much as Rank admired Freud's work and company, growing differences were evident. Rank thought of the ego not as a derivative of drives, a by-product of frustration and failed gratification, but as primary self-seeking building blocks for growth and development. As Esther Menaker explains, for Rank

> The ability to act creatively – that is to choose to alter or have an impact on the external environment as well as on the self – is implemented through the human capacity for internalization: the taking in of the experiences of the outer world, be it with persons or events, and having it become via memory

images, a part of the self ... Identifications are added to what is originally the individual's own ego and that together they form an independent power. The force of this power is projected onto the outer world and is expressed as will.
(Menaker, 1996, p.70)

In *The development of psychoanalysis* (1925), with Sandor Ferenczi, Rank championed living and reliving affective experience in therapy. Emphasizing the therapeutic experience and the viability of action over verbal memory, they rejected the Berlin school's criticism that repetition by the patient is predominately resistance. Later, Rank expanded this work into what he would call 'relationship therapy'. *The development of psychoanalysis* anticipates Rank's lifelong emphasis on the curative effect of emotional experience (*Erlebnis*) over privileged intellectual understanding (*Einsicht*). As Kramer says about Rank's insight: 'It is not the infantile past but the living present – the *Erlebnis* of one's own difference, the consciousness of living, with all its painful feeling, thinking, and acting – that patients deny, forget, or wish to escape.' (Kramer, 1996, p.20)

Rank believed neurosis is the result of an individual's inability to affirm his or her difference, his or her unique idiom, given from birth. This is a failure in creativity rather than sexuality. Affirmation of one's difference is a manifestation of the will toward individuation that introduces the dilemmas of separation and relatedness (Barbre, 1997). Difference is the *Erlebnis* the patient has never before been willing to accept, fully and consciously, without feeling overwhelmed by angst or guilt (Kramer, 1996, p.20). As Rank said, 'The feeling of experience (*Erlebnis*), purposefully and with intent, is made the central factor in the therapeutic task ... The therapist registers the patient's slowly emerging, inarticulate, unvoiced feelings ... The therapeutic experience is ... a process in which the individual learns to develop emotions.' (Rank, 1936, p.165)

Having realized that willing leads to guilt, Rank began searching for the origins of anxiety that he thought he found in the experience of birth. In *The trauma of birth* (1924) Rank first attempted to conform his thinking to Freud's biological determinism. In this work he considered initial physiological separation from mother as the prototype of future anxiety. Later, he departed from this literal interpretation, suggesting birth is a metaphor for the struggle for psychological separation and self-discovery. In short, the nurturing, protective, powerful birth mother – relatively neglected by Freud – became central in Rank's theory.

Rank's self-creation, in life and writing, created tensions with Freud. Although at first Freud was pleased with Rank's efforts, the emphasis on mother–child interaction as primary clashed with Freud's patricentric theory of the Oedipus complex and castration anxiety. Hence, *The trauma of birth* (1924) was construed as challenging libido theory. After publishing it, Rank sailed to New York to lecture on pre-Oedipal theory. As Kramer points out, 'although Freud introduced the word "pre-genital," Rank coined the word "pre-Oedipal," and was first to employ it in the modern relational sense' (Kramer, 1996, p.43). However, his creativity became his burden. Because of envious attacks by Ernest Jones, Karl

Abraham and other Committee members, he struggled to maintain his connection to Freud. In a letter from the United States, Rank denied Freud's charges that he had 'excluded' the father, saying: 'Naturally that is not the case and absolutely cannot be, it would be nonsense. I have only attempted to give him the correct place' (Kramer, 1996, p.xiv).

In 1926, after publishing *The technique of psychoanalysis*, Rank lectured again in New York. He suggested Freud represses the castrating pre-Oedipal mother's role: 'the bad mother he has never seen, but only the later displacement of her to the father, who therefore plays such an omnipotent part in his theory ... The strict mother thus forms the real nucleus of the super-ego' (Kramer, 1996, p.xiv). Rank's modification of theory and therapeutic procedure (later developed in *Will therapy* [1929], *Truth and reality* [1929], *Psychology and the soul* [1930], *Modern education* [1931], *Art and artist* [1932] and *Beyond psychology* [1941]) contributed to his break with Freud in 1926. From 1926 to 1934, his most productive years, he resided in Paris. From 1934 to 1939, he lectured, wrote and saw patients in New York. Responding to his 1930 dismissal from the American Psychoanalytic Association, Rank said he had 'stopped calling himself a *psychoanalyst*. I am no longer trying to prove that Freud was wrong and I am right ... It is not a question of whose interpretation is correct – because there is no such thing as *the* interpretation or only *one* psychological truth' (Kramer, 1996, p.xv).

In 1939, Rank divorced Tola Rank, and in July of that year married Estelle Buel. They planned to move to California in the coming year. Unfortunately, Rank died at New York Hospital from a massive reaction to an injection of a sulfa (antibacterial) drug, on the morning of 31 October, Hallow's Eve. Rank's last word was '*Komisch*', meaning 'comical, strange, uncanny, peculiar'. By the time of his death, Rank had contributed extensively to the study of the role of creativity, the meaning of birth and separation, the fear of mortality and the wish for immortality, and the nature of the will.

Rank's development reveals a lifelong fascination with existential dualities, paradox, and the contrapuntal play of likeness and difference. In a lecture entitled 'The anxiety problem' (1926/1996), Rank points out that the trauma of birth is the most stressful but also the most triumphant experience in all human life. At the same time, it brings with it a heavy burden: the trauma of self-awareness or self-consciousness. Rank observes that the source of human suffering is simply 'the fact that we have a psychical life' (Rank in Kramer, 1996, p.124), the strange awareness that we are alive. This is the angst for self-consciousness itself: 'It is simply anxiety in the I and for the I (*Angst im Ich und um das Ich*' (ibid.). The tendency to get free from this angst is perhaps the strongest psychic force in the individual. The human being becomes at once creator and creature, or actually moves from creature to creator, and in the ideal case, creator of himself or herself, his or her own personality. The evolution of consciousness and the birth of the creative self, a process of continual learning, unlearning and relearning, is never complete.

Infants' earliest experiences concerning the emerging sense of their bodies (individuation, autonomy, movement, vitality and a new form of existence) and connections with others are often associated with a positive sense of life. Death intimations are also present, with threats of separation and disintegration, introducing a lifelong struggle between life and death forces. With too much trauma, the balance may be tilted toward death imagery and anxiety (Walsh, 1996; Barbre, 2004), a perspective that resonates with Robert Jay Lifton's 'death imprint' left by overwhelming encounters with death (Ross, 1997). As Rank points out:

> There is in the individual a primal fear, which manifests itself now as fear of life, another time as fear of death. The fear in birth, which we have designated as fear of life, seems to me actually the fear of having to live as an isolated individual – a fear of separation from the whole (too much difference) – although it may appear later as fear of the loss of this dearly bought individuality, as fear of death, of being dissolved again into the whole (too much alikeness and enmeshment in the other). There is included in the fear problem itself a primary ambivalence which must be assumed, and not derived through the opposition of life and death instincts.
>
> (Rank, 1936, p.124)

Individuals live paradoxically in the space between alikeness and difference, striving to emerge from the influence of others, only to seek validation of their creative products and acts from the collective (Rank, 1932). Freedom of will abides in the crucible of likeness and difference.

In *The thinking heart*, Anne Alvarez (2012) cites Broucek's (1997) research concerning babies' delight discovering they can be causal agents, smiling and cooing at contingent relationships between their spontaneous behaviour and events in the world, and their subsequent ability to produce these happenings 'at will'. Alvarez suggests that 'Broucek stresses the importance of the will – a relatively unexplored subject in psychology and psychoanalysis' (p.30). In fact, the nature of the will was explored in great depth by Otto Rank, and was central to his therapeutic work: 'The problem of willing ... had come to be the central problem of ... personality, even of all psychology' (Rank, 1945, p.260). As Rank stressed, 'The individual ego is the temporal representative of the cosmic primal force – the strength of this force represented in the individual we call the will' (1945, p.212). He called his clinical approach Will Therapy. Therapy's aim, rather than remembering the traumatic past, is to help patients learn to will in the present.

Rank's theory underscores that willing is always accompanied by degrees of guilt and anxiety because not only does it necessitate some aggression in the service of self-assertion and striving; it also means that the individual must separate from the experience of the group and the security of collective affirmations. This tension presupposes an existential opposition of wills. Rank is clear that our differentiation includes both an identity with the 'other' and an experience of separateness. This paradoxical phenomenon introduces a dramatic dilemma: how to live out one's unique expression when it opposes the wishes and needs of another. Rank understood that relatedness is jeopardized by self-assertion, and guilt arises when separation creates a presumption of injury to the other's need for togetherness. He calls this dynamic 'ethical guilt', an inner reaction from the fear of hurting the other through separation. Because of the fear of retribution, this inevitable struggle is also a source for death anxiety as well. Guilt, then, is a natural consequence of the creative urge toward individuality, a by-product of the experience of separateness – an existential guilt. Succinctly put, 'Guilt is a confession of the narcissistic origin both of self-assertion through separation and of empathy through union' (Menaker, 1982, p.60).

Rank suggested the child's early oppositional 'No' (e.g. 'counterwill', 'negative will') toward primary caretakers constitute a 'Yes' to the emerging sense of self. 'Impulse' is a creative aspect of will, not simply a Freudian drive. He argued that inhibition is conscious 'denial', seeing this dynamic as a more constructive equivalent of the psychoanalytic concept, repression. Since inhibition as negative will can be transformed therapeutically into positive will, Rank (1930) sees it less as 'resistance' (a term Rank disliked) and more as valuable, rudimentary will: 'If the resistance is not utilized in this way, the patient will become guilty' (p.51). Hence, therapy affirms the counterwill's right to resist, giving voice to the entire person, negative and positive. This approach resembles Winnicott's positive view of aggression that can fuel love. Caretakers must survive this aggression for the world to become more real for the child as she learns the limits of omnipotent control fantasies.

Between fears of individuation and loss of his or her dearly bought individuality, 'the individual is thrown back and forth all his life' (Rank, 1936, p.124). In each individuating step, someone or something is left behind. Humans pay for their life (creation) through death fear, punishing themselves through symptoms pertaining to guilt about attempting to construct a life. They 'refuse the loan (life) in order to escape the payment of debt (death)' (ibid., p.126). Neurotics try to buy freedom from death by daily, partial self-destruction – or as Stenslie says, summarizing Rank, 'People start with an active, engaging attitude toward life, are then made passive under the thrall of death, and finally become active again by punishing themselves through their neurosis' (Stenslie, 1984, p.193).

We see throughout history the attempt to deal with death anxiety revealed in myth and legends, in religion and in the artistic products of creative individuals with whom the collective world can identify. As Menaker says, summarizing Rank's thinking, 'Paradoxically, the fear of death and its counterpart, the wish for immortality, lead to the fullest expression of life in the form of the creative expression of the will. That is not to say that the wish for immortality is the *cause* of creative action and its consequent product, but rather it motivates and mobilizes the striving for the expression of individuality which is a given and is there at the outset' (Menaker, 1982, p.47). As Rank understood well, self-actualization, so necessary to each person, can only be attained through separation, which symbolizes death. The more we become self-conscious of our unique personality, the greater the urge to eternalize it. Thus, the tension between mortality and the wish for immortality is part of the life process. Further, an artist uses 'the given cultural forms; but in so doing he also adds or alters something so that his product differs sufficiently from the cultural cliché as to be his own individual creation ... Interplay between creative personality and cultural form, ideology, and institutions, advance socio-cultural evolution' (Menaker, 1982, p.32). Struggling for immortality fuels creative strivings, including creating children to carry out projections and connecting ourselves to groups, causes or ideologies seen as surviving the self. Religious and social institutions are communal immortalities, Rank believes.

In later years, Anna Freud's first child patient, Peter Heller, criticized the psychoanalytic movement for its disregard of cosmic, spiritual or religious dimensions in a way that limited and diminished humanity. In my child analysis this is suggested by the manner in which religious themes were ignored or set aside, and by blindness or withdrawal *vis à vis* major non-sexual aspects of existence, the prime instance being the interpretation of my preoccupation with and fear of death as 'nothing but' the expression of fear of the father and of my (aggressive, guilt-laden) relationship to him (Heller, 1992, p.57).

In comparison, Rank remarked that our civilization

> and with it the various types of personality representing and expressing it, has emerged from the perpetual operation of a third principle which combines the rational and irrational elements in the world view based on the conception of the supernatural (or spiritual essence in the person) ... What we have in common with our remote ancestors is a spiritual, not a primitive self, and this we cannot afford to admit because we pride ourselves on living on a purely rational plane.
>
> (Rank, 1941, pp.62–63)

Fear of irrational forces results from unsuccessful attempts to deny them especially, Rank argues, in scientific psychology.

Rank did not like the term therapeutic 'technique', which, he felt, imposed a point of view. He preferred notions of 'process', 'constructive therapy' and a 'philosophy of helping' where patients find self-acceptance by accepting their difference, their uniqueness (Rank, 1936, p.2). Like Rollo May, Rank distinguished the analytic situation from the transference. The therapeutic relation is not merely a new edition of the past. The analyst's personality and the emotional relationship with the analyst determine what will happen as much as the patient's past. Instead of uncovering the past, the patient's ego is the focus. Creative will is liberated. This perspective denies resignation to one's character understood only by past determinants. Accepting will means embracing self-creation – or, as Rank emphasized, 'The artist appoints himself or herself artist' (Menaker, 1982, p.35). The therapist participates in this recognition and renegotiation of the merging self-acceptance.

Rank points out that neurosis often begins in the individual when artistic temperaments miscarry and fail to achieve artistic expression. Neurosis represents a failure in creativity essentially rather than a failure in normal development. Rank thought of the neurotic type as an *artist manqué*, a failed artist, the artist against him or herself. For Rank, neurosis is the pathological indicator of the failure both to accept and transcend the 'responsible level of consciousness' through 'the volitional affirmation of the obligatory'. Neurosis is a failure of creativity. This means that the individuals who suffer may be seen as blocked artists in the creation of the self, caught in-between the need wilfully to oppose the will of others (counterwill) and the failure to construct or affirm self-ideals. In contrast, the artist type can find a form creatively to project his or her suffering into the work, a direct projection of the self into the form that reworks his or her suffering into the emotional use of creative production. The neurotic individual is inhibited from expressing his will, is instead stuck with him or herself in a hyperconsciousness introspection that prohibits spontaneity. Rank stresses that neurotic persons punish themselves through their symptoms, and often this punishment is in the form of guilt feelings associated with acts of will and the attempt to construct a life. The neurotic symptom occurs when the strong will is in service of obstructing the flow of vitality.

Overall, Rank saw neurosis as a will disturbance in the ego in terms of self-acceptance and acceptance of what life offers: the 'obligatory' of life and death. Therapy can be a place where we learn 'the volitional affirmation of the obligatory', meaning that we must learn to willingly affirm the tragic nature of life, and that our thrownness into life is such an obligatory. The obligatory also means the inevitability of death and limitations, and suffering is the human lot in regard to this death consciousness. Rank believed that therapy helps a person adapt to this inevitability, to be able to affirm and say 'Yes' to the tragic nature of life instead of denying it.

Rank's notion of the 'volitional affirmation of the obligatory' is beautifully illustrated in a fragment of Friedrich Schiller's poetry that serves as an epigraph to Rank's chapter 'Soul and Will' in *Psychology and the soul* (1930). The fragment reads: 'Nehmat die Gottheit auf in euren Willen / Und Sie Steigt von ihrem Weltentron' ('Take the Divine into your will / And she'll step down from her starry throne'). The language here has a wonderful ambiguity: the word-meanings in German suggest that the 'stepping' can be up or down, that is, 'up from her worldly throne' *and* 'down from her starry throne'. 'Taking' the starry or divine will to strive toward a creative ideal means also to identify with the nature of life, affirming an existence which also includes earthly limitation and death. When you affirm death you take it into your own, suggesting that God's will or the ideal becomes more human. The creative will emerges out of the ground of being and rises toward an ego-ideal. Our humanity, then, contains a transcendent potential in immanence and contingency. The poem depicts Rank's powerful awareness of the paradoxical nature of life, and the transformation of the compulsion of will to the freedom of will that abides in the crucible of likeness and difference.

Rank believed that psychotherapy can constitute a positive will toward the person's ability to grow and change through the initiation of new thinking. This perspective denies a resignation to one's character understood only by past determinants, while also affirming a capability in the person of unfolding birth and becoming. The will expresses the uniqueness of each individual, and learning to accept the will means a self-recognition or self-creation. In contrast, 'psychoanalysis, by describing the impulses as unconscious and universal, thus absolving the individual from them by declaring them universal, and thus absorbing the individual from responsibility for them, becomes one-sided' (Menaker, 1986, p.105). Rank contends that there is a limited therapeutic value in such reassurance from the therapist that the will impulses are not necessarily evil, especially for individuals '"who always seek some kind of excuse for their willing and find it now (in modern times) in the id instead of in God" (Rank, 1945, p.223). All too often the casual use of the past offers the patient the opportunity to justify his neurotic symptoms or character structure in terms of his history, and causes him to remain bound to his caretaker, insufficiently differentiated – unborn' (Menaker, 1986, p.119). Rank contends that the crucial issues may be missed in the psychoanalytic method of emphasizing the past as the most important aspects to make conscious of in this context. The patient's ego may not be able to make use of the understanding, and this stuckness may be in regard to the mother bond that is recreated in the actual situation of the analysis. The process of differentiation in the analytic setting became paramount for Rank. By helping the clients affirm their individuality, their distinctiveness, the hope is to help them accept their own will as the individuated function of the ego toward life itself.

In a tour de force, Rank argues that neurosis itself is a creative process. The therapeutic intervention is to see that a person's creative process, even if it is difficult and laboured, is successful in its refusal to condemn the will by affirming the counterwill's right to resist, and by doing so give voice to the entire person, negative and positive alike. In the acceptance of emotional suffering as an existential fact of life, the illusion that suffering can only be avoided through proper upbringing is dispelled, and the individual is called upon to assume responsibility for his or her own adaption to the painfulness of certain aspects of life.

Rank thought that Freud limited the functions of the ego, arguing instead that the ego is actually *acausal*, and can creatively transcend historical influences, emphasizing the individual responsibility of his or her own will and the self-adjustment potential to adapt to the social environment. Heinz Hartmann, Edith Jacobson, W.R.D. Fairbairn, Harry Guntrip, Carl Rodgers and Leslie Farber – to name a few theorists – would later revise and add to the understanding of ego functions reflective of Rank's earlier view of the ego's autonomy and creative will, and the importance of the environment. In addition, Rank points out that the neurotic person who has stressed a one-sided individuality that is too exclusive of the social influences is trapped between the will to express autonomy and the wish to love others. He contends that the neurotic struggle exemplifies the psychology type 'whose tormenting self-awareness blocks his or her own apotheosis with destructive interpretation that crowd out creative celebrations of the soul' (Rank, 1930, p.37). Rank thinks that neurosis in general is a refusal of life because the individual fears his own life force or libido, and this fear is traced to the fear of birth, which he designates as a fear of separation.

Rank underscored frequently that people often suffer because their striving for separateness precludes the possibility of a living relationship to the 'thou' or 'other' in the world and has thus, to some extent, distorted the individual's perception of the world. Rank underscores that willing and loving must be restored in a functioning balance – the contrapuntal play of creative, potential, paradoxical space between likeness and difference. This occurs in helping a person experience his own will possibilities instead of interpreting the problem only. Reconstructing the self must be achieved through the relationship experience between patient and therapist. As Rank said 'The human being is not only an individual but also a social being – the ego needs a Thou in order to become a Self' (Rank, 1941, p.8). Hence, throughout his writing Rank stresses that individuals suffer from inhibitions in regard to their capacity and ability to will. This inhibition Rank saw largely as the result of the interaction of the original endowment with a primary environment which failed to affirm the will of the growing child. But due to the presence of the will in each person, the task of therapy is to address this developmental deficit in order to support and affirm the patient's creative possibilities to structure a self and make an art of one's life. As James Lieberman says, 'Rank saw the therapist as midwife to a psychological rebirth that occurs when one moves from creature to creator, not passively accepting the gift and burden of life but taking it up actively ... This is psychopoesis, soul-making' (Lieberman, 1998, p.xv). Rank emphasized that we need the irrational as much as the rational forces for our guide – that we need illusion and play not only as an antidote to too much reality with its death awareness and life fears, but 'partly as a rehearsal for change in one's own identity, one's narrative' (Lieberman, 1998, p.xv). We need to be aware of the contrapuntal play of likenesses and difference. Rank returns this soul-force, this creative activity, into the life of his therapeutic vision.

Let us conclude with a clinical example. Forty-year-old William was referred due to depression brought about by his struggle with infertility. 'God must hate me to put me through such misery,' he began. Feeling broken, inadequate, unmanly, William says: 'The only thing I create is death. Maybe I should leave my wife so she can be with someone else.' He feels unable to accomplish much. 'I was building my family like an ark, then I learned of my infertility. We continue trying to build. Getting older brings weather of all kinds, so we work harder. And nothing happens – except the catastrophe. Rain every day. I feel like I'm treading water and Noah is sailing by with a wave on a wave.' William's image of fighting death, while Noah has been given opportunities and life, reflects William's envy, hurt, rage, anxiety, loss, sadness and sense of personal defectiveness. Noah's waving suggests the sadistic triumph of William's projections on to a world that denigrates his manhood and creative efforts. God and Noah, like life itself, have it in for him. Since he can only create death, he imagines scenarios where he is 'out of the way', rejected, absent like the progeny he cannot produce.

Although there is much literature about infertility and its psychological effects in women, comparable material about males is lacking. Reproductive endocrinologists report that the male factor accounts for 45 per cent of infertility. One in four men is infertile. Keylor and Apfel (2010) point out that male infertility 'is characterized by anxiety about sexual adequacy, potency and manliness. This assault on a man's sense of self revives feelings of competition, castration, and experiences of developmental trauma' (Keylor and Apfel, 2010, p.60). In accord with those observations, William feels 'cut off' from the world, competing with others who are fathers or 'more creative, smarter'. Similarly, Keylor and Apfel describe a man who found his ability to function sexually and at work compromised from the moment his doctor described his defective, sluggish sperm.

Early in treatment, William brings a dream: 'I am stumbling in the darkness in the basement of a house. There is deep mud on the floor, and I am struggling to walk. Someone is calling me from the top of the steps, where there is light, but I am stuck. I slowly pull myself toward the bottom of the steps.' After exploring the dream with him, we begin to see that the dream reflects William's depression in his day-world, with a hopeful addition symbolized by the call and light. His 'defect' triggers shame and banishment, withdrawal from the world, to the basement, the lower realm, where he is stuck. In his house, often analogous to the self-structure, the voice calling him from 'where there is light' suggests another direction associated with vision and movement – a will to advance from the muddy world of self-criticism toward the difficult work of extricating himself from his dark perspective. The dream may also point to unconscious feelings of being dirty and cloying, compensated by an inner healing momentum manifested in seeking therapy.

William often speaks of his experience-distant relationship with his father. He blames him for genetic infertility, but protects him from rage and hurt by praising his way of providing for the family (being a man, unlike William). Ambivalence toward father appears in transference doubts about 'the good of talking about any of this stuff', twinned with appreciation that he can. These dynamics mirror Keylor and Apfel's point that male infertility can reactivate developmental conflicts:

> While the great majority of men diagnosed with infertility are capable of withstanding this assault on their self-state, and have sufficient loving support in their intimate relations and friendship communities not to need intensive psychological help, for others the infertility intersects with previous conflict or trauma in a way that can overwhelm the psyche.
>
> (2010, p.5)

William and I worked with these feelings that assaulted his sense of masculine potency and the anxiety that it created. As William became more trusting of the therapeutic relationship, he became more aware of his rage and resentment in regard to the difficult reality of his infertility. As Keylor and Apfel say poignantly: 'Men and women are entirely unprepared for infertility; it is usually a shocking event for both partners' (2010, p.22). William uses the therapy well to express the shock of his continual inability to father a child, and in doing so begins to recognize that this chronic challenge, painful as it is, does not mean that he is marginalized as a creative person.

During this period, William had a dream:

> I am on an old clipper ship moored off an arctic or polar port – the kind that Shackleton might have sailed. The ice is breaking up in the port, and we are preparing to set sail. I have a bag in my hand, and I open it to find pearls. Strangely, I throw the pearls across the deck, sadly satisfied by my action. The wind is up, and the breaking ice reflects the blue sky vividly. I last remember seeing the horizon and open sea.

This dream expresses William's struggle with sadness and loss, twinned with growing hope and confidence. His situation had been frozen ('stuck'), but is thawing. He identifies with Shackleton's crew, or the hero himself, who, despite being stranded and nearly left to die, is rescued by an enormous will toward life.

In William's association to the bag of pearls, recounting many visits to doctors, he sometimes felt he was casting pearls before swine. I wondered if the pearls might reference his sperm ('thrown from the bag'). I pointed out that he described the wind as 'up' – a sense of spiritual movement and potency. 'Sadly satisfied' might mirror his feelings about ejaculation. Although pleasurable, it could remind him of infertility. When I asked about the blue ice and horizon, he said he was beginning to feel in the world again, though self-contempt still 'blocked the harbour at times'. From our discussion it appeared that William was 'breaking' out of his depression, the frozen port, beginning to feel emergent will, feel part of a crew of others indicative of life itself. He reported that he had begun 'making love again' – something that had been curtailed by feelings of castration and humiliation.

Rank explored in his social–cultural writings that from ancient beliefs in the male–father as the progenitor in procreation, patriarchal ideology emerged in the 'sexual era/religious era' (Rank, 1930). Archaic humanities thought that sexuality could be everything but procreation since procreation was thought to steal the soul and threaten immortality. As cultures developed, moralistically re-evaluated non-reproductive sexuality was understood as evil, a cause of death. Sexuality became solely for procreation. Offering children to the community, church and God justified the act. From a Rankian perspective, we can see that, finding himself abandoned by the life-force that should be his inheritance, William relates his inability to father a child to having 'bad will', which God condemns. His infertility is viewed as inactive and destructive, a reason for wife and God to forsake him.

We recall in Rank's theory that creativity attempts to materialize something illusory, spiritual or transcendent, 'to prove the existence of the soul by concretizing it' (Rank, 1932, p.96). William's feeling that he is condemned to drown while God's minion 'goes by with a wave' reflects Rank's notion of self-condemnation in the wake of the inability to make real the ideal through creative production (progeny). William's infertility connotes loss of immortality, preceded by perceived rejections by community and family. If he cannot create, life becomes unreal, broken, frozen, death-dealing. Sexuality becomes fraught with ambivalence and 'sad satisfactions'.

William's psychotherapy focused on revitalizing his will to help him discern that he is capable of actualizing a unique, creative idiom. His dream of the ice-thaw in the arctic port, and the hope of embarking toward the blue horizon, suggested gathering will, striving toward immortality. This vision offered him a glimpse of his desire to separate from transferential paradigms and inherited collective beliefs to continue individuation, letting the self set sail. Breaking ice inaugurated a different kind of flood than his ark analogy. It unburdened him from the numbing stasis of bereavement, leading to flooding grief, opening a passage for his life to resume its course. He and his partner began considering other opportunities toward parenthood and co-creating a life together.

Individuals' difficulty bearing separation and individualization led Rank to see human suffering as related to feelings of difference, a feeling William had to confront in the therapeutic crucible. In fact, Rank called his psychology 'a psychology of difference' (Rank, 1941), meaning that he empathized with our human fear of separation and alienation. In consequence of feeling different and isolated, humans exhibit a strong urge to identification and likeness. As Rank underscores,

> The individual traces his difficulties, his sufferings, back to difference. Whether this difference has belonged to the individual from childhood, whether it first appeared through painful experiences of later life, or whether it does not come to full consciousness at all, it exists, is given in the very fact of his individuality, which apparently he can neither accept nor affirm, but must deny ... The individual suffers from his difference, from his individuality.
> (Rank, 1936, pp.46–47)

William communicated his fear of difference, of not belonging, not being 'like' his father, even as he longed to be different, a son becoming a self, not a reflection of father. His suffering was connected with his struggle to affirm his difference. It is important to note that the word 'difference' has the same etymology as the word 'suffer', being the Latin *ferre*, 'to bear' (*Oxford English Dictionary*, p.722). 'To bear' refers to birth and carrying. William's suffering is connected with his struggle to affirm his difference, and this connotes both a birth and a burdening, which the process of therapy allowed.

Echoing this Rankian wisdom, the psychoanalyst Adam Phillips observes, 'Psychoanalysis tells us in short, that our lives depend on our recognition that other people – those vital others that we love and desire – are separate from us, 'beyond our control' as we say, despite the fact that this very acknowledgment is itself productive of so much violence. Difference is the one thing we cannot bear' (Phillips and Bersani, 2008, p.viii). However, as Phillips concludes, sounding very much like Rank, perhaps the acknowledgement of difference is the beginning of 'a new story of intimacy' that will 'prefer the possibilities of the future to the determinations of the past' (ibid.). As we see in the clinical case of William, a new story of intimacy does prevail in the tragic nature of life where, evoking Rank, the affirmation of the obligatory can paradoxically transform the creature to creator, and the hope to construct a life can become a creative will to both bear the burden of difference and transcend it. Or, as Rank says succinctly, 'Therapy is a process in which a person who has been unable to go on living without more fear and guilt than he is willing or able to bear, somehow gains the courage to live again' (Taft, 1933, p.283).

References

Alvarez, A. (2012). *The Thinking Heart*. London: Routledge.

Barbre, C. (1997). Reversing the crease: Nietzsche's influence on Otto Rank's concept of creative will and the birth of individuality. In J. Golomb, W. Santaniello and R. Lehrer (eds), *Nietzsche and depth psychology*. New York: State University of New York Press, pp.247–267.

—— (2004). The wages of dying: catastrophe transformed. In F. Kelcourse (ed.), *Human development and faith: life-cycle stages of body, mind, and soul*. St Louis: Chalice Press, pp.285–307.

Bersani, L. and Phillips, A. (2008). *Intimacies*. Chicago: University of Chicago Press.

Bollas, C. (2003). Introducing Edward Said. In E.W. Said, *Freud and the Non-European*. London and New York: Verso, pp. 2–9.

Burchfield, R.W. (ed.) (1972–1986). *A supplement to the Oxford English Dictionary*. Wotton-under-Edge: Clarendon Press.

Freud, S. (1953). *Beyond the pleasure principle*. In J. Strachey, *The standard edition of the complete psychological works of Sigmund Freud*, vol. 18. London: Hogarth Press.

Heller, P. (1992). Reflections on a child analysis with Anna Freud and an adult analysis with Ernst Kris. *Journal of the American Academy of Psychoanalysis*, 20: 48–74.

Homans, P. (1989). *The ability to mourn*. Chicago: University of Chicago Press.

Keylor, R. and Apfel, R. (2010). Male infertility: integrating an old psychoanalytic story with research literature. *Studies in Gender and Sexuality*, 11: 60–77.

Kramer, R. (ed.) (1996). *A psychology of difference: the American lectures*. Princeton: Princeton University Press.

Lieberman, E.J. (1995). *Acts of will: the life and work of Otto Rank*. Amherst: University of Massachusetts Press.

Menaker, E. (1982). *Otto Rank: a rediscovered legacy*. New York: Columbia University Press.

—— (1996). *Separation, will, and creativity: the wisdom of Otto Rank*. Northvale: Jason Aronson.

—— and Menaker, W. (1984). *Ego in evolution*. New York: Da Capo Press.

Rank, O. (1903) Unpublished diary, 1903–1905. New York: Columbia Library Rare Books Collection. Selected entries in Taft, J. (1958). *Otto Rank: a biographical study based on notebooks, letters, collected writings, therapeutic achievements and personal associations*. New York: The Julian Press.

—— (1924). *The Trauma of Birth*. New York: Harper & Row Torchbook (original English translation 1929).

—— (1907). *Der Kunstler: Ansatze zu einer Sexual-Psychologie*. Vienna and Leipzig: Hugo Heller & Cie.

—— (1909). The myth of the birth of the hero. In Robert Segal (ed.), *Quest of the hero*. Princeton: Princeton University Press, pp.1–86.

—— (1911). *Die Lohengrinsage: Ein Beitrag zu ihrer Motivgestaltung und Deutung* (*The Lohegrin Saga*). Leipzig and Vienna: Franz Deutike.

(1914). *The double: a psychoanalytic study*, H. Tucker (trans.). London: Maresfield Library, 1989.
—— (1924). *The trauma of birth*. New York: Harper & Row Torchbook (original English translation 1929).
—— (1930). Seelenglaube und Psychologie. In Gregory C. Richter and E. James Lieberman (trans.), *Psychology and the soul: a study of the origin, conceptual evolution, and nature of the soul*. Baltimore: Johns Hopkins University Press, 1998.
—— (1931). *Modern education*, M. Moxon (trans.). New York: Knopf.
—— (1932). *Art and artist*. New York: Knopf.
—— (1936). *Will therapy*. New York: Knopf (originally published as *Technik der Psychoanalyse*, vol. 1, 1926, Vol. 2, 1929, Vol. 3, 1931).
—— (1941). *Beyond psychology*. New York: Dover.
—— (1945). *Will therapy and truth and reality*. New York: Knopf
Rank, O. and Ferenczi, S. (1925). *Entwicklungsziele der Psychoanalyse: Zur Wechselheziehung von Theorie und Praxis*. Leipzig, Vienna, Zürich: Internationaler Psycho-analitischer Verlag, no. 40. Published in English as *The Development of Psychoanalysis*, C. Newton (trans.). New York: Dover, 1956.
Ross, L. (1997). The meaning of death in the context of life. In H.R. Polio, T. Henley and C.B. Thompson (eds), *The phenomenology of everyday life*. Cambridge: Cambridge University Press, pp.298–333.
Said, E.W. (2001). *Reflections on exile and other essays*. Cambridge: Harvard University Press.
—— (2003). *Freud and the Non-European*. London and New York: Verso.
Stenslie, C.E. (1984). The contribution of Otto Rank's psychology to the critical understanding of the psychoanalytic concept of narcissism. Dissertation, The Pennsylvania State University.
Taft, J. (1958). *Otto Rank: a biographical study based on notebooks, letters, collected writings, therapeutic achievements and personal associations*. New York: The Julian Press.
Walsh, N. (1996). Trauma and death. In C.B. Strozier and M. Flynn (eds), *Trauma and self*. Lanham, MD: Rowman and Littlefield, pp.245–254.

Conclusions
The universal and the particular in the therapeutic encounter

Rebecca Coleman Curtis

As Yoshimo (2006) stated in a book called *Covering*, when human lives are described with enough particularity, the universal is revealed through them. Identity and difference are two sides of the same coin that have played a role in the development of Western philosophy at least since Plato composed the *Sophist*. Heidegger (1969) wrote a book translated as *Identity and difference*, Hegel wrote extensively on this subject (Grier, 2007) and early Vedantic philosophical systems are also concerned with the topic. For psychologists, however, identity usually refers to the ways in which individuals are unique. For sociologists, identity usually pertains to social roles and categories. The present volume deals with both senses of the word. For psychoanalysts and therapists, we see in these chapters the attempt to understand people's unique identities while bridging the distance between them.

Peter Brook (2014, p.14) has written that when we go to the theatre we want to be surprised, 'And yet we can only be concerned if we can feel a strong link with ourselves.' We want to feel that we have our feet firmly planted on the ground as we move into the unknown. We all like a degree of novelty. Yet, as Milner (1969) put it, we want to find a degree of 'the familiar in the unfamiliar'. We see something familiar, although different, in the characters of such writers as Katherine Mansfield, Tennessee Williams and Carson McCullers. Psychoanalysts are trained to tolerate uncertainty, to be curious. These qualities may make us even more interested in what is different than many average people are. Yet to engage in this work, like in method acting, we have to find a part of ourselves in another person.

Freud (1919) even wondered at one point, seeing 'an elderly gentleman in a dressing gown and traveling cap', who the old man was. Thinking the man was not at all like himself, he came to realize that this was his own reflection in a mirror. He noted there is something at once familiar and unfamiliar about similarities and differences that is unnerving and disrupts our usual sense of self-definition, our theories of ourselves. Stern, in his chapter, discusses how we all become different through aging, and many of us through marriage and divorce, pregnancy, relocation and illness.

Confronted with difference, there can be an immediate response of fear or anxiety. A vast psychological literature exists on how primates are simply frightened by those in their own species who look different (Hebb, 1946). Another extensive literature exists about how people like those better whose attitudes and values agree with their own and dislike those who seem to disagree with them (Byrne, 1971; Curtis and Miller, 1986; Griffitt, 1974, Kaplan, 1972). But yet in regard to romantic attraction, people prefer and are more excited by those with different pheromones (Wedekind et al., 1995). Sameness leads to stagnation. Ultimately, the absence of difference is psychological death. And, although people are first to take care of their own kin in times of emergency, there is an increasing number of people who are seen as family (Davies, Wright and Aron, in press).

In Solomon's (2012) book *Far From the Tree*, parents of children who were different, such as deaf or dwarves, later said that they wished their child had not been otherwise (parents of schizophrenics were an exception). As people get to know one another in a caring relationship, the qualities of the individual become familiar, and in general we know that familiarity increases liking (Zajonc, 1968).

This book shows how psychoanalysts and psychotherapists find similarities in their feelings of vulnerabilities, develop an appreciation of cultural values different from their own and get in touch with aspects of themselves that, if nor disavowed or part of 'not-me', find contact hearing the experiences of another and identify with those feelings in those situations. They often find limitations and defects within themselves. There is always a risk of rejection, but also of a new self recovered. As the relationship and new understandings grow, people begin to feel what Gadamer (1960/1975) referred to as a 'fusion of horizons'. For Gadamer, our understandings and interpretation always comes from within a particular 'horizon'. The fusion with another's horizon means that we exist neither in a closed horizon, nor within a unique one. The process requires a speaker and a listener. Through encounters with others, the horizon of our own understanding is susceptible to change.

It is estimated that in the United States between 2040 and 2050 the majority of the population will be people of colour (Ortman and Guarneri, 2009, from the United States Census Bureau, 2008). Simple contact with those who are different does not reduce prejudice, but intimate and cooperative situations do. Attitudes trump race. Although there are some exceptions, whites prefer associations with blacks who have attitudes like their own, rather than whites who have opposing attitudes (Byrne and Wong, 1962; Rokeach, 1968; Stein, Hardyck and Smith, 1965).

As opposed to focusing upon prejudices, our volume examines the growing liking for people who are different, what has been referred to as allophilia. We see analysts becoming fond of someone on the autism spectrum, someone suffering from psychosis, someone transgendering, of someone facing a serious criminal charge, of people from oppressed indigenous populations, and, presumably, the patients sharing similar fond feelings. Although our media focus on discrimination, a serious problem to be sure, there are multiple examples of people seeking to get to know those who are different. For example, 431 million people in 170 countries have watched the Discovery Channel. Millions of young people each year choose to be foreign exchange students and millions of families host them (Pittinsky 2012).

The process of identity formation involves both identifying with others and disidentifying, and as Guarton pointed out, becoming differentiated yet connected.

Fromm (1964) had suggested that relying on the preferences of others is an escape from freedom and Sartre (1943/1956) considered doing so to be living in bad faith. Belnap describes the move in adolescents from identification to identity, a taking on of one's own values. Fucheck shows that even ruptures in the therapeutic alliance can help patients distinguish their own desires from those of the analyst. Developing a good relationship with an analyst is not always an easy route and sometimes fails. Patients sometimes come in with a prejudice against a group of people that is hard to overcome. The analyst may be part of such a group. O'Leary emphasizes the need for more diversity in analysts themselves.

As Willock demonstrated, sometimes, when we dislike someone, the person reminds us unconsciously (or consciously) of someone who has mistreated us. And sometimes we must disidentify with a parent. In therapy, a negative identificatory process can be revised. Sometimes, as Belnap pointed out, even psychotic symptoms function to communicate identity and therapy can help move these symptoms into a more functional identity. Similarities can be quite hard to find. Sapountzis had difficulty sitting with a strange young man who would not communicate but who brought in notebooks of words in Urdu and letters of different alphabets until Sapountzis recalled his own difficulty learning German and not being accepted at a German school. Over time, the boy brought in his interest in other cultures, and they were able to relate, both sharing in this enjoyment.

In many of these chapters, authors struggle with listening to the experiences of others so that they might have the feelings of the other person in that situation while still struggling to maintain their own perspectives. Or, they endure their own sense of difference while keeping in mind the perspective of another or a broader society. As Buber (1923/1958, p. 62) noted, 'All actual life is encounter.' For Buber, there are 'I–it' relations when we relate to others as members of categories or 'I–Thou' (or 'I–You') encounters when we relate with the entirety of our being to another whole person. Persons appear by entering into relation with other persons – by touching the You. It is this 'I–You' relation that occurs in the therapeutic encounters described in this book. The physicist David Bohm (1996) also promoted the necessity of real dialogues if we are to understand and get along with others who are different. Those of us in the Western world are intensely aware of a desire to do this instead of being in yet another war. Intimate interactions, including those in psychoanalysis, are one way to help us navigate the divides between peoples.

References

Bohm, D. (1996). *On dialogue*, L. Nichol (ed.). London: Routledge.
Brook, P. (2014). Programme notes to *The valley of astonishment*. New York: Playbill, Inc.
Buber, M. (1958). *I and thou*. New York Scribner, originally published 1923.
Byrne, D. (1971). *The attraction paradigm*. New York: Academic Press.
Byrne, D. and Wong, T.J. (1962). Racial prejudice, interpersonal attraction, and assumed dissimilarity of attitudes. *Journal of Abnormal and Social Psychology*, 65: 246–253.

Curtis, R.C. and Miller, K. (1986). Believing another likes or dislikes you: behavior making the belief come true. *Journal of Personality and Social Psychology*, 51: 284–290.
Davies, K., Wright, S.C. and Aron, A. (in press). Building positive relations between groups from close relationships between members of those groups. In L.R. Tropp and R. Mallett (eds), *Beyond prejudice reduction: pathways to positive intergroup relations*. Washington: Psychology Press.
Freud, S. (1919). The uncanny. *Standard Edition*, 17: 217–252.
Fromm, E. (1964). *Escape from freedom*. New York: Holt (original work published 1941).
Gadamer, H.G. (1975). *Truth and method*, G. Garden and J. Cumming (eds and trans). New York: Seabury.
Griffitt, W. (1974). Attitude similarity and attraction. In T.L. Huston (ed.), *Foundation of interpersonal attraction*. New York: Academic Press.
Hebb, D.O. (1946). On the nature of fear. *Psychological Review*, 55: 259–276.
Heidegger, M. (1969). *Truth and identity*, J. Starnbuagh (trans.). New York: Harper & Row.
Kaplan, M.F. (1972). Interpersonal attraction as a function of relatedness of similar and dissimilar attitudes. *Journal of Experimental Research in Personality*, 6: 17–21.
Milner, M. (1969). *The hands of the living God: an account of a psycho-analytic treatment*. London: Hogarth Press.
Rokeach, M. (1968). *Beliefs, attitudes, and values*. San Francisco: Josey-Bass.
Sartre, J.P. (1956). Being and nothingness, H.E. Burns (trans.). New York: Philosophical Library, original work published 1943.
Solomon, A. (2012). *Far from the tree*. New York: Scribner.
Stein, D.D., Hardyck, J.A. and Smith, M.B. (1965). Race and belief: an open and shut case. *Journal of Personality and Social Psychology*, 67: 281–289.
Wedekind, C., Seebeck, T., Bettens, F. and Paepke, A.J. (1995). MHC-dependent mate preferences in humans. *Proceedings of the Royal Society of London Series B: Biolo*.
Yoshimo, K. (2006). *Covering: the hidden assault on our civil rights*. New York: Random House.
Zajonc, R. (1968). Attitudinal effects of mere exposure. *Journal of Personality and Social Psychology*, 9: 1–27.

Index

abandonment 99, 130–131, 180, 182
Aborigine 5, 92, 96; Aboriginal Elders 97, 107
absence 12, 15, 32, 48, 53, 89, 110–112, 138, 160, 167, 184–185, 194, 209
abstraction 136
abyss 18, 107, 112, 116
acting out 20, 41, 44–45, 174
adaption 147
adaptive challenge 91
addiction 106
ADHD 83
Adler, Alfred 193
Administration for Children's Services 69
adolescence 3, 14, 28–46, 111, 144, 193
adolescent development 30, 34
adulthood 28–46, 138, 148, 166
affect 22, 31, 49, 50, 51, 56, 115, 137, 141, 142, 145, 147, 166; competency 31; regulation 145–146, 148
affective attunement 145
affective colouring 53
affective involvement 80
affectivity 168
age, age-appropriate 3, 13, 17, 28, 30, 35, 45–46, 56, 77, 80, 83, 89, 95, 97, 99, 111, 114–115, 116, 136, 138, 139, 140, 155, 174–175, 193
aging 174–175
alcohol abuse 99
alienation 45, 129, 149, 205
alike, alikeness 2–6, 16, 22–26, 49, 50, 57, 64–65, 72, 95, 102, 144, 190, 197
alike/different divide 72
allophilia 209
aloneness 78
alpha function 13
American Psychiatric Association 137

American Psychoanalytic Association 89, 92, 196
American Psychological Association 91
analysis, psychoanalysis 5–6, 11, 13–15, 19–20, 23, 25–26, 72, 87–93, 153, 159, 165, 168–169, 171–172, 174, 180, 182–190, 193–197, 199, 201, 205, 210
analyst as patient 179–190
analytic objects 79
analytic third 76–83
anger 14, 16, 24, 33, 42, 63, 98, 100, 123, 130, 140, 173, 181, 185, 186
annihilated self 111
annihilation 96, 99, 111,
anomalous experiences 132–133
anxiety 20, 25, 31, 36, 51, 95–96, 98, 100–102, 140, 142, 143, 150, 154, 184–187, 193, 195–198, 202–203, 208
Asperger, Hans 136
Asperger's Syndrome fn. 143
association 16, 73, 74, 78–82, 153, 157, 158, 204
atonement 114
attachment 20, 23, 99, 111, 144–146, 148, 154, 166–167, 169, 192
'attacks on linking' 129
attraction 32, 142, 175, 209
attunement 3, 23, 26, 145
Austen Riggs Center 152
Australian Aboriginal people 95–103
Australian Dreaming 109
authority 31, 34, 36, 40, 41, 126, 150, 151, 171, 183
autism, autistic 5, 105–116, 136–138, 142, 149, 154, 209
autistic cut-out 105
autistic defence 105–107
autistic psychopathy 136

Index

Autistic Spectrum Disorder 136–138
autonomy 22, 23, 26, 156, 196, 201

B4U-ACT 71
Baranger and Baranger 78, 79
Barinya 116
Baron-Cohen, Simon 137, 138
Belnap 3, 28–46, 210
Benjamin, Jessica 12, 20
bi-nocular perspective 158
bi-personal field 78, 79
biculturalism 130, 132
Billow, R.M. 78
Bion, W.R. 110
bipolar disorder 130
birth defects 165
'Black Psychoanalysts Speak' 90
Blanco, Matte 79, 81
Blatt, S.J. 22
Blos, P. 30
Bollas, Christopher 49, 192
borderline 69
borromean knot 150
brain damage 138
Brandchaft, B. 14, 133
British Object Relations Theory 12
Bromberg, P.M. 22
'bullet mind' 38
bullying, bullied 39, 132, 144, 146–149, 154–155

cancer 30, 140
caregiving, caregivers 22, 145, 146
caretaking 141
Casey, B.J. 28, 32
central trauma 112
child-caregiver system 166
Childhood Disintegrative Disorder 137
childrearing 11, 95
Christianity 131
chronic psychotic disorder 148
classical autism 137
cleft palate, cleft lip 6, 166, 168
co-construction 92
colonization of otherness 119
commedia'dell arte 49
community 31, 46, 57, 62, 63, 71, 98, 99, 101, 105–107, 109, 110, 116, 152, 154, 155, 157, 185, 190, 204
companionship 141
Comparative-Integrative Psychoanalysis 13, 20
compassion 17, 169, 188

concretization 106
Cooper, A.M. 172, 175, 176
coping 146, 148
coping mechanisms 146
counter-transference 22, 24, 63, 70–72, 74, 75, 99–101, 114–115, 174, 175, 181, 182, 187; countertransference enactments 24, 174; countertransferential reactions 82
creativity 6, 144–160, 193, 195, 196, 199, 200, 204
cultivation 31, 96
culture 1–3, 5, 6, 36, 41, 71, 78, 92, 95–97, 101, 102, 105–110, 118, 119, 121–124, 130–134, 138, 151, 192, 204, 210; cultural competence 123, 125; cultural difference 92, 95, 101; cultural genocide 4, 96, 97, 129; cultural identity 123; cultural superego 96; cultural supervision 5, 118–121, 123, 125
curiosity 3, 33, 38, 39, 45, 87, 119, 128, 143, 147, 149, 159, 181, 183, 185, 186

Dadirri, or 'healing circle' 105–107, 112–114, 116
dark abyss 107
dating 138, 141, 142, 147
deadened mother 98
Dearing, R.L. 23
death 1, 5, 13, 52, 97, 99, 107, 112, 114, 140–142, 166, 168, 193, 194, 196–200, 202, 204, 209
death drive 13
defensive processes 14
defensiveness 174, 183, 185–187, 189–190
delusion 28, 32–34, 37, 39–41, 43
demoralization 132
denial 90, 91, 131, 165, 169, 198
dependence, dependency 26, 46, 100, 102, 114, 158–160
deprecated otherness 144
depression, depressed 23, 57, 69–72, 74, 80, 98, 100, 139, 149, 166, 202–204
depressive position 12, 13
deprivation 145
Derrida, Jacques 53
Delusion 32
desire 17, 22, 24, 26, 33, 34, 38, 43, 50–52, 54, 76–78, 83, 99, 100, 102, 110, 131, 138, 139, 141, 142, 144, 149–152, 154–157, 160, 175, 181, 187, 194, 205, 210; Desire of the Other 154, 156
despair 51, 110, 119, 121, 149

development 3, 6, 19, 22, 23, 26, 28–46, 51, 54, 61, 82, 102, 119, 121, 123, 131, 136–138, 144–149, 153–154, 156, 159, 165, 166, 171, 173, 192, 194–196, 199, 202, 203, 208; developmental achievement 31, 33, 38, 39, 41, 45; developmental dynamics 28
diagnosis 46, 76, 136, 138, 140
difference 2–6, 36, 41, 43, 56, 59, 61, 64, 65, 89, 92, 95, 101–103, 119, 124, 125, 128–134, 137, 144, 146, 159, 187, 188, 192–206, 208–210
differentiation 22, 26, 34, 43, 197, 201
disappointment 53, 168, 182,
discomfort 51, 73, 77, 101, 119, 149, 150
disidentification 11–20, 209
disorganized attachment 145, 146
disruption 22, 35, 145, 188
dissociation, dissociated experience 14, 22, 131, 145, 167, 168, 189
diversity ('diverse') 2, 4, 87–93, 210
divorce 14, 17, 69, 155, 173, 196, 208, 240
Djarada 109–110
Dobson, Mick 103
doer/done-to relationships 12
domestic violence 99, 101, 110, 113
dream 16–18, 20, 41, 53, 54, 70, 72–74, 103, 105–109, 112, 114, 115, 125, 126, 129, 157–159, 194, 203–205; The Dreaming 105, 107–109
drug abuse, drugs, stimulant abuse 98, 110–114, 116, 154; see also 'addiction'
DSM 137; DSM-IV 137
dyad ('patient/therapist dyad') 4, 78, 92, 131, 179, 189
dystonic behaviour 55

Early Infantile Autism 136
early relationships 145–146, 148
echolalia 136
effective presence 176
ego 11, 12, 17, 71, 96, 106, 110, 111, 114, 130, 194–197, 199–202; antilibidinal ego 12, 17
emotional stability 31
emotional valence 53
empathy 6, 15, 16, 42, 43, 82, 101, 106, 142, 193, 198; empathic attunement 145
enactment 14, 16, 24, 26, 64, 79, 106, 109, 174, 182, 187, 189
enmeshment 20, 197
envy 63, 106, 110, 175, 202
exclusion 144–160

Erikson, Erik 11, 23, 34
Ewens, T. 28

failure 23, 41, 42, 60, 80, 87–89, 100, 131, 141, 146, 149, 150, 153, 154, 175, 185, 187–190, 195, 199, 200
Fairbairn, W.R.D. 12, 17, 20, 201
false memories 158
false self 14, 24, 34, 57, 65
family 1, 11, 14–17, 23, 25, 26, 28, 33, 34, 36, 38, 41–45, 59, 60, 69, 71, 76, 96, 98–102, 110–114, 121–123, 126, 129, 131–133, 138, 140–142, 150, 155, 165, 166, 172, 173, 187, 193, 194, 202–204, 209
fantasy 13, 14, 36, 51, 52, 54, 70, 149, 154, 175, 180–182, 189, 198
father 5, 12, 15, 16, 19, 25, 38, 56, 57, 69, 70, 80, 82, 83, 97, 98, 108, 109, 114, 121, 122, 125, 130, 139–143, 150, 157, 166, 173, 193, 196, 199, 203–205
fear 12, 15, 24–26, 33, 39, 40, 42, 51, 74, 77, 95–100, 112, 114, 125, 141, 146, 155, 157, 159, 160, 166, 167, 173, 175, 182, 187, 189, 193, 194, 196–199, 201, 202, 205, 206, 208
feelings 13, 16, 18, 22, 24, 25, 29, 33, 36, 38, 41–44, 62–64, 70, 74, 76, 80, 91, 98, 101, 131, 138–143, 145, 147–149, 152, 154–157, 159, 160, 166–169, 175, 180, 181, 183, 195, 200, 203–205, 209, 210
feminism 120
Ferenczi, Sandor 12, 195
Ferro, A. and Basile, R. 79
Fiscalini, J. 79
foetal self 112
Fonagy, P. 12, 52, 133, 137, 147, 148
forgiveness 114
foster care, foster family, 'fostered' 98, 114, 130
four pillars of wellbeing 131, 133
Fragile Spielraum, The 48
free association 153
Freud, Sigmund 6, 12, 13, 17, 19, 20, 90, 96, 183, 192–196, 198, 201, 208
Freud, Anna 12, 30, 129, 199
Frith, Uta 137, 138

gender identity disorder 4, 76
gender identity issues 78
genealogy 121, 126
genital warming 18
genocide, genocidal 2, 4, 92, 96, 97, 129

Gerson, M. 80
globalization 2, 129
'good-enough holding' 132
Grandin, Temple 138, 140
grandiosity 44, 45
Greenhill 120
Guarton, Gladys 3, 6, 22–26, 209
guilt 22, 23, 26, 40, 42, 43, 50, 71, 73, 75, 100, 101, 114, 130, 147, 158, 169, 172, 193–195, 197–200, 206

hallucinations 33, 45
hapu 121, 125, 126
healing circle, see '*Dadirri*'
hell 57
hierarchy of needs 28
hinengaro 128, 131, 134
Hitler, Adolf 18
Hoffman, Irwin 183, 185, 186
holding 17, 37, 102, 106, 112, 129, 132, 133, 168
Holocaust 92, 129
home 3, 15–17, 48–65, 69, 87, 95–103, 109, 110, 113, 114, 122, 131, 133, 136, 138, 139, 167, 168, 179, 192, 194
homelessness 52, 101, 168
Homes, A.M. 48
homosexuality, gayness, gay 5, 17–19, 56, 59, 61, 62, 64, 90
humiliation 147
hyper-identification 37, 39
hypomanic state 167

identification 34, 35
identification 4, 11–20, 33, 36, 37, 39, 42, 43, 46, 56, 59, 64, 66, 67,70,73, 74, 75, 80–81, 97, 99, 121, 126, 131, 145, 182, 186, 190, 200, 209, 210
identity 2–4, 11, 17, 23, 29–31, 34–36, 42, 45, 62, 63, 76–78, 83, 87, 89, 95–97, 102, 110, 121, 123, 128–134, 144–160, 171, 176, 177, 180, 189, 193, 194, 197, 198, 202, 208–210; identity crisis 45; identity development 3, 23; identity diffusion 36; identity formation 30, 35, 209; identity in crisis 42; lost identity 102
immigration 173
impasse 24, 44, 131, 148, 153, 156, 180
imprisonment, imprisoned 49, 99, 114, 187; imprisonment in smothering passivity 114
inadequacy 25

incest 122
independence 26, 102, 140, 160
individuation 6, 20, 22, 28–30, 34, 36, 40–46, 52, 192, 195, 196, 198, 201, 205
inferiority complex fn., 170
inner life 52–54
innocence 71, 73–75
insecurity 139
integration 22, 26, 40, 91, 102, 129, 132, 136, 173
interpersonal dyad 92
intersubjectivity 14, 131; intersubjective space 133; intersubjective third 80
intervention 5, 30, 56, 123, 132, 148, 166, 168, 172, 173, 201
intimacy 23, 26, 141, 159, 179, 190, 205
introjective personality configuration 22
introjective/projective processes 12
irrational beliefs 45
isolation 3, 19, 158, 167, 169, 176
Issacs, Susan 51, 54
iwi 121, 125, 126, 131

Jesus 37, 44, 46, 126
Journal of the American Psychoanalytic Association 92

Kanner, Leo 136, 137
kanyini 96, 102,
Klein, Melanie 12, 13, 51, 96, 99, 130
Kohut, J. 12
Kunapipi cult 108

Lacan, J. 131, 150, 151, 154, 156
Laing, R.D. 18
language delays 83
learned helplessness 99
learning 26, 28, 29, 31, 33–37, 39–41, 44–46, 83, 120, 124, 147, 149, 153–156, 196, 201, 210
Leary, K. 89, 91
Levenson, E. 22, 172
Lewis, Helen Block 23, 91
libidinal ego 12, 17
libido 20, 195, 201
Lichtenberg, J.D. 15
likeness 2–6, 59, 64, 95, 101, 102, 145, 192, 193, 196, 197, 200, 202, 205
Likierman, M. 82
literal thinking 141
literalness 136
loneliness 55, 56, 83, 129, 139, 141, 147, 169

loss 26, 28, 35, 48, 51, 69, 73, 88, 91, 96, 101, 102, 105, 106, 109, 110–114, 125, 131, 142, 145, 146, 197, 198, 202, 204
loud silence, the 87
love 14, 16–20, 26, 45, 74, 83, 90, 93, 99, 109, 110, 124, 141, 174, 193, 198, 201, 204, 205
Lynd, H.M. 22

Mahler, M.S. 20
Main M., and Hesse, E. 145, 146
malattunement, misattunement 22, 166
mana 118, 124–126
'manifest content' 129
Maori 5, 118–126, 128–134
Maori Mental Health Services 5, 128, 130, 133, 134; Maori Mental Health Model 131
Maori Sovereignty 120
marginalization, marginalized 65, 72, 73, 91, 101, 147, 203
Margolis, Marvin 89
Markham, Edwin 93
Markson, E.R. 57
master-slave dialectic 22
mastery 46, 146–150,
Mathelin, K. 82
Meares, Russell 48
memory 12, 25, 48, 49–56, 131, 145, 155, 158, 160, 192, 194, 195
mentalization 137, 147
mentalizing 133, 137, 138
Merkin, Daphne 50
metacognition 147, 148
metaphor 32, 38, 48, 49, 53–57, 120, 123, 137, 158, 195; embedded metaphor 49, 53–55,
metapsychology 49
mind 28–31, 33–35, 37–40, 43–46, 49, 52, 63, 73, 82, 95, 105, 107, 115, 132, 134, 137, 138, 143, 145, 148, 152, 153, 158, 159, 167, 168, 187, 188
minority representation 90, 91
mirroring 133, 166, 168
misrecognition 12
moemoea 125, 126
molestation, molested 69, 70, 72, 111
mood disorder 129
moral defence 17
moral masochism 50
mother, mothering 3, 5, 11–20, 33, 34, 42–44, 49–52, 54–57, 63, 69 70, 80, 82, 83, 96, 98–102, 105–108, 110–115, 125, 126, 130, 131, 138–142, 154, 155, 158, 159, 166, 167, 172, 173, 193, 195, 196, 201
mother-child bond 12
mother-infant attachment 99
murder 80, 98, 106, 110, 112, 115
mutual regulation 166
mutuality 168
myth 42, 45, 65, 103, 108, 109, 124, 126, 130, 188, 194, 198

Name of the Father 150
narcissism, narcissistic 17, 116, 151, 155, 156, 175, 194, 198
neonatal surgery 166, fn. 169
neurosis 3, 11, 48–57, 195, 198–201
neutrality 70, 74, 75, 80, 92, 171, 176
New South Wales 96
non-existence 110

O'Carroll, Tom 70–72, 75
object 3, 11–14, 17–20, 23, 40, 48–57, 78, 79, 81–83, 96, 100, 110, 111, 114, 145, 150, 154, 158, 174, 179; object concept 50; object constancy 150; object free 51; object relations 48; Object Relations Theory ('object') 12, 154; object-seeking ('object seeking') 50, 51
omnipotent projections 12
'One People, One Land' 103
other, otherness 2, 3, 6, 12, 16, 19, 23–26, 28, 49, 52–54, 69–75, 76–83, 101, 119, 124, 133, 144–147, 151–154, 156, 158, 159, 167, 168, 190, 192, 197, 198, 202, 205, 209, 210
'other mind' 167–168

paedophilia 4, 74
Paedophilia: The Radical Case 70, 71
pakeha 5, 118, 122, 126, 128–130, 133
panic 25, 167, 187
Papatuanuku 123, 126
paralysis 23, 24, 26
paranoia 33, 34, 39, 41, 44, 98, 100, 130, 154, 155; paranoid psychosis 153; paranoid schizophrenic 114; paranoid-schizoid 12, 13, 96–97, 100, 102; paranoid-schizoid anxiety 102
parenting 48, 145, 173
parents 2, 5, 6, 11, 14, 15, 17, 25, 30, 34, 36, 37, 41–45, 50, 56, 69, 82, 97–99, 136, 138, 139, 141, 145, 148, 154, 155, 166, 167, 169, 209

passive influence/interference 16
pathological accommodation 14
patient-therapist dyad 78
peer relationships 146–148
peer victimization 146, 148
persecution 96, 111, 158
Pervasive Developmental Disorder (PDD) 137
phenomenology 165
play 6, 19, 33, 45, 69, 77, 139, 141, 142, 192–206
pleasure 12, 50, 51, 55, 77, 90, 156, 159, 174
political correctness, politically correct 89, 128, 130, 131, 133
Pollock, Jackson 53
post-partum depression 57
post-traumatic stress disorder, PTSD 23, 70, 71, 74
Pound, Ezra 48
pre-sexual response 18
pregnancy 64, 112, 173, 208
presence of absence 53
primitive superego 130
projection 12, 33, 35, 78–80, 129, 199, 200, 202
projective processes 12
psychic canvas 52–55
psychic death 97
psychic holding 106
psychic isolation 19
psychic space 19, 107
psychic uniqueness 82
psychoanalysis, see 'analysis'
psychoanalytic listening 32
psychoanalytic psychotherapy 3, 4, 39, 149, 152
psychoanalytic treatment 30, 80, 88, 91, 153, 176
psychopathology 144, 146–148
psychosis 5, 28, 29, 31, 34, 35, 37–46, 106, 130, 131, 144–146, 148–153, 209
psychosis NOS 130
psychosocial development 153, 154
psychotherapy, see 'therapy'
psychotic 3, 5, 28–43, 45, 46, 55, 56, 106, 109, 115, 144, 146, 148, 149, 152–154, 157, 159, 210
psychotic communication 35–41
psychotic experience 40, 144
psychotic illness 32
psychotic obsession 38
psychotic self 35

psychotic spectrum disorders 148
psychotic state 29, 34, 35, 38, 39, 43; acute psychosis 37–38
psychotic symptomatology 30
psychotic symptoms 3, 5, 28–34, 40, 41, 45, 144, 146, 159, 210

racial bias 88, 92
racial integration 91
racism 96, 130
rage 15, 80, 98, 106, 188, 193, 202, 203
Rainbow Serpent 108
rape 92, 97, 106, 110
realistic object usage 12
reality testing 31–34
reanimation 168
reason, reasoning 30, 31
recidivism 75
recognition 12, 13, 23, 25, 40, 44, 62, 102, 139, 145, 149, 153, 156, 159, 171, 173, 199, 201, 205
reconciliation 102–103, 113
reenactment 182, 189
rehabilitation 75, 116
relatedness 22, 23, 175, 195, 197
relational home 168
relational processes 13
relational trauma 22, 145
relationship 22–24, 26
relocation 173, 208
remembering 12–15, 103, 137, 197
repeating 12–14, 33, 39, 109, 115
repetition compulsion 12
resilience 29, 41, 46, 145, 148, 149, 152, 173, 174
resistance 20, 63, 73, 132, 139, 145, 195, 198
reverse repetition 15
Ringstrom, Philip 169
Rorschach responses 153
rupture 6, 112, 131, 183, 185, 187, 210

sadomasochistic 12, 13
schizophrenia 30, 31, 33, 129, 130
schizophrenogenic mother 172
Schore 22, 23
Searles 4, 80, 81
seeking 51, 55, 56
Segal, Hanna 50
self 2–6, 11–20, 22–26, 29, 30, 32, 34–37, 40, 41, 46, 54, 57, 60, 62, 63, 81, 82, 90, 92, 107, 110–112, 144–147, 149, 150, 152, 153, 183, 187–190, 192–196,

198–205, 209; childhood self 12, 16–18; divided self 17; libidinal self 17; rejected self 16; self-continuity 41; self-destruction 111, 113, 130, 167, 198; self-development 145–146; self-disclosure 173; self-doubt 23; self-esteem 11, 25, 26, 147; self-experience 3; self-hatred 16, 19; self-humiliation 168; self-image 19; self-loathing 19; self-mutilation 168; selfobject 52, 55; self-presentation 16; self-regulation 145, 146; self-sabotage 18; self-state 11, 12, 20, 203
separation 6, 13, 20, 28–30, 34, 36, 40, 41–45, 98–101, 188, 193, 195–198, 201, 205; separation-individuation 20
'Sex Monster, The' 74
sexual abuse 75, 97, 112, 131
sexual assault, see 'rape'
shamanism 129, 132, 133
shame 3, 22–26, 28, 35, 40, 44, 45, 56, 57, 87, 91, 97, 102, 112, 131, 146–148, 150, 154–157, 159, 160, 176, 203
sinthome 151
Smith, Linda Tuhiwai 1
Stein, Abby 74
Stockholm Syndrome (for survival) 19, 20
Stolen Children 97, 99, 105
Stolen Generations 97, 99
stress 23, 31, 70, 98, 145–147, 184, 196
Subject Caught by the Desire of the Other 154
subject-object dualisms 81
subjective experience 81
subjective object relating 12
substance abuse 69, 72, 131
suffering 4, 57, 100, 102, 106, 153, 168, 169, 196, 200, 201, 205
suffering in the suffering 106
suicide 23, 24, 99, 106, 110, 112, 114, 122, 167, 193
superego 96, 110, 130
symbolization 136

tangata whai ite ora 132
tangata whenua 118, 120, 123, 125, 126, 128
Te Whare Tapa Wha 131–133
telepathy 133
terror 48, 95, 97, 99, 101, 106, 107, 111, 112, 114, 115
The Patient as the Therapist to the Therapist 80

Thematic Apperception Test 17
theory of mind 138
therapeutic action 57
therapeutic dyad 179
therapeutic frame 142
therapeutic interaction 49, 57, 176
therapeutic stance 77, 78
therapy 3–5, 24, 29, 30, 32, 33, 39, 40, 43, 45, 48, 50, 55, 57, 59–64, 69, 71, 72, 77, 79, 81, 88, 92, 105–107, 109, 111, 116, 119, 131, 132, 136, 144, 149, 152, 155, 168, 171, 172, 174, 182, 190, 192, 195–200, 202, 203, 205, 206, 210
tohunga 132–134
transcendent function 133
transference 22, 24, 34, 48, 49, 63, 70, 72–75, 80, 99, 114, 115, 142, 174, 175, 181–183, 185–187, 190, 199, 203
transference-countertransference 22, 175
trauma 2, 5, 6, 12, 13, 22–24, 53, 69, 70, 72, 75, 80, 97–101, 103, 105–116, 129, 131, 144–146, 148, 149, 153, 165–166, 168–169, 179, 182, 185, 189, 190, 195–197, 203; trauma, Aboriginal 105–116; trauma breakout 107; trauma, developmental 165, 166, 203; trauma, enobling 169; trauma, intergenerational 97, 101, 115; trauma of dislocation 142; trauma survival, trauma survivor 165
treatment 2–6, 15, 19, 20, 22–26, 29, 30, 38, 45, 49, 50, 55, 57, 59, 62, 63, 69, 70, 72–75, 78–80, 88, 90–92, 116, 128, 136, 138–140, 151–154, 156, 157, 159, 160, 168, 169, 174–176, 180, 182–190, 203
Treaty of Waitangi 120, 125, 126, 129
'tricky ground' 119
true self 60, 183
trust 23, 26, 29, 31, 34–37, 40, 44, 70, 78, 101, 102, 157, 159, 160, 173, 176, 180, 182, 183, 187, 203
Tustin, Frances 116

unconscious 3, 20, 23, 26, 38, 39, 42, 44, 49, 52, fn.2 p. 66, 82, 88, 90, 91, 110, 113, 120, 123, 153, 166, 174–176, 201, 203, 210
Ungunmerr-Baumann, Miriam Rose 106–108
unresolved trauma 107, 145, 146
unthought known 49
urbanization 131

'vagabond mind' 38

Index 219

valence 53, 56
validation 41, 168, 197
victimization 146–148, 169
Visit, The 11–12

waiata 125, 126
wairua 131–134
weaving 120
whakapapa 120, 121, 123, 124, 126

whanau 120–122, 125, 126, 129, 131–1
William Alanson White Institute 88
work 2–6, 12, 19, 20, 23, 31, 37, 42, 45, 53, 63, 72–73, 110, 111, 115, 119, 122, 123, 128, 129, 132, 139, 150, 153, 154, 155, 160, 175, 176, 182, 183, 186, 187, 188–189, 190, 193–195, 197, 203

zone of indivisibility 79

Taylor & Francis eBooks

Helping you to choose the right eBooks for your Library

Add Routledge titles to your library's digital collection today. Taylor and Francis ebooks contains over 50,000 titles in the Humanities, Social Sciences, Behavioural Sciences, Built Environment and Law.

Choose from a range of subject packages or create your own!

Benefits for you

- Free MARC records
- COUNTER-compliant usage statistics
- Flexible purchase and pricing options
- All titles DRM-free.

Benefits for your user

- Off-site, anytime access via Athens or referring URL
- Print or copy pages or chapters
- Full content search
- Bookmark, highlight and annotate text
- Access to thousands of pages of quality research at the click of a button.

REQUEST YOUR FREE INSTITUTIONAL TRIAL TODAY

Free Trials Available
We offer free trials to qualifying academic, corporate and government customers.

eCollections – Choose from over 30 subject eCollections, including:

Archaeology	Language Learning
Architecture	Law
Asian Studies	Literature
Business & Management	Media & Communication
Classical Studies	Middle East Studies
Construction	Music
Creative & Media Arts	Philosophy
Criminology & Criminal Justice	Planning
Economics	Politics
Education	Psychology & Mental Health
Energy	Religion
Engineering	Security
English Language & Linguistics	Social Work
Environment & Sustainability	Sociology
Geography	Sport
Health Studies	Theatre & Performance
History	Tourism, Hospitality & Events

For more information, pricing enquiries or to order a free trial, please contact your local sales team:
www.tandfebooks.com/page/sales

Routledge — Taylor & Francis Group
The home of Routledge books

www.tandfebooks.com